RECOGNITION AND MODES OF KNOWLEDGE

RECOGNITION AND MODES OF KNOWLEDGE

Anagnorisis
from Antiquity to
Contemporary Theory

TERESA G. RUSSO, *Editor*

THE UNIVERSITY OF ALBERTA PRESS

Published by

The University of Alberta Press
Ring House 2
Edmonton, Alberta, Canada T6G 2E1
www.uap.ualberta.ca

Copyright © 2013 The University of Alberta Press

LIBRARY AND ARCHIVES CANADA CATALOGUING IN PUBLICATION

Recognition and modes of knowledge : anagnorisis from antiquity to contemporary theory / Teresa G. Russo, editor.

Based on papers presented at the Centre for Comparative Literature's annual conference at the University of Toronto, April, 2008.
Includes bibliographical references and index.
Issued also in electronic format.
ISBN 978-0-88864-558-6

1. Recognition in literature—Congresses. 2. Recognition (Philosophy)— History—Congresses. 3. Knowledge, Theory of, in literature—Congresses. 4. Literature—History and criticism—Theory, etc.—Congresses. 5. Comparative literature—Congresses. I. Russo, Teresa G., 1972– II. University of Toronto. Centre for Comparative Literature. Conference (2008)

PN56.R33R43 2013   809'.9338   C2012-908217-1

First edition, first printing, 2013.
Printed and bound in Canada by Houghton Boston Printers, Saskatoon, Saskatchewan.
Copyediting and proofreading by Joanne Muzak.
Indexing by Judy Dunlop.

All rights reserved. No part of this publication may be produced, stored in a retrieval system, or transmitted in any form or by any means (electronic, mechanical, photocopying, recording, or otherwise) without prior written consent. Contact the University of Alberta Press for further details.

The University of Alberta Press is committed to protecting our natural environment. As part of our efforts, this book is printed on Enviro Paper: it contains 100% post-consumer recycled fibres and is acid- and chlorine-free.

The University of Alberta Press gratefully acknowledges the support received for its publishing program from The Canada Council for the Arts. The University of Alberta Press also gratefully acknowledges the financial support of the Government of Canada through the Canada Book Fund (CBF) and the Government of Alberta through the Alberta Multimedia Development Fund (AMDF) for its publishing activities.

This research was supported by the Social Sciences and Humanities Research Council.

For Giovanni and Bernardina

CONTENTS

PREFACE IX
ROLAND LE HUENEN

ACKNOWLEDGEMENTS XI

INTRODUCTION XIII
A Rising of Knowledge
TERESA G. RUSSO

1 | SOMETHING DIVINE IN RECOGNITION 1
PIERO BOITANI

2 | RECOGNITION AND IDENTITY IN EURIPIDES'S *ION* 33
NAOMI A. WEISS

3 | ETHICAL EPIPHANY IN THE STORY OF JUDAH AND TAMAR 51
RACHEL ADELMAN

4 | BIBLICAL RECOGNITION 77
Seperation From Bestiality and Incestuous Relationships as Resistance to Hellenization
HARRY FOX (LEBEIT YOREH)

5 | ENTER JOB, WITH FEAR AND TREMBLING 101
RHIANNON GRAYBILL

6 | THOMAS AQUINAS ON CHRISTIAN RECOGNITION 123
The Case of Mary Magdalene
KEVIN FREDERICK VAUGHAN

7 | NARRATIVE IDENTITY 141
Recognizing Oneself in Augustine and Ricoeur
JENNA SUNKENBERG

8 | THE INTERRUPTION OF TRAUMATIC DOUBLING IN THE INTERPOLATED TALE OF DOROTEA 155
JEFFREY NEIL WEINER

9 | SPENSER'S BAD ROMANCE 179
"First, Astonishments; Then, Consolations" in The Fairie Queene
JOSEPH RING

10 | THE HOME, THE PALACE, THE CELL 219
Places of Recognition in Le rouge et le noir *and* Great Expectations
ROSA MUCIGNAT

11 | RECOGNIZING OUR MISRECOGNITIONS 241
Plato and the Contemporary Politics of Recognition
CHRISTINA TARNOPOLSKY

CONTRIBUTORS 261

INDEX 265

PREFACE

ROLAND LE HUENEN

IN APRIL 2008, several literary scholars as well as a number of graduate students gathered at the Centre for Comparative Literature, University of Toronto to reflect on the notion of *anagnorisis* or recognition in literary works from antiquity to the postmodern. This international conference was the nineteenth that the students of the centre were organizing, contributing to maintain a tradition that is a testimonial to continuity, determination, and scholarship. Those nineteen years encompass many generations of students who have played an active and essential role in the building of Comparative Literature at the University of Toronto, as a unit and as a locus of knowledge and research.

In his *Poetics*, Aristotle, who was the first to theorize on recognition, defines anagnorisis as "a change from ignorance to knowledge, leading either to friendship or to hostility on the part of those persons who are marked for good fortune or bad" (1452a). More recently, in his *Recognitions: A Study in Poetics* (1988), Terence Cave shows that the term develops from its initial meaning of family recognitions, as in *Oedipus* and the *Odyssey*, to all these plots that engage in representing the loss and recovery of knowledge, that is, literature in general from its classic origin to the postmodern. In the proceedings of the conference, the notion is approached from various angles and from a wide spectrum of periods and authors ranging from Euripides to Paul Ricoeur, with studies devoted to the Bible, Augustine, Aquinas, Cervantes, and nineteenth-century novels.

Appearing with increasing frequency in current academic debates and scholarly works, the very notion of recognition invites a reflection on forgetting, memory, and identity, as it is the case with Ricoeur's *Memory, History, Forgetting*, for which the necessity of forgetting is stressed as a condition for the possibility of remembering, as a way to keep memory and curiosity for the past alive. Since the Greeks, the link between memory, imagination, and identity provides a founding element of Western culture. The originality of Ricoeur's line of reasoning rests in the proposition that oblivion as a separate level of thinking releases fundamental capacities of remembering. Forgetting is the other side of recognition, but also its prerequisite, whereas both concepts are necessary to an understanding of oneself and of the past, but also of the present and the future alike, and thus acquire a dimension that is unavoidably historical. In Ricoeur's account the mastery of recognition and the power of oblivion lead to an exposition of an historical condition of existence. However, such an attempt seems to overlook the traditional distinction between *anamnesis* (recollection) and *anagnorisis* (recognition), between a more simple way of recall and a more disquieting questioning of the self.

ACKNOWLEDGEMENTS

I WOULD FIRST OF ALL LIKE TO THANK the Social Sciences and Humanities Research Council of Canada (SSHRC/CRSH) for supporting the conference, "From Ignorance to Knowledge: Recognition from Antiquity to the Postmodern and Beyond," held at the Centre for Comparative Literature at the University of Toronto in the spring of 2008, and funding this publication with a generous grant that made this volume possible, providing us with the opportunity to share this research and scholarship.

I would like to acknowledge Professor Roland Le Huenen, the director of the Centre for Comparative Literature at the time of the conference, for his assistance and advice throughout this project, and Professor Jonathan Locke Hart for initiating the idea of this publication and supporting the work of the conference committee. With Professor Le Huenen, he has been instrumental in guiding this volume. I am also grateful to Professor Hart for introducing me to Peter Midgley of the University of Alberta Press, who has become a great coach in the editing of this volume and provided great editorial support throughout the preparation of the manuscript.

I am thankful to all the peer reviewers and experts in various academic fields for reading the submitted articles and for all their recommendations. Anonymous assessment was implemented. Thus, these scholars go unnamed, but they were essential in the process of refereeing and revision during the initial stage of selecting the chapters and preparing the manuscript. In addition, I am grateful to the editorial staff at the University of Alberta Press. The readers provided recommendations that strengthen the style and cohesion of the volume, while Mary Lou Roy, Duncan Turner, and Joanne Muzak were valuable at the copyediting stage.

I express my thanks to my colleagues at the Centre for Comparative Literature, David Dagenais and Jonathan Allan, for their advice and valuable assistance during the early phase of this project. I need to also mention the great support I received from the staff at the Centre for Comparative Literature, Aphrodite Gardner and Bao Nguyen, Sarah Scott from University of Toronto's grant office, and from Linda Cameron, director of the University of Alberta Press and her staff at UAP, including Sharon Wilson and Monika Igali.

I would like extend a heartfelt thank you to all the contributors who I had a pleasure to meet or see again at the conference. I enjoyed working with them and discussing various concepts of the theme of this publication. I am extremely grateful to Piero Boitani and Christina Tarnopolsky for reading an early draft of my work and for their helpful recommendations that enhanced the final version of the publication.

And I finally want to thank my family for their moral support, my husband Gaetano Di Pietro, my sisters, Grace Juanillo and Laura Matar, and my parents, to whom this volume is dedicated, who have always shown endless support, patience, and understanding through the years.

INTRODUCTION
A Rising of Knowledge

TERESA G. RUSSO

THE CENTRE FOR COMPARATIVE LITERATURE at the University of Toronto held its annual conference on the theme of recognition, entitled "From Ignorance to Knowledge: Recognition from Antiquity to the Postmodern and Beyond," in April 2008. The conference was inspired by a seminar offered in the fall of 2006 when Amilcare Iannucci introduced Piero Boitani, one of Italy's distinguished professors of literary criticism from Sapienza University of Rome, to the centre to lecture on the theme of *anagnorisis*. The seminar, Anagnorisis: Scenes and Themes of Recognition, aimed at exploring the functions of recognition both as a structural device and in its emotional and cognitive aspects from ancient classics to twentieth-century texts. The conference expanded the idea to bring together a diverse group of scholars to discuss the theme of recognition in a wide variety of literatures, examining not only Aristotelian anagnorisis but other forms, such as post-Aristotelian models of recognition, Hegelian, and post-Hegelian models of recognition in critical theory in an effort to provide a forum fostering dialogue and cross-fertilization of different theoretical approaches. I had the pleasure of organizing this conference with David Dagenais, Keavy Martin, Pouneh Saeedi, and Elisa

Segnini; and it was the well-written abstract of David Dagenais, with the contribution of the committee, that drew so much attention to the conference and so many submissions. The goal of the conference was to bring scholars from a wide range of disciplines who employ various approaches and perspectives in their examination of the term of recognition and its relationship to self, society, ideology, and culture. We were honoured to have Boitani return to our campus and to have Philip Kennedy (New York University, Middle Eastern Studies), Christina Tarnopolsky (McGill University, Political Science), and Jonathan Locke Hart (University of Alberta, English and Comparative Literature) as guest speakers, discussing the classical and modern theories of recognition.

The conference as well as this volume initiates with *classical* recognition, defined in the *Poetics* (1452a) as a discovery and gain of knowledge, moving from ignorance to knowledge (gnōsis), or, as Boitani explains the Greek prefix in his work: *ana*—upward, a rising of knowledge, which includes a set of family recognitions and recognition of persons where one recognizes his or her or someone else's true identity (see *The Tragic and the Sublime* 117–18). Sophocles's *Oedipus Rex* is considered one of the finest and more artistically satisfying examples of anagnorisis because, as Aristotle explains, it is accompanied by a reversal of events or *peripeteia*. The simplest type of anagnorisis discussed by Aristotle is recognition by scars, birthmarks, or tokens, as in the story of Odysseus. In other literary conceptions, recognition takes place and leads to a revelation and a gain of knowledge: here we encounter Thomas Aquinas's *quidditas-claritas*, James Joyce's notion of epiphany, T.S. Eliot's concept of the "objective correlative," William Wordsworth's "spots of time," Ernest Hemingway's "moment of truth," W.B. Yeats's "great memory," Giuseppe Ungaretti and Giorgos Seferis's "moment," and Marcel Proust's "petite Madeleine."

The study of Aristotelian recognition began with four seminal works: *The Tragic and the Sublime in Medieval Literature*, *The Bible and its Rewritings*, and *The Genius to Improve an Invention* by Boitani, and *Recognitions: A Study in Poetics* by Britain's eminent scholar, Terence Cave. Kennedy follows the tradition of Boitani and Cave while examining anagnorisis in the Qur'an and Arabic Literature in his most recent volume, *Recognitions in Arabic Islamic Literature: Anagnorisis in Arabic Narrative Tradition* (Routledge / Curzon Press 2011). Boitani, in his last work on the subject, demonstrates how Aristotle's codification of anagnorisis becomes a central element of complex plot in works of literature from Euripides to T.S. Eliot, framed as a problem of knowledge (*The Genius*, x–xi). Cave also shows how the term in the twentieth century shifts from a classical model to a set of plots structured around the loss and recovery of knowledge; the mode of knowledge in recognition plots operates by synecdoche and even accidentally or by default (9, 497).

Distinguishable moments of classical recognitions are notable in Dante's *Commedia* and successfully represented in his staging of recognition scenes—Francesca da Rimini, Piccarda Donati and her brother Forese Donati, Brunetto Latini, and the gathering of past poets in Limbo to name a few. Dante's recognition scenes demonstrate one of Boitani's intriguing claims about anagnorisis: recognition brings people together. Thus, recognition comes to mean "life as knowledge of each other" (*Tragic and Sublime* 145). Knowledge is given and received, an exchange staged in the *Commedia* as pilgrim and souls recognize, identify, testify, and understand. In the wider spectrum of anagnorisis in the poem, Dante's crossing into the afterlife is for his own attainment of true knowledge (cf. *Tragic and Sublime* 149–50). The journey moves the pilgrim from a mode of self-ignorance to a state of knowing thyself and humanity—a movement framed by Dante the poet within a theological and philosophical understanding of fall and salvation.

Other literary terms include a sense of discovery or have a built-in meaning of knowing that closely resembles traditional recognition's progression from nothingness to a moment of absolute truth or a marvellous discovery, such as literary epiphany first coined in Joyce's *Stephen Hero*. His definition, interestingly, requires three moments of recognition before an epiphany or spiritual manifestation. Stephen states that, first, one recognizes the object, then, one will recognize "a thing in fact," and, finally, there is a recognition: "that it is that thing which it is" (*Stephen Hero* 213).

This is the moment when the object leaps out and is marked with radiance; an epiphany is achieved. *Epiphaneia* initially developed a religious meaning in the early Christian period as a "visible manifestation of a hidden divinity either in the form of a personal appearance, or by some deed of power by which its presence is made known" (Walzl 436). Even in Greek drama, there are manifestations of Zeus, Venus, Athena, and other deities. Etymologically, the word in Greek means an appearance; the verb means to display or show forth or even to shine forth. Emmanuel Levinas describes the face-to-face encounter as an epiphany, even the gaze is an "epiphany of the face"; the "other" recognized as a matter of ethics (75–76, 150). In literature, epiphany is a moment of luminosity, a sudden unsought realization as to the nature about something, someone, or oneself. In Dante's *Purgatorio*, anagnorisis occurs in the course of an epiphany or moment of manifestation with Sordello's revelation of Virgil and the triumph of Beatrice (Boitani, *Tragic and Sublime* 156, 163).

Joyce, further, uses the term in *A Portrait of the Artist as a Young Man* with Thomas Aquinas's *quidditas-claritas* definition to highlight the stages of apprehension. Stephen states:

> *You apprehend it as one thing. You see it as one whole. You apprehend its wholeness. That is* integritas….*you pass from point to point, led by its formal lines; you apprehend it as balanced part against part within its limits; you feel the rhythm of its structure. In other words the synthesis of immediate perception is followed by the analysis of apprehension. Having first felt that it is one thing you feel now that it is a thing. You apprehend it as complex, multiple, divisible, separable, made up of its parts, the result of its parts and their sum, harmonious. That is* consonantia….*I thought he [Aquinas] might mean that* claritas *is the artistic discovery and representation of the divine purpose in anything or a force of generalization which would make the esthetic image a universal one, make it outshine its proper conditions. But that is literary talk. I understand it so. When you have apprehended that basket as one thing and have then analyzed it according to its form and apprehended it as a thing you make the only synthesis which is logically and esthetically permissible. You see*

> that it is that thing which it is and no other thing. The radiance of which he
> [Aquinas] speaks is the scholastic quidditas, *the* whatness *of a thing.*
> (213, emphasis original)

Recognition is presented as a temporal sequence achieved in phases, as Stephen's first definition in *Hero*, a moment of apprehension and psychological movement from unknowing to seeing and understanding or the act of arriving at knowledge. Aquinas introduces the terms—*integritas*, *consonantia*, and *claritas*, which many scholars demonstrate are misused by Stephen, shovelling Aquinas's meaning—in the *Summa Theologica* to describe the three persons of the Holy Trinity (1 Q39 a8respondeo). *Quidditas-claritas* comes to mean a moment of clarity or recognition; "the mind comes to know" such quality of things rather than a sequential movement to knowledge (Noon 22).

Joyce's definition caused a revolution in the way illuminating moments were studied. However, before him other authors discussed moments of manifestation, using various terms to describe a moment of manifestation or revelation that brings about a type of recognition, an occurrence of discovery. Constance Vassiliou Tagopoulos equates "objective correlative," "spots of time," "moment of truth," "great memory," and Seferis's "Moment" to Joyce's literary epiphanies, stating that all these moments have "image-strings" that stimulate the memory and, in a sense, capture the imagination (231). And one can include the significance of truth arising and established from such moments the same as truth springs forth and is constituted from an epiphany. Proust's "petite Madeleine," for instance, similarly functions as a visual thread for the memory, inspiring an awakening and a moment—a process of cognition begins in order to "discover the truth" (49). The narrator finally recognizes the Madeleine dipped in tea as the catalyst, stirring the consciousness; the little cake stimulates the memory and helps the narrator recognize the past. In fact, memory will be a reoccurring theme in some of the following chapters; memory insofar as recalling the past in one's sudden revelation that transforms the future and initiates the passage from ignorance to knowledge. Some scholars, such as Morris Beja, believe that Joyce's epiphany is different from Aristotle's term of recognition in that the result of the sudden and emotional illumination results in a mystical enlightenment or an experience of conversion (Beja 716). Some of the following chapters may challenge the idea that epiphanies alone cause spiritual conversions as certain defining recognitions result in "sudden illuminations" after a moment of self-understanding and self-analysis. However, we can agree that both anagnorisis and epiphanies in addition to many "moments" of manifestations (whether it be a "rational" discovery or "spiritual" conversion) lead to an insight or revelation, a knowledge, following an acknowledgement of a sign, cognition, or apprehension.

The term recognition has also been debated in contemporary philosophical and political debates underlined by Hegel's theory of self-consciousness itself. Hegel, initially following Aristotelian notions of recognition and Aristotle's ontology with Johann Gottlieb Fichte's model of "reciprocal effect," outlined by Fichte in *The Foundations of Natural Law* (2 vols., 1796–1797), develops a "mutual recognition" (and various forms of "reciprocal recognition") that ensures a complementary agreement and mutuality of differing subjects—a process of reconciliation and conflict occurring in alternating stages within an ethical and social concept of a community (*System of Ethical Life*, 1802; see Honneth 11–30; see also Fitche 33–34). Hegel develops a theory of "interpersonal recognition" based on the "natural ethical life" of realizing a first stage of one's dependence (including the need for individuals or certain relations, emotional needs, or vital care) and a second stage that includes the claims of possessions. And "intersubjective recognition"—a person transitions into a "whole person" by gaining their identity (*System of Ethical Life*)—emerges from his work as Hegel defines struggles of personhood and honour first by following Hobbes and Machiavelli's political philosophies and then later moving to identifying social struggles within an ethical or moral growth of society, perfectly outlined in Axel Honneth's *The Struggle for Recognition* (1995). Hegel later replaces Aristotle with a theory of consciousness and makes a shift to a model of recognition that included the understanding of human interaction based on the master/slave dialectic of human struggle, which has influenced Søren Kierkegaard, Karl Marx, and Friedrich Nietzsche. Simon Blackburn explains that individuals know themselves by incorporating their understandings of how they are viewed by others, which results in a "fight for recognition" (162; see also Honneth 82). This Hegelian metaphor for the struggle of recognition emerges from *The Phenomenology of Spirit* (1807) (see ch. iv, sec. A), but Hegel also defines recognition as freely undertaken by two parties, requiring reciprocity. In this pure manifestation of recognition one has to bear in mind the agency of one as he/she attempts to demonstrate his/her own agency on that person: "he attains his self-awareness only by regarding the other as other" (*Philosophy of Right* [1820] 40). In both Hegelian paradigms, knowledge of self is significant, as seen in Aristotelian recognition, in which one not only attains self-awareness or develops a defined identity, but also attains (or "rises" to) a knowledge of oneself to be recognized by someone else in regards to one's own abilities and qualities, first laid out by Hegel in *System of Ethical Life*.

Hegel's philosophy influences contemporary theories of recognition that include a phenomenology of selfhood. This gives rise to a phenomenology of judgement, especially in Honneth's analysis of social recognition, and it accounts for the importance of social relationships and the understanding of how social relationships impact recognition in Paul Ricoeur's analysis of the chief moments of recognition. Hegel's ideas of recognition influenced the fields of political philosophy, ethical politics and philosophy, natural law, property rights, and most recently the philosophy of education. And his concepts of recognition affected thinkers from a wide variety of disciplines, including Georges Bataille, Jacques Lacan, Jean-Paul Sartre, Emmanuel Levinas, Frantz Fanon, Drucilla Cornell, and Francis Fukuyama. The term recognition has spurred recent debates in social and political theory, for instance, in the field of recognition in multicultural societies, where identity politics and the distribution of recognition are considered. Christina Tarnopolsky represents this new development of recognition—the contemporary politics of recognition—as she examines misrecognitions and the place of shame in democratic politics in her article, "Prudes, Perverts, and Tyrants: Plato and the Contemporary Politics of Shame," and elsewhere in her work, entering a debate with both critics and defenders of the politics of shame, such as Michael Warner and Jean Elshtain. Suddenly, we see a shift in the theory of recognition; whereas anagnorisis was initially—and it continues to be—used to analyze Greek drama, and all literature and poetry (and ideal for examining opera), it has now also become valuable in modern politics with Hegelian philosophy to discuss identity politics, cultural politics, and multiculturalism. Canadian scholar Charles Taylor states in *The Politics of Recognition* (1995) that identity has become the most important aspect of recognition. And these are not just theoretical concepts. Political leaders have already attempted practical uses of the contemporary theories of recognition and most recent a practice of a type of politics of shame in foreign relations to produce peaceful resolutions in conflicts of nuclear power. Israeli President Shimon Peres expresses the use of shaming when asked how to achieve goals in a peaceful manner; he states that a solution must be created where one (its citizens) may be shamed to be in the same room with leaders who support nuclear warheads and that "We have to bring back the importance of being ashamed" (Peres, Transcripts, Sept. 24, 2010, 00:26:39).

Both Aristotelian and Hegelian recognition, as well as other contemporary theories of recognition, emerged from the conference presentations and are represented in this volume. The importance of this undertaking was best described by Tarnopolsky when she told the committee that this was the first time that Aristotelians and Hegelians entered into a dialogue on the subject of recognition: "While there have been many conferences exploring recognition (anagnorisis) in Aristotle and its relationship to other literary works and genres, and there have been many conferences exploring recognition in Hegel and its relation to the contemporary politics of recognition, including Charles Taylor, Axel Honneth, Nancy Fraser, etc., I believe that your conference was the first to systematically bring together Aristotelians and Hegelians to explore the issue of recognition and to do so across so many different genres: literary works, works of political philosophy, the Old and New Testament, Islamic literature, etc." This was also an opportunity, she expressed, for Hegelians to trace back the classical roots of their theories of recognition. Moreover, the three-day conference became the venue to encounter scholars one generally would not have the opportunity to meet and where Cave's student, Kennedy, and Boitani met for the first time and discussed the issues of recognition with one of Northrop Frye's students, Jonathan Locke Hart, and with Tarnopolsky, a Canadian political theorist. This volume offers a selection of those papers and does not seek to represent every author, plot, or instance of recognition, or all the theoretical changes anagnorisis underwent from period to period, but includes examples of both classical and modern recognitions and the use of the term after Aristotle.

We begin with classical anagnorisis in Boitani's article "Something Divine in Recognition," in which he examines the role of faith in the acquisition of knowledge of the "other." Seeing is not necessarily believing, and one may have to awake their faith to believe, to recognize what they see. Boitani discusses all three aspects of Aristotelian recognition—surprise or wonder, pity and fear, and its mechanism, culminating to the question of proof and the lack of signs, flesh, and blood. Boitani demonstrates how in some cases it is not material proof but the divine that comes into play in recognizing the beloved and shows how the divine is placed within the process of recognizing. Can one suspend disbelief, experience, suffering, certainty? Discussing classical romance to Old and New Testaments, Boitani points out the leap of faith involved with recognition, an element missing from Aristotle's definition and that goes beyond just recognizing to a miraculous event.

Naomi Weiss focuses more fully on the classical genre and takes a psychoanalytic approach in her reading of Euripides's *Ion*. She identifies a set of repetitions of scenes and preoccupations of the past that fit Freud's analysis of trauma patients and the "compulsion to repeat." This chapter, "Recognition and Identity in Euripides's *Ion*," examines the classical scenes of recognition between son and mother in Euripides's play and highlights the changes of memory and identity that occur throughout the drama for a final self-recognition and understanding to transpire at the end of the play. Kreousa, so concerned with "ancient memory," fails to recognize the many proofs so evident in the present, while her son's focus on a stagnant present will be interrupted with questions of the past and finally causing a rebirth. The Athenian audience also plays a crucial role in the recognition process and in the discovery of their very own self-identity from past events. Euripides's play represents the best of anagnorisis, while placing recognition within a psychological experience.

Weiss's chapter is followed by Rachel Adelman's discussion of ethical epiphany in the Hebrew Bible and Christianity's Old Testament story of Judah and Tamar. By examining rabbinic sources and drawing on the theory of recognition and Levinas's ethics of substitution, Adelman claims that the peripeteia in this story is crucial in shaping a redemptive outcome of the Joseph story. Deception and veiling of truths lead to misrecognitions and misunderstandings. But, such processes are necessary in some cases for strengthening an understanding of self and role in the world. In this case, Tamar's deceit affected Judah's character that led to an understanding of his greater role in leading Canaan out of famine. The reversal of events in Aristotelian terms led to an ethical epiphany and confession of truth, discovery of identity, and a clearer recognition of one's relations and errors. In "Ethical Epiphany in the Story of Judah and Tamar," Adelman demonstrates how the events in this story bring forth a "recognition of responsibility," a reversal of roles, and an ethical act of substitution.

Harry Fox, also examining the Hebrew Bible in "Biblical Recognition: Separation From Bestiality and Incestuous Relationships as Resistance to Hellenization," compares exegetical readings of two biblical accounts of creation and the cravings of the Israelites (Numbers 11), both verses important in the history of Jewish and Western sexual mores, and discusses various types of recognitions—natural, spiritual, mutual, self—and the struggle for recognition in light of Aristotelian anagnorisis, Hegel's *Anerkennung*, Ricoeur's analysis of gift giving, and Tarnopolsky's definitions of shame in connection to the establishment of transgressive behaviour in these verses. Fox begins by outlining the importance of identity and discusses the understanding of oneself from meeting one's opposite, but also from the discovery of one like "you": Adam and Eve demonstrate a mutual recognition that he links to language and speech and that establishes a heteronormative sexuality. A moment of complete mutuality is achieved between the created and creator, only to be ruptured with the act of gift giving the forbidden fruit—a moment of recognition, Fox explains, that creates destruction and a struggle for recognition. But Fox discusses how, on the other hand, the act of recognition actually saved humanity from living in a constant state of unhappiness and distress. And finally in Numbers, Fox demonstrates through rabbinic sources that the complaints of the Israelites are not only gluttonous cravings, but complaints against Moses over martial matters. Both Genesis and Numbers establish sexual norms, ending bestiality and consanguineous marriages and privileging heterosexuality.

In "Enter Job, With Fear and Trembling," Rhiannon Graybill reads an Old Testament story, the Book of Job, as a philosophical narrative in conversation with Søren Kierkegaard's *Fear and Trembling* and Jacques Derrida's *The Gift of Death*. She discusses Kierkegaard's teleological suspension of the ethical in an analysis of Job's speech as a scene of address, one of recognition, attesting to the role that language and silence play in recognizing oneself and one's lack of knowledge or understanding. Graybill explains Job for Kierkegaard and Derrida in the mist of their silence and mere suggestion of Job's role in their works. Abraham stands out as a hero of faith, who was tested in private, only before his son, and who favoured "an absolute relationship with God" in *Fear and Trembling*. But, how does Job function in the question of being tested by God and in one's struggle of faith? What violence has he suffered? Graybill addresses this struggle under Kierkegaard's terms of faith, ethics, and the religious realm.

Kevin Frederick Vaughan discusses the concept of recognition within a Christian experience in one of Thomas Aquinas's biblical commentaries, which focuses on a controversial scene in the New Testament, the appearance of the risen Jesus to Mary Magdalene in the Gospel of John. So many scholars and commentators have questioned why Mary at first mistakes Jesus for the gardener. Is this a lack of faith, or did Jesus not want to be recognized, and why is she prohibited to touch him? In "Thomas Aquinas on Christian Recognition: The Case of Mary Magdalene," Vaughan examines the connection of faith and recognition, offering a discussion of the transformation of recognition and the nature of Mary's recognition according to Saint Thomas. Recognition in this case is understood within Mary Magdalene's *visio Christi*, and the case of seeing and believing is taken up within a Christian theory of anagnorisis. Love and faith become two conditions in recognition moved by grace.

Following a philosophical critique of Aquinas's Gospel of John is Jenna Sunkenberg's analysis of Augustine and Ricoeur, concerning the idea of understanding within Ricoeur's notion of "narrative identity." This chapter, "Narrative Identity: Recognizing Oneself in Augustine and Ricoeur," examines how the past, present, and future shape one's own self-understanding, a picture of the past stored in memory for self-analysis and account for one's future. Memory has been discussed in other chapters, but here memory and the images created of one's own experiences play a pivotal role in the understanding of self within a hermeneutics of the self and of text. She claims that both Saint Augustine in his *Confessions* and Ricoeur in *The Course of Recognition* establish a relationship between time and narrative within the phenomenon of self-recognition, and she discusses self-understanding and the changing of self or conversion as reconfigured through textual interpretation.

We then move from Greek tragedies and sacred texts to the theme of recognition in the novel and poetry by canonical authors. First, Jeffrey Weiner explores the many facets of recognition scenes and self-recognition in *Don Quijote*'s tale of Dorotea. The story projects two underlining themes that Sunkenberg outlines in Augustine and Ricoeur's philosophies—the importance of time in narrative and experiences performed in narrative. Here, we see how Dorotea personifies her own lived and repetitive trauma to a male audience. Lived experience turns into a narrative, and forgotten memory remembers the trauma of the past and present. Weiner explores the term of anagnorisis in a renaissance comedy, which like so many classical tragedies provides an important role in the plot for the audience. In Cervantes's story, the male audience will assist in affirming a public recognition. This comedy has all the elements of a classical tragedy, but it is the element of confession where the final and important recognition will take place for Dorotea and cease the repetition of trauma. Confessions have already been considered by Boitani, Vaughan, and Adelman: Boitani demonstrates how, in Hebrew and Christian recognition, to recognize is to acknowledge and confess; Vaughan shows Thomas Aquinas's linkage of recognition and confession; and in Adelman's chapter, Judah is compelled to confess upon recognizing the tokens that belonged to him. In the same manner as in the recognition scenes of Judah and even Job, confession will become the catalyst of a re-cognition scene analyzed by Weiner in "The Interruption of Traumatic Doubling in the Interpolated Tale of Dorotea." Weiner explains the Spanish verb *admirar* and its fixed meaning of knowing; *admiración*, like concepts of "great memory," "moment," and "moment of truth" discussed previously, imparts a sense of the Aristotelian principle to discover truth and gain knowledge. *Admiración* will play a key role in the reconciliation scene and recognition of one's own duty.

Similarly, "moment of astonishment" and traumatic shock or modes of trauma that result in a sudden recognition of truth and identity are introduced in Joseph Ring's reading of *The Faerie Queene*. In "Spenser's Bad Romance: 'First, Astonishments; Then, Consolations' in *The Faerie Queene*," Ring explores several related moments of astonishment in Spenser's epic poem, highlighting instants of "sublime blockage" and the middle ground of wonder, which leads towards "true knowledge." Ring suggests that the moments of astonishment that arise during epic combat in *The Faerie Queene* equal the sublime tradition of blockage and associates it with epic and tragic anagnorisis. The scenes of epic combat considered here produce different recognition scenes or a shock moment of knowing, which also in some cases is shifted to the audience.

The reader, like the Athenian audience in Weiss's analysis of the *Ion* (in effect here the audience of the battlefield) shares in the astonishment, as Ring explains, while poetic activity is transported to the reader. In other words, "the displacements of recognition," to borrow Cave's term, occurs to the outside of fiction and a movement of discovery is repositioned to the audience (Cave 196; Frye 289). Ring additionally examines the process of transformation both physically and psychically during battle. While in another battle scene he explores astonishment and the emergence of knowing someone or something during the state of wonder; memory emerges beyond any sense of comprehension. Ring discusses astonishment in ethics and religious terms, demonstrating the fear and consolation associated with sudden wonder.

Finally in this collection of literary paradigms, Rosa Mucignat presents "The Home, the Palace, the Cell: Places of Recognition in *Le rouge et le noir* and *Great Expectations*" in which she explores how two nineteenth-century authors adopt the theory of anagnorisis with concerns for localization, so that one discovers the self in not only a figural, but a real place. Mucignat defines three stages and places in the hero's road to recognition, marked with confusion and crisis that finally drives the hero into confinement. She navigates between the various "places" to demonstrate the conditions that force one into isolation where the process of self-understanding begins. Mucignat examines how Stendhal and Dickens use the theory of recognition to mediate between social and geographical realities. She discusses the trope of recognition as a point of reassessing and discovering spatial values. The hero's last place, the cell, becomes "a haven for thought," according to Mucignat. It is also *to* the "cell" of memorial storage where the hero returns to his past or, in mnemonic terms, to the cell of memory, a place where inventory and the past is stored and thought and invention initiates. The hero enters a phase of discovery in Frye's definition of the "recognition of the hero" (187), and Mucignat defines the locus for the occurrence of true reflection and the staging of the final phase of the hero. In other chapters, trauma and fear bring forth revelation and an uncovering. In *Le rouge et le noir* and *Great Expectations* the process of realization begins within a place of alienation—a place where one wonders and awakens and where self-recognition is achieved.

The volume ends by returning to a classical Greek text, Plato's *Gorgias*, to analyze three models of a "politics of shame" and how they might be useful to politics today. Tarnopolsky presents a piece on the contemporary politics of recognition, the theory's criticisms of its own misrecognitions, and the problematic form of mutual recognition. She introduces in her chapter, "Recognizing Our Misrecognitions: Plato and the Contemporary Politics of Recognition," the key theorists who turned to Hegel for their debates on recognition and misrecognition and discusses the character of intersubjective recognition by turning to Plato. Starting with a close reading of the *Gorgias*, she outlines Plato's "politics of shame" and examines the kinds of intersubjective recognition that can characterize democratic deliberations. Tarnopolsky demonstrates, as other situations of recognition discussed throughout the chapters, that fear and suffering accompany the process of recognition and even more so in a politics of shame, which involves the discomfort of the gaze and a seeing of defects before the transformation; the politics of shame can also require charity to move respectfully between disagreements and shared ideals as the mutual recognition suggested in the *Summa theologiae* formed by charity. The prompting of misrecognitions in the probing manner of Socrates can assist one in knowing thyself in order to have a fuller understanding and respect for other citizens and to achieve one's own potential in society.

We see in some of these chapters that, as in literary epiphany and Stephen Hero's *quidditas-claritas* definition, one can undergo a process of several recognitions before arriving to a state of knowing or a discovery of knowledge, while others experience a sudden agnition and shock. The newly obtained knowledge is essential in the moment of transformation as Joyce's epiphany illustrates. The function of memory in recognizing is paramount as the authors demonstrated in these various moments of anagnorisis and modern recognitions. The presence of trauma, fear, or terror brings one to the past to reconcile the future—a going back into memory or into what Augustine terms an "act of remembrance." Dante's entire journey, for example, is a going back to the past, remembering classical and historical events during various recognition scenes while acquiring knowledge from these revelations—"memory of mankind" for both the pilgrim and the reader (Frye 346)—and then, at last after confession, drinks from the stream of "good memory" to prepare himself for his final recognition of God. Recognition can recall past events, "our own buried life"—a past as Augustine reminds us is stored in memory to be retrieved for that "moment of truth"—resurrected within a revelation, epiphany, a moment that brings about a knowledge crucial for growth and change.

The present volume demonstrates the different ways recognition operates in sacred texts, literature, politics, and philosophy among reoccurring themes of repetition, space, loss and gain, confession, the narrating of experiences or recalling of past events, trauma, rupture, separation and reunion, and faith. While it does not say the final word on the role of recognition in society, ideology, and culture, we hope it may represent the first of many dialogues between Aristotelians and contemporary theorists.

Works Cited

Beja, Morris. "Epiphany and the Epiphanies." *A Companion To Joyce Studies.* Ed. Zack Bowen and James F. Carrens. London: Greenwood Press, 1984. 707–25. Print.

Blackburn, Simon. *Oxford Dictionary of Philosophy.* Oxford: Oxford University Press, 2005. 161–62. Print.

Boitani, Piero. *The Genius to Improve an Invention: Literary Transitions.* Notre Dame, IN. University of Notre Dame Press, 2002. Print.

———. *The Tragic and the Sublime in Medieval Literature.* Cambridge: Cambridge University Press, 1989. Print.

Cave, Terence. *Recognitions: A Study in Poetics.* Oxford: Clarendon Press, 1988. Print.

Fichte, Johann Gottlieb. *The Foundations of Natural Right.* 1796–1797. Ed. Frederick Neuhouser. Trans. Michael Baur. Cambridge: Cambridge University Press, 2000. Print.

Frye, Northrop. *Anatomy of Criticism.* 1957. Princeton, NJ: Princeton University Press, 1971. Print.

Hegel, Georg W.F. *Philosophy of Right*. 1820. Trans. Howard P. Kainz. The Hague: Martinus Nijhoff, 1974. Print.

Honneth, Axel. *The Struggle for Recognition: The Moral Grammar of Social Conflicts*. Trans. Joel Anderson. Cambridge: Polity Press, 1995. Print.

Joyce, James. *A Portrait of the Artist as a Young Man*. 1916. New York: Viking Press, 1956. Print.

———. *Stephen Hero*. 1904–1907. New York: New Directions, 1944. Print.

Levinas, Emmanuel. *Totality and Infinity: An Essay on Exteriority*. 1969. Trans. Alphonso Lingis. Dordrecht, NL: Kluwer Academic Publishers, 1991. Print.

Noon, William T. *Joyce and Aquinas*. New Haven, CT: Yale University Press, 1957. Print.

Peres, Shimon. Interview by Sean Hannity. *The Sean Hannity Show*. FNC. September 24, 2010. Transcript, http://www.livedash.com/transcript/hannity/5202/FNC/Friday_September_24_2010/459190/.

Proust, Marcel. *Swann's Way, Remembrance of Things Past*. 1934. Trans. C.K. Scott Moncrief and Terence Kilmartin. Vol. 1. New York: Random House, 1981. Print.

Tagopoulos, Constance Vassiliou. "Myth, Memory, and Love in Plato, Seferis and Joyce: Quest for Language and Balance." Diss. City University of New York, 1997. Dissertation Abstracts International 50: 01A, 1997. Print.

Walzl, Florence L. "The Liturgy of the Epiphany Season and the Epiphanies of Joyce." *PMLA* 80.4 (Sept. 1965): 436–50. Print.

1

SOMETHING DIVINE IN RECOGNITION

PIERO BOITANI

I

Helen, whose face launched a thousand ships and burnt the topless towers of Ilium, never went to Troy. Paris never swept her into his chamber. It was not Helen the city leaders contemplated on the walls. Furious at her defeat in the most fatal beauty contest of all time, Hera fobbed Paris off with a phantom, an image made out of air: a quasi-living-and-breathing, identical copy: Helen's double. The flesh-and-blood Helen had been carried off by Hermes and hidden in a cloud in some tuck in the ether, then removed safely to Egypt, to the house of the chaste Proteus, to preserve Menelaus's bed inviolate. The first ever East-West clash, the First World War—the Trojan War—was fought for an illusion. Zeus simply wanted to ease the earth of some of its burden by thinning out the human population and, at the same time, give the most heroic of heroes, Achilles, the chance to shine.

This is Helen's own account when she appears at the opening of the play Euripides devoted to her a few years before dying, not a tragedy in the modern sense of the word, but the enacting of an astonishing rehabilitation of the first adulteress, the story of her reunion with Menelaus, and their return to the marital bed and home: a romance play with a happy ending.

In the course of his wanderings on the way home (almost as long as those of Ulysses), Menelaus, bringing with him Helen's double, arrives in Egypt and finds the true Helen. What interests us here is not the general plot of the play, but the recognition scene proper. When Helen (the real one) first appears to Menelaus, he is shaken. As soon as he sees her emerging from the king's palace, he is turned to stone, unable to pronounce a syllable. In her turn, Helen, seeing a man in rags approach her, runs to the tomb of Proteus to implore protection. Paradoxically, it seems to be Menelaus who first recognizes her, while she is as if blinded: the supreme moment hanging by a hair's breadth. But seeing is one thing, recognizing quite another. Helen has no need of secret signs, reasoning, or memory: she simply observes and understands. At the same time, each asks the other who he/she is: the one is too similar to Helen; the other to Menelaus! Helen is more open to recognition, and immediately accepts that her husband is he, exclaiming, "Come to me—I am your wife!" (*Helen* 566). He, however, is far from ready to reciprocate: "Wife? What do you mean? Leave my clothes alone!" (567). The facts simply fail to square, and when Helen asks him to believe his own eyes, he replies that while it is most certainly true that she resembles Helen, the evidence prevents him from believing it: he already has one Helen. And when the real Helen informs him that the other is an image created out of air by some god, and that there are not two Helens, as he seems to believe, but only a name endowed with ubiquity, Menelaus decides to leave her: "The memory of what I went through at Troy is more convincing than you are" (593).[1]

Seeing is most certainly not knowing, nor believing: what speaks directly is life, experience, suffering felt on the pulse, in the soul, and in the flesh. What is certain, for Menelaus, are the long years spent doggedly battling to win Helen back: defamation, death, destruction. This constitutes life. Accepting *this* Helen means believing in the unknown, in the unowned: accepting as one's own a different story invented by the gods, and another level of existence independent of oneself. In a word, it means making the leap of faith.

In Euripides's *Helen* Menelaus can afford not to run this risk. The Messenger informs him of the "prodigy": the Helen he had left in a cave before reaching the palace has vanished into the air, explaining the divine plan as she departed. And he who was skeptical of the evidence of their eyes, faced with this wonder, can now yield: "Then all concurs, and the woman speaks the truth! Ah long-desired day that brings you back into my arms!" (622–23). "That is this," is what Menelaus says literally: a paradox indeed, that two divergent realities are now recognized as one ("all concurs"), when one of the two is annulled by a "miracle," and a *thauma* is accepted as proof! Helen had required considerably less. After a moment's hesitation, given the stranger's condition, she was more than ready to welcome him back. Bursting with desire and longing ("Oh, Menelaus, when will you come? How I yearn for your arrival!" [540], she had exclaimed on leaving the palace) Helen looks and believes. "Oh gods!" she murmurs, "because to recognize those we love is a god" (560).

To recognize those we love is a god. The original, *theos gar kai to gignoskein philous,* leaves no room for doubt: in recognizing our loved ones (and the sentence could also be translated, "it is a god that makes us recognize those we love") there is, or there comes into play, something divine (*theos* could also be an adjective). It makes little difference whether the divinity is the cause or the thing: what Helen proclaims when she understands who is standing in front of her is that to love is human, to recognize divine: that the agnition[2] between two human beings linked through love has something of the life of the gods in it and is in itself a *numen*. This is a truth of no small significance. It places the divine within the process of awareness and the love between husband and wife, and at the same time makes that awareness, when accompanied by this love, an emanation of the divine—apparently, a small, but in reality a huge certainty. Helen has no need of the leap of faith: prepared by desire and longing, she perceives the divine immediately, within herself, an instant flood of feeling the moment she perceives her husband. Helen has no need of the leap of faith because she herself represents faith: that between husband and wife, which here is a seamless part of her faith in god.

II

Aristotle, who was the first to theorize on recognition, has absolutely nothing to say about this particular, stunning scene. Perhaps it seemed to him slightly ridiculous, or excessive, or perhaps it did not fit into his own, much more rational, scheme for what he called *anagnorisis*—recognition.[3] For Aristotle, anagnorisis is a key element of plot in both tragedy and the epic, together with *peripeteia* (reversal) and *pathos* (catastrophe). It generates pity and fear (*eleos* and *phobos*), which is the purpose of the mimesis inherent in tragedy, and it produces a shock of surprise and emotion tied to wonder. It is—thus his own definition—a change from ignorance to knowledge, and although this knowledge is of a particular person (or at times an object or an event), yet, because poetry is more philosophical than, say, history, and is concerned with universals, the knowledge that recognitions leads us to is universal. Several combinations of ignorance, knowledge, error (*hamartia*), and anagnorisis, are possible. And several forms of anagnorisis are also possible. Indeed some scholars have seen in the list of types of recognition that Aristotle gives in chapter 16 of the *Poetics* a mirror of the ascending kinds of knowledge—senses, memory, intellect, and "intuition"—he describes in the *Metaphysics* and the *Posterior Analytics*.[4] In the *Poetics* we have, in ascending order: (1) recognition through signs—birthmarks, scars, rings, necklaces, the main example here being Odysseus recognized by the nurse when she feels on his thigh the scar produced by the boar's wound; (2) recognition contrived by the poet, i.e., not stemming naturally from the plot; (3) recognition through memory (Odysseus, who cries when the bard sings of Troy, is recognized by Alcynous); (4) recognition based on reasoning (*syllogismos*: Electra and Orestes in Aeschylus), with its parallel type, that based on mistaken inference on the part of the audience; and finally, best of all, (5) recognition that arises from the events themselves and coincides with peripeteia (*Oedipus Rex* is the model).

Aristotle leaves out other instances, though they are present in the literature known to him: for example recognition "de facie," without complicated processes behind it (in the *Odyssey*, the people, who inhabit

Hades, recognize and are recognized by Odysseus at first sight once they drink the blood of the sacrifice), or recognition "by instinct" (such is the case of the dog, Argos, with Odysseus), or recognition by "exchange of words" (I am—I am; Glaucus-Diomedes in the *Iliad*), or recognition-revelation of gods (Athena in the *Iliad* and the *Odyssey*). And of course we do not know what Aristotle thought of anagnorisis in comedy, as the second book of the *Poetics*, if he wrote it, has not come down to us. What seems clear is that Aristotle is interested in three concomitant aspects of recognition: the blow of surprise and wonder it produces, the feeling of pity or fear it arouses, and its mechanism. Aristotle knows that recognition is an essential aspect of knowledge. At the very beginning of the *Poetics*, when he talks of imitation and says that human beings feel a particular pleasure before mimesis, he states that the reason for this is in fact recognition. When one sees a statue of, say, Pericles, one is struck by surprise and wonder at recognizing Pericles in the work of art: "this is that," *toutos ekeinos*, Aristotle says. Recognition, for him, is never neutral. It leads to either *philia* or *ekhthra*, that is to say either to friendship or hostility, and above all it produces either *eleos* or *phobos*, i.e., pity or fear or both. When a spectator watches Oedipus recognize himself as the very man who has killed his father and lain with his mother, he feels both pity towards the character and horror at what he has unwittingly done and now comes to know. Good recognition scenes are never cheap plot devices. They concern human beings and knowledge; they represent the acquisition of knowledge, not of abstractions or theoretical truths, but either of oneself or of another human being. They are charged with all the emotion and the ethical tensions this implies. One would be tempted to say, against Euripides, "There is something supremely human in recognition." If metaphysical inquiry is the search for prime causes and essential truth, anagnorisis is metaphysics in the flesh. This is why its mechanisms are so important for Aristotle and why in elaborating his kinds of recognition he stays so close to his theory of knowledge. The processes of sense perception, memory, and reasoning become dramatic, anguishing scenes. One needs but to read Eurykleia's washing episode, or Odysseus crying when the bard sings of Troy in the *Odyssey*, or watch Electra try to reach a rational conclusion on the identity of the person who has left a footprint and a lock of hair on her father's tomb in Aeschylus's *Choephoroi* to realize the immense power a good recognition scene holds.

Of course, there also exists a type of anagnorisis that is not just bad because of the way the artist organizes it, but that is potentially bad for the very reason the poet has contrived it rather than working it properly into the plot, the chain of events. Umberto Eco, for instance, has examined recognition in nineteenth-century popular novels, the so-called *feuilletons*, whose place has been taken in the latter part of the twentieth century by TV serials ("L'agnizione" 19–26). Eco starts with Aristotle and his definition of anagnorisis, but goes on to introduce a distinction the Greek philosopher never made, namely between double and simple recognition. The former, he says, must surprise not only the character but also the reader. The latter takes place when the character is totally dismayed, but the reader already knows what is happening (this is the case, for instance, of Edmond Dantès's multiple revelation scenes in Dumas's *Count of Monte Cristo*). Eco then introduces a third type of recognition, which he calls "the village-fool agnition" ("L'agnizione" 23–25). Of this, there exist according to him two subtypes—when the village fool is a real idiot and when he is only a maligned idiot. The first takes place when the author has provided both the character and the reader with all the clues necessary to solve the puzzle, but both are so stupid they do not come to the conclusion, i.e., the recognition. In the second case, the village fool is a maligned idiot because the events of the plot do not really tell him anything and what makes the reader aware is the tradition of popular novels. In Eugene Sue's *Les mystères de Paris*, the hero, Rodolphe, meets la Goualeuse, i.e., the defenceless, innocent prostitute Fleur-de-Marie. As soon as it becomes known that Rodolphe's child-daughter has been taken away from him, the reader of course understands that Fleur-de-Marie is that daughter. But why on earth should Rodolphe think he is the father of a young woman he has casually met in a dirty inn? He will, quite rightly, come to know this only at the end of the novel. But Sue knows the reader already suspects the solution, and thus anticipates it for him already at the end of the novel's first part. In other words, the plot is subject, Eco says, to the "conditioning of literary tradition and mercantile distribution" ("Edmond Dantès" 38). "Useless recognition" is what Eco terms this kind of anagnorisis, and one would naturally tend to associate it with Aristotle's recognition contrived by the poet, were it not for the fact that Eco adds a final type, the topos of "the false unknown."

> At the opening of a chapter, popular novels often present a mysterious character who should be unknown to the reader, but after making him act as much as it is necessary, the author warns: "The unknown man, in whom the reader will have already recognized X...." The protagonist of the recognition, be it noted, is not the character (the unknown figure knows perfectly who he is and generally appears in a dark lane or a private room without anyone else having seen him), but only the reader. If he is well acquainted with feuilleton, the reader understands immediately that the unknown figure is a false unknown and normally guesses straightaway who he might be, but the author insists in making him play the part of the village fool—and perhaps succeeds with some less knowledgeable readers. (Eco, "Edmond Dantès" 38)

When Eco's later piece appeared in the Italian daily, *La Repubblica*, on 1 February 2008, it was accompanied by a wonderful *collage* of recognition scenes concocted by him and stitched together so as to form a continuous whole in which one scene was, as it were, fitted into, or presented as the sequel, of another. Dumas's *Three Musketeers* merged into Ponson du Terrail's *Rocambole*, and this in turn into the novels by Garibaldi, Xavier de Montepin, Victor Hugo's *Les Misérables*, and Dumas's *Count of Monte Cristo*. But one could also elaborate a different typology based on Aristotle and mainstream, "high" literature, thematically, and diachronically organized. In other words, each section would be devoted to a theme and would span from antiquity through the Middle Ages to modernity.[5]

The *first* section is devoted to "return"—*nostos* as the Greeks called it. This is the world of the *Odyssey*, which in many ways represents the entire cosmos of recognition. There are something like thirty recognition or misrecognition scenes in the poem, including of course the two singled out by Aristotle, Alcynous's and Eurykleia's. But return necessarily implies anagnorisis; for a man who comes back home after twenty years has obviously changed and must eventually be recognized as the same who left. Thus, in the *Odyssey*, Odysseus recognizes his Ithaca after being landed there, and then reveals himself to Telemachus, is recognized by the dog, the nurse, the swineherd, the Suitors, Penelope, and finally his father Laertes. There are, in addition, a number of scenes of misrecognition, notably the first meeting between Odysseus disguised as a beggar and his wife, or the many times the protagonist presents himself with a different identity. The theme of recognition between gods and between gods and human beings is also present, and at least two scenes here, between Calypso and Hermes and between Athena and Odysseus, are capital. Another set involves Telemachus on his journey to Pylos and Sparta, when he is recognized by Nestor, Menelaus, and Helen (who also recounts a recognition scene between herself and Odysseus disguised as a tramp spying in Troy during the war). Finally, an absolutely essential series of recognition scenes takes place in Hades, the other world, when Odysseus arrives there to consult Tiresias. Agamemnon, Achilles, and Ajax—Odysseus's old companions during the Trojan War—appear to him, and the moving anagnorisis between Odysseus and his mother, Antikleia, who has in the meantime died, is also described. Most of these scenes are staged with supreme artistry and charged with amazingly intense emotion— suffice it to think of those that involve Odysseus with his mother, wife, and father. They also always point to something deeper: a rediscovery of the self, the finding of one's real and most profound roots, the discovery of truth (for instance, about death, love, the divinity, memory, poetry, narrative). After the *Odyssey*, return continues to inspire wonderful scenes of recognition, or misrecognition, in reality as well as literature. When someone returns after a war pretending to be the husband of a well-to-do woman, he can be recognized by her as her true husband. The case of the French Martin Guerre is a famous one thanks to Montaigne and Natalie

Zemon Davis,[6] but the Bruneri-Canella one occupied Italy for two decades in the 1920s and 1930s, and the vicissitudes of the Russian Pseudo-Dmitry, or of the various Lost Dauphins of France, had some serious historical consequences. In the novel, it will be enough to recall Dumas's *Count of Monte Cristo*, Tolstoy's masterful scene between Pierre and Natasha at the end of *War and Peace*, and Pirandello's *The Late Mattia Pascal*. But a special place is occupied here by modern works that rewrite the *Odyssey* or sections of it, such as Jean Giono's *La naissance de l'Odyssée*, Joyce's *Ulysses*, and Proust's *Recherche*.

In the final section of the latter, *Time Regained*, the famous matinée at the Guermantes, when Marcel finds some of his old acquaintances after a long time, is described with precise reference to the Hades episode in *Odyssey* XI (Proust, *À la recherche du temps perdu* 518, 523).[7] The scene opens up a discussion on the relationship between memory and recognition, draws out a space for the distinction between what Proust here terms *penser*, *savoir*, and *comprendre*, and establishes an illuminating connection between agnition and death. It would constitute the modern example of a *second* theme in an organic treatment of anagnorisis, which one would have to devote to memory—Aristotle's *mneme*—and which would begin with the recognition of Odysseus triggered by the bard's singing in *Odyssey* VIII. Touching on Plato's theory of knowledge as memory, the discussion here would have to include some of the Dante's capital examples, such as Forese's and Piccarda's, and later, Romantic instances.

In Joyce's novel one would pay particular attention to the way the Irish author has transformed the recognition, or misrecognition, scenes in Homer's poem. Macintosh, the raincoat-man, is never quite recognized by Leopold Bloom, but the novel ends with two stunning pieces of anagnorisis between husband and wife, Penelope and Ulysses. In the first, Bloom finally reaches the nuptial bed (the *Odyssey*'s sign for recognition and the place where Ulysses and Penelope are finally joined) where his unfaithful Penelope, Molly, lies. She is half naked after the day's exertions with her lover, and half asleep. What is above all visible of her is her beautiful bottom. Then the signs invoked by Aristotle for anagnorisis begin to show:

"visible signs of antesatisfaction," Joyce writes, "an approximate erection: a solicitous adversion: a gradual elevation: a tentative revelation: a silent contemplation." A few seconds later, they have become "visible signs of postsatisfaction" and "a silent contemplation: a tentative revelation: a gradual abasement: a solicitous aversion: a proximate erection." And finally, anagnorisis takes place: "somnolent invocation, less somnolent recognition, incipient excitation, catechetical interrogation" (Joyce 484–86). *Ulysses* will then culminate and end with Molly's final recognition and acceptance of her husband, her life, and the universe: "And yes I said yes I will Yes" (Joyce 644).

A *third* theme, which coincides with one of Aristotle's types, is that of reasoning, *syllogismos*. Reasoning in this particular form—logical deduction based on clues—comes into being with Greek philosophy and is immediately staged by Greek dramatists. To study recognition by reasoning from classical Greece down to modern times means, then, to test the belief in reason that subsequent ages have held, and it is fairly important here to establish links with contemporary philosophies—for instance, between recognition scenes built by playwrights in the seventeenth and eighteenth centuries and the theories of knowledge by Descartes or the English empiricist thinkers, or to follow the different meanings recognition takes in the thought of Kant, Hegel, Ernst Bloch, and Ricoeur.[8] The Electra-Orestes recognition scene in Aeschylus's *Choephoroi*, discussed by Aristotle, is the progenitor of this type. In it, Aeschylus shows himself fully aware of the difficulties reason encounters when trying to reach a firm conclusion, but he also affirms a strong belief in the power of reason. The recognition scenes in the Electra plays by his successors—both in fact rewritings of his archetype—qualify that faith. Euripides, for instance, ridicules both Aeschylus's clues and his *syllogismos*. Sophocles turns both upside down with amazing skill. But the story reaches our own day and age. Translations of Aeschylus (for example, Robert Lowell's) transform key elements in the scene so as to make the scene palatable to modern audiences.[9] Electra plays by Enlightenment writers such as Voltaire or pre-romantics like Alfieri rely on anything but reason. Likewise, the scene is either eliminated (thus Marguerite Yourcenar) or completely changed by authors such as Hofmannsthal (and Strauss in his opera version), Jean Giraudoux, Eugene O'Neil, and Sartre in *Les mouches*.[10] But the great paragon of modern reasoning in drama is Shakespeare's *Hamlet*, and a comparison between this and the Electra plays of antiquity (Pirandello, who knew something about the theatre, wrote in *The Late Mattia Pascal* that if you take the paper sky out of Sophocles's *Electra*, Orestes turns into Hamlet) shows a great turning point in Western belief about the power of reason. Hamlet can argue *ad libitum* and with great Scholastic, logical precision about whatever he fixes his mind upon, for instance, about Alexander's body eventually turning into the loam stopping a beer barrel. But he cannot reach any conclusion whatsoever on the three most urgent questions that anguish him, namely whether the ghost that has appeared to him really is that of his father, whether Claudius is guilty of his brother's murder (the evidence he chooses, Claudius's reaction to the play, just will not work), and whether death is preferable to life ("To be or not to be," a question analyzed with Scholastic subtlety but that eventually bangs, once more, against the wall of conscience). The quasi-recognition scene between Hamlet and his father's ghost is staged by Wilhelm Meister in Goethe's *Lehrjahre*, and if anyone needs any proof that anagnorisis is an unfathomable mystery, that there are more things in heaven and earth than our philosophy ever dreamt of, and that reason works only up to a certain point, then Goethe's scene would be the best evidence.

For Aristotle, the best type of anagnorisis is that which takes place at the same time as the peripeteia, the reversal, in a plot where the protagonist acts without knowing the truth about himself or event. In this case, the plot is built like perfect clockwork, and the release of emotion, the *explexis* or shock, is greatest. The knowledge one acquires with this kind of recognition, critics have maintained, does not simply match Delphi's motto, "Know thyself," but also resembles that which is attained in Aristotle's last and supreme way of knowing, where the mind, after having gone through sense perception, memory, and reasoning, apprehends all as it were in a single intuition. Several times in the *Poetics*, Aristotle indicates clearly that Sophocles's *Oedipus Rex* incarnates for him the best tragic plot and the best anagnorisis. But one of the main themes of *Oedipus* is the way in which knowledge leads to annihilation of the protagonist as a ruler and human being, to his blindness and self-exile. The coming together of artistic perfection and nothingness deserves, I think, a special section—the *fourth*—in an ideal treatment of recognition, particularly in view of modern pessimism. One could therefore examine here the many rewritings of *Oedipus Rex* that have occupied Western artists since antiquity: Statius's *Thebaid* and many medieval versions, Seneca, Corneille, Calderon's *La vida es sueño*, Voltaire, Hofmannsthal, Cocteau's *La machine infernale*, Renzo Rosso, Pasolini; in opera, Leoncavallo, Mussorgsky, Stravinsky. Yet here again there is one exemplary modern play that can, from its very title, be associated and usefully compared with *Oedipus Rex*—Shakespeare's *King Lear*, the story of a man, and of his follower in misfortune, Gloucester, who lose their kingdom and dukedom because of their own foolishness, have to go through humiliation, madness, loneliness, blindness, and defeat to know themselves, and experience three astonishing recognition and self-recognition scenes (Lear's with his daughter Cordelia being the supreme one) before their final annihilation.

III

In *King Lear*, one is forced to note a series of elements that are basically foreign to classical antiquity, namely the presence of a Job plot and of a subtext represented by Paul's dictum in I Corinthians 3.18, "If any man among you seemeth to be wise in this world, let him become a fool, that he may be wise." This opens up an entirely new perspective; for there is a whole world of biblical recognition—I mean both in the Hebrew and the Christian Bible—that critics have not really tackled. I offer here only a few remarks. The Bible does not theorize on anagnorisis, but exhibits quite a few recognition scenes, especially in Genesis and in the New Testament. And in a sense, from Genesis to Exodus to the very first words of John's Gospel, one of the central themes of the Bible is precisely that of God who struggles to be recognized by Israel and fails to do so except by recourse to exceptional means, such as theophanies or through exceptional human beings like Abraham, Jacob, Joseph, Moses, David, Solomon, the prophets, and later the Apostles. The Bible stages this theme much more consistently and much more mysteriously than, say, does Euripides in the *Bacchae*, where Dionysus wants to be recognized by the Thebans and plays illusion tricks on Pentheus to achieve his purpose, with the final result that, after the god's epiphany, the true recognition is that by which Agave becomes aware that she is carrying the head of her own son and that she has killed him.[11]

The Bible goes one step further—it shows us with obsessive insistence two essential features: first, that in order to recognize God, man must have an inner readiness to do so and, as it were, a knowledge of himself as a human being, a capacity to turn inwards constantly, and to be constantly open outwards and upwards. Secondly, the Bible tells us that, when it comes to the recognition of God by man, there is ultimately no proof. You have just got to believe it; you cannot rely either on signs, memory, or inference. In New Testament, Greek *pistis* does not mean "proof," but "faith," and *semeia* (signs) are Jesus's miracles. In Hebrew, *haker*—to recognize—is much less important, though by no means insignificant, than *jada'*, to know. But *jada'* in the sense of knowing God always implies recognition, acknowledgement, confession, and gratitude, or, as one German commentator puts it much more neatly, *Erkenntnis, Anerkenntnis, Bekenntnis*, and *Erkenntlichkeit* (Botterwerk 503). The most astonishing example of this is Job, who, after listening to the voice of God exploding out of the whirlwind, exclaims, "I had heard of thee by the hearing of the ear; but now mine eyes seeth thee...I know thee." Job re cognizes, acknowledges, and "confesses" his God (Job 42.5–6).

However, if I were to choose the best recognition scenes in the Hebrew Bible, I would unhesitatingly pick Genesis 18, Abraham's meeting with the three beings traditionally identified as angels, and Genesis 37–45, the story of Joseph. When, in Genesis 19, does Abraham understand that one of the three is Yahweh himself, as the reader has been informed in the very first sentence of the chapter? Halfway through the episode, Abraham acts as the village fool indeed. He uses singulars and plurals seemingly without any consistency, is made to address his guests indifferently, because of the consonantal nature of the Hebrew language, as lords or lord or Lord. Then, suddenly, he finds himself alone face to face with the Lord, seemingly knows his mind to destroy Sodom and Gomorrah (but how, since He only discloses his intention to "go down, and see"?), stands up to God, negotiates with him as to the number of just people needed to save the cities, and teaches him an unforgettable lesson on the nature of justice: "That be far from thee to do after this manner, to slay the righteous with the wicked: and that the righteous should be as the wicked, that be far from thee: Shall not the Judge of all the earth do right?" (Gen. 18.25). There is no doubt that at this point Abraham has recognized Yahweh. But perhaps he was a maligned idiot from the very beginning and he just wanted to be sure before addressing this man (for the three are simply called "men" at the beginning of the chapter) as God. The anagnorisis remains a total mystery, but at least two things are clear, that Abraham recognizes the Lord inasmuch as he in a sense creates God, appointing him Judge of all the earth, and because he, Abraham, knows himself, a mere human being of "dust and ashes" now standing before his incommensurable Divinity.

In the case of Abraham's great-grandchild, Joseph son of Jacob, recognition is a much more complex phenomenon. In fact, it constitutes a theme and a continuous play that begins at the beginning, when both Jacob and his ten sons refuse to recognize the prophetic truth of Joseph's apparently foolish dreams of superiority and command. Later, Jacob is forced to acknowledge the coat dipped in the blood of a goat's kid as evidence that Joseph has been devoured by an "evil beast"; Judah has to publically recognize that the signet, the bracelets, and the staff he had given his Tamar, believing her to be a prostitute, are in fact his and that he has lain with his daughter-in-law and is the father of her child. Further along in the narrative, the disastrous outcome of the episode of Joseph and Potiphar's wife is based on the (false) recognition of Joseph's garment. Then, the brothers' descent into Egypt to buy grain sets off a momentous and at first mysterious deployment of agnitions and misrecognitions rarely matched in literature. Throughout, the brothers are the maligned idiots and Joseph of course an all-knowing God. They cannot recognize in this Egyptian potentate the brother they had sold into slavery; he of course recognizes them immediately and weeps. He plays with them like a cat with mice, accusing them of being spies and detaining one until the others bring Benjamin down to him (they, and Ruben in particular, confess aloud their guilt towards Joseph, who understands them, but they do not understand him because he has so far used an interpreter). He has the precise amount of money they have paid for corn placed in their sacks, then, when they return with Benjamin, he arranges them around the table according to their ages, and, when they depart again, he has the payment for the corn put into their sacks again and his special silver divination cup placed in Benjamin's sack. When they are brought back to his palace, he decides that Benjamin, who is apparently guilty of having stolen the cup, should stay as his prisoner. And at this point, Judah rises and makes a speech in which he personally takes full responsibility for Benjamin's life. Joseph can no longer restrain himself. He orders all Egyptians out of the room and reveals himself, crying, "I am Joseph. Doth my father live?" (Gen. 45.3), and, a few minutes later, as final evidence but with a threatening touch, "I am Joseph your brother, whom ye sold into Egypt" (Gen. 45.4).

It is a glorious story, which uses signs as wonderfully ambiguous clues, plays with dreams and their foreboding and interpretation, touches the innermost chords of human feeling, and leads to a final apotheosis. The whole story of Joseph and his brothers constitutes a process of anagnorisis, the passing from ignorance to knowledge (in Aristotle's definition), based on three basic, complementary, and interconnected devices: sign, recognition, and revelation. Totally human, they at the same time project a divine shadow over events. This part of Genesis, for example, organizes its signs to construct a discourse, not in analytical but in *narrative* philosophy, which constantly adumbrates the meeting point between human and divine. It explores the material, evidential value of signs intentionally created by human individuals, and foregrounds the importance for their correct reading of the context of the events embedding them. It also underscores the psychological resonance generating and being generated by them. This resonance originates in the memory and the feelings—pain, amazement, fear, terror—and awakens in the addressee self-knowledge, moral awareness, gratitude, and confession. Without the paradigm created here, the *Comedy* as it stands would have been impossible for Dante, and Dostoevsky could not have written *The Brothers Karamazov*. Here everything becomes sign: objects, words, gestures, actions, and even knowledge itself (for example Joseph's in arranging his brothers according to age). Then, through doubt and wonder, the human sign provokes the crucial question, and *allows us to glimpse God*: "What is this that God has done to us?" (Gen. 43.28), the brothers ask on finding the money in the sacks.

There can be no agnition without signs: Judah needs all the objects given to Tamar; Joseph's brothers need his sentence, "I am Joseph your brother, whom you sold into Egypt," his weeping, and his embrace. However, while later midrash gives a decisive weight to this, Genesis considers it necessary but insufficient: here agnition is not possible without a recognition of personal responsibility, without which the sign is open to misinterpretation and the agnition becomes méconaissance and ultimately ruin. This recognition once again involves God: "God has found out the crime of your servants," Judah proclaims in his great speech (Gen. 44.16). Lastly—and this is the real key to the narrative's anagnorisis—agnition is impossible without revelation, and vice versa. The brothers cannot recognize Joseph until he is ready to reveal himself; when he does decide, he must do it through signs, however oblique. "I am Joseph your brother, whom you sold into Egypt" is a symbolic fusion of the two procedures. Neither agnition nor revelation occurs by chance: they are born, as Aristotle rightly states for those of *Oedipus Rex*, "out of the events themselves." But those events are orchestrated by man and willed by God.

This kind of anagnorisis ultimately points, of course, to the revelation-recognition process of God himself. Not only does the opening formula—"I am Joseph"—recall that through which God reveals himself to the patriarchs, but Joseph's next statement points explicitly, for a full three times, to a recognition of the divine plan: "God has sent me before you to preserve life" (Gen. 45.5). The story of Joseph, his brothers, and the elderly Jacob reveals exactly how the anagnorisis becomes a further stage in the discovery of God, God-centric discourse, *theo-logy* as history of salvation, *Heilsgeschichte*, in which the individual recognizes his or her true role, that of other individuals, and that of the Lord: "God has found out the crime of your servants," Judah admits, applying the manifestation of God to the sphere of personal responsibility. "Am I in the place of God? While you meant evil toward me, God meant it for good, for the survival of many people" (Gen. 50.20–21), Joseph chides and comforts his dismayed brothers, extending the question from personal sins to the ways God uses them to act in the world.

Any critical treatment of recognition in the Joseph story would of course be incomplete without a comparison with its later rewritings. If I had the space, I would deal with great personal delight with Flavius Josephus and Sura XII of the Qur'an, where the plot is recreated in a new light, and above all with Thomas Mann's massive and beautiful tetralogy *Joseph and his Brothers*. I will simply point out a couple of important features. Firstly, the theme and problem of recognition pervades Mann's gigantic amplification of the Bible story both because it comprises, in itself, the ultimate point of the story, and because the story offers itself as re-writing. Mann immediately underlines that recognition begins in Genesis long before the story of Joseph, when, at his mother Rebecca's instigation, Jacob tricks his father Isaac into giving him the blessing of his brother Esau. While in Genesis Isaac fails, falteringly, to "recognize" Jacob because his arms are hairy like Esau's, in Mann's *The Tales of Jacob* (the first of his four volumes), Isaac is both more uncertain and at the same time convinced by the evidence of the material sign offered him. His "sighted blindness" is played on more openly, and Jacob's reply, which glances at Christ's words to Pilate, "Thou sayest," foregrounds it even more. "'Yea,' said he, 'these are thy hairy limbs and Esau's red fleeces,

I see them with my seeing hands and must be convinced. The voice is the voice of Jacob, but the hands are the hands of Esau. Art thou then my very son Esau?'" Upon which Jacob answers, "Thou seest and sayest it" (Mann, *Joseph und seine Brüder* 207; Lowe-Porter 137). This is just the first of the tetralogy's many recognition scenes, which will end not with Joseph's revelation of himself to his brothers, but with a moving anagnorisis between Joseph and Jacob. Secondly, the recognition theme is tied to Abraham's discovery of God, which is in fact presented as both an "invention" (*inventio* or finding out) and a recognition, and to Jacob's subsequent development of that discovery. Thirdly, Mann works into the recognition scenes of the novel clear echoes of the New Testament, particularly from the Passion and Resurrection sequels. Fourthly, recognition soon becomes a cosmic law: of myth, of time, of the relationship between the human and the divine, and of narrative itself. But Mann, who comes over two thousand years after Aristotle, writes his novel when Freud is still alive. And *Joseph and his Brothers* relies heavily on Freud for a final feature of its recognition theme. At one point in the novel, Mann stops using the word *erkennen* for recognizing, and begins to employ *wiedererkennen*—re-cognizing, a term that mirrors a whole ontology and aesthetics. In *Joseph in Egypt*, the third of the four novels, Mann wonders whether he knows his story or not, and his reply lies in the mystery of Abraham's recognition of God. The same mystery, however, holds for the story, the characters, and not least the narrator himself. Shortly before, in the same chapter, Mann had stated: "I feel indeed as though I had once already reached this point in my story and told it once before; the special feeling of recognition (*des Wiedererkennens*), of having been here before and seen it all (*des Schongesehen*) and dreamed the same dream (*des Schongeträumt*), moves me and challenges me to dwell upon it—and such precisely were the feelings, such the experience of my hero" (*Joseph und seine Brüder* 654; Lowe-Porter 612). At the same time, life is but a repetition of what has already taken place, "for we move in the footsteps of others, and all life is but the outpouring of the present into the forms of the myth" (Mann, *Joseph und seine Brüder* 657; Lowe-Porter 465). The *Wiedererkennen* is inseparable from this way of being, since it is the awareness of forming part of the process of imitation. The only recognition is a re-cognitive process. But this *déjà-vu*, this *Schongeträumt*, this re-cognition, are the feelings of the narrator, too; he has already "told it once before," he tells us. And it is here that the process of re-cognition joins life with narrative. In "Freud and the Future," Mann writes that if older schools of biography seek self-endorsement and verisimilitude through the fact of narrating "as it always was" and "as it has been written," it is precisely because "man sets store by recognition" (*dem Menschen ist am Wiedererkennen gelegen*). In the new, we seek the old; in the individual, the type. It is from that recognition that man draws "a sense of the familiar in life" ("Freud and the Future" 243).[12] Mann, clearly here in sympathy with the Freud who, in *Jokes and their Relation to the Unconscious*, posits the "joy of re-cognition" (*Freude am Wiedererkennen*) as one of the central impulses of the human being, would seem to share this comfort, and does everything in his power—and how could he not, given the nature of re-writing?—to involve us in the same emotion. For, if Mann is the re-writer, we are re-readers. We too, then, are the addressees of the answer given by Aristotle (or one of his close followers) to the question, in the *Problems*, as to why we enjoy familiar music so much more than a new piece: "because in the one instance we simply acquire knowledge; in the other we use it in a form of *recognition* (*anagnorizein*)" (XIX, 5 and 40; 918a 5–9 and 921a 32–39).

If the Hebrew Bible and its rewritings thus present us with the *fifth* section of our treatment of anagnorisis, the *sixth* would inevitably include the New Testament. The key pre-Passion scene of recognition in the Gospels occurs when Jesus asks his disciples who they think he is. Peter—the same Peter who will later deny knowledge of Jesus—replies, "Thou art the Christ, the Son of the living God." Jesus's answer to this is very interesting: "Blessed art thou, Simon Bar-jona: for flesh and blood hath not revealed it unto thee, but my Father which is in heaven" (*Novum Testamentum Graece et Latine*, Mark 8.27–30; Matthew 16.13–20; Luke 9.18–21). Peter's recognition of the Christ has rightly been called a "confession," *Petri Confessio*. This is not based on material signs, on flesh and blood, but on God's direct *revelation*, to which evidently Peter the man has responded.

During the Last Supper we have a mysterious scene in which the disciples play the role of the village fools while the readers understand everything. When Jesus says, "One of you shall betray me," the disciples fail to recognize Judas as the traitor in spite of the indications Jesus gives (Mark 14.17–21; Matthew 26.20–25; Luke 22.21–23; John 13. 21–26). But it is after the Resurrection that recognition attains its climax in the New Testament. All Gospels present crucial, startling scenes of misrecognition or anagnorisis after the Crucifixion. Only in Mark's original text there is none, because the women gone to the tomb only see a man in white and they flee in terror.[13] In Matthew, Jesus appears to the women after the angel has told them he is risen, and they, recognizing him, worship him. However, the three most beautiful scenes are of course to be found in Luke and John. The episode of Emmaus in the former (24.13–35) is totally unexpected and admirably poignant, so much so that Dante will use it in *Purgatorio* XXI and T.S. Eliot in *The Waste Land*. The fact that the disciples do not recognize Jesus for a long time and only do so when he breaks and blesses the bread in a repetition of the Eucharist is a mystery of primary theological import. Yet it is John's treatment of recognition after the Resurrection that has made readers and artists throughout the ages gasp with surprise and wonder. Mary Magdalene and Doubting Thomas have become paragons of the Western imagination. Why does Magdalene not recognize Jesus when he appears to her and speaks, and she takes him for the gardener? Why does she recognize him only when he calls her by name? What exactly is the point of Peter's and the Beloved Disciple's rush to the tomb, a scene within the scene? The dramatic artistry that goes into John 20 is extraordinary. The puzzles I have just pointed to are underlined in the same chapter by Jesus's apparition to the disciples and finally to Thomas. Thomas doubts that Jesus has really risen and appeared to the others and says that he will not believe it unless he sees his hands with the print of the nails and puts his finger into those prints and thrusts his hands into his side. What Thomas wants is material evidence, like the scar Eurykleia washes on Odysseus's thigh. And he would get it, for Jesus, who appears once more now, invites him to do precisely what the disciple would wish. But, as things are, John will not have a traditional recognition scene. In the lines that follow, the text nowhere states that Thomas touched Jesus's wounds. Instead, it simply makes Thomas pronounce the New Testament version of the Old Testament faith formula: *ho Kyrios mou kai ho Theos mou*, "My Lord and my God" (John 20.28). The whole point is further clarified by what Jesus says immediately afterwards: "Thomas, because thou hast seen me, thou hast believed: blessed are they that have not seen, and yet have believed" (John 20.29). Even the evidence of sight is denied value.

It is this scene that gives rise to a Christian theory of anagnorisis. John Chrysostom, Gregory the Great, and Peter Lombard (who quotes them and whose *Sentences* are universally known in the later Middle Ages) maintain that "de visis enim non est fides, sed agnitio" (Chrysostom, *In Hebrew* 21, 2; *PG* 63, 151) and "apparentia non habent fidem, sed agnitionem" (Gregory, *Hom. In Evangelia* II, xxvi; *PL* 76, 1201–202). Things that appear, which can be seen, do not involve faith, but recognition.[14] Gregory, whose relevant passage is reproduced by Peter Lombard, solves the problem with a stroke of genius that picks up the substance of an argument developed by Augustine. Both Augustine and Gregory maintain that Thomas did touch his Master's wounds, and Gregory adds that this was allowed by the Lord himself so that we can have solid faith. Faith, says Gregory quoting the Epistle to the Hebrews (11.1), is "the substance of things hoped for, the evidence of things not seen" (*Hom. In Evangelia* II, xxvi; *PL* 76, 1201–2). So Thomas's was not an act of faith, but one of recognition. "Tactus est, et agnitus est," he was touched and recognized, says Augustine. But then, asks Gregory, why does Jesus tell Thomas, "because thou hast seen me, thou hast believed"? The answer that both Augustine and Gregory give to this question is subtle and fundamental. Thomas, says Gregory, "saw something, but believed something else" (*Hom. In Evangelia* II, xxvi; *PL* 76, 1201–202). A man cannot see the divinity, the divine nature. "Thomas saw a man, but confessed God": my Lord and my God. "Hence by seeing he believed, because considering true the man (realizing he really was Jesus the man), he proclaimed him God, whom he could not see" (Augustine 327). Thus, what we have here is a double scene: first, one of anagnorisis, with the right signs (Jesus's wounds, which, says Gregory, "heal the wounds of our lack of faith"); then one of faith. This interpretation—a splendid fusion of Greek rationalism and Hebrew-Christian mystery—will condition medieval versions of the episode, for instance, in the Mystery Plays. And if we wanted to see what modern authors do with the theme, we would have to consult Klopstock's *Messias* (where the conflict between recognition and faith is brilliantly solved by means of Joseph's—the Joseph of Genesis—intervention) and the conversation between the Devil and Ivan in Dostoevsky's *Brothers Karamazov*. Furthermore—and here we would enter our *seventh* section—we should examine in detail the recognition scenes in Dante's *Comedy*, which represents the medieval universe of anagnorisis as the *Odyssey* contained the totality of recognition for classical antiquity. Virgil, Francesca, Brunetto, Casella, Forese, Statius, Beatrice, Piccarda are supreme examples of this in the poem and will become paradigmatic for modern writers, such as T.S. Eliot and Seamus Heaney.

However, the best rewritings of John's scenes come in Shakespeare's romances. Shakespeare, as one would expect from a playwright, has experimented with anagnorisis throughout his career, and admirable recognition scenes are present in the comedies as well as in, for instance, *Romeo and Juliet*, *Twelfth Night*, and, as we have seen, *Hamlet* and *King Lear*. It is precisely the scene between Lear and Cordelia that constitutes the stunning archetype of the recognitions Shakespeare stages in *Pericles*, *Cymbeline*, and *The Winter's Tale*.[15] In all these plays, recognition involves an old father and a young daughter lost and found (in two, *Pericles* and *Winter's Tale*, the old man is also a husband who after a long time finds his wife again). The recognition (at times double) takes place after infinite vicissitudes ultimately inspired by Greek romance—and takes the form, as indeed in that kind of romance and in John's Gospel, as a miraculous event. In each of the plays, the anagnorisis scene (or the two anagnorisis scenes) comes at the end of the action, so that recognition and denouement coincide in a summit of emotional tension. In all three plays, the scene is organized with unbelievable slowness and extraordinary delay, so as to lead from ignorance to knowledge through partial clues and revelations as if in a musical crescendo (and music plays an essential role in all three plays).

In *Cymbeline*, where recognition involves not only the old father Cymbeline and his daughter Imogen, but also her brothers Guiderius and Arviragus, their stepfather Belarius, her husband Posthumus, and the Roman general Lucius, the scene, over five hundred lines long, is composed of sixteen movements, which pick up and conclude all the plot's threads in the new light that surrounds everything. In *Pericles*, the two final scenes—the two agnitions between Pericles and respectively his daughter Marina and his wife Thaisa—appear like stages of a single epiphany. In the former, through words that sound like fragmentary clues, Marina's identity slowly penetrates, and then explodes in Pericles's mind. The revelation makes him hear the music of the spheres. In the latter, Diana's appearing *ex machina* prepares the ground for a recognition based on voices (as in the case of Jesus and Mary Magdalene) and brings Pericles to an acme where happiness and annihilation coincide. In the *Winter's Tale*, the scene between Leontes and his daughter Perdita (of which the spectator only learns indirectly) is a preparation for that in which all characters witness the return to life of the statue of Hermione, Leontes's dead wife. But, having discussed the *Pericles* and *Cymbeline* scenes at length elsewhere,[16] I would like to explore the *Winter's Tale* here.

Leontes's jealousy makes him lose at the same time his newly born girl, Perdita, and his wife, Hermione. Yet to the contrast between appearance and reality, to the vicissitudes, the shipwreck, the pastoral scene of the other romances, Shakespeare adds in the *Winter's Tale* the opposition between Nature and Art, and the debate on this occupies the whole play. It is not by chance that while the recognition between Leontes and Perdita is presented indirectly, through the account of three Gentlemen of the Court, that between Leontes and Hermione, carefully prepared in the previous scene, takes up much greater space and closes the play. For in the sixteen years (time is perhaps the play's main theme) which separate Perdita's birth and Hermione's "death" from the child's blooming into a beautiful flower, Hermione has been "preserved" by her friend Paulina in a way Shakespeare never clarifies, and suddenly appears as a statue, a work of art just completed by the renowned Italian artist Giulio Romano. Giulio is the author of a statue that is such a perfect replica—a *mimesis*— of the original, of Hermione, that one can think in the statue Art beats Nature, and Life is more alive than the life that was. It is not just a question of living statues, of which there is a long tradition. This statue is a miracle, a piece of wonder, as the three Gentlemen say using the highly charged word "grace."

In order to understand what kind of statue Giulio Romano has made, we need to follow the three Gentlemen into the gallery full of rarities and watch the scene that unfolds before us. All the play's characters are present. Suddenly, Paulina draws out the curtains and reveals the statue. She asks the spectators to "prepare / To see life as lively mocked as ever / Still sleep mocked death" (*The Winter's Tale* 5.3.18–20). Whether, in fact, this be sleep or death the *Winter's Tale* never clarifies, but the revelation produces among the onlookers total silence, the sign of a stupefied recognition. "I like your silence," Paulina says, "it the more shows off / Your wonder" (5.3.23–24). For indeed this is the moment Aristotle speaks of at the beginning of the *Poetics*, when, in discussing the pleasure human beings feel in contemplating images that imitate real figures, he states that the instant one recognizes that "this is that," i.e., that the image corresponds to the figure, is supreme (15–19; 1448b).

By degrees now, with incomparable slowness, recognition and resurrection begin. Hermione's imitation, Leontes exclaims, is perfect: she was "tender as infancy and grace," the stone, now, is "dear"; yet, it has wrinkles, it looks "aged" in a way his wife was not. "So much the more our carver's excellence," Paulina replies, "Which lets go by some sixteen years and makes her / As she lived now" (5.3.30–32). Art, then, imagines Time, reads life through it, imitates Nature. Yet it also passes over Time and life by concentrating into an icon—"warm life, as now it coldly stands"—what was subjected to death. While Leontes sees in the statue the "life of majesty" he knew in the lady when he wooed her and a "magic" that prompts in him memory and repentance, Perdita wants to kneel, implore her blessing, take her hand and kiss it. Both are now Leontes remarks, "standing like stone" with the statue. Husband and daughter have, through a wonder that is stupor, become statues. Paulina, who several times in the scene threatens to close the curtain, invites them to be patient, replying that the image has just been finished, her colours are not dry yet. But Art enchants: it looks as if the statue were breathing, its veins pulsing with real blood, the "very life," as Polixenes notes, "seems warm upon her lip" (5.3.66). "No longer shall you gaze on't," Paulina rejoins, "lest your fancy / May think anon it moves" (5.3.60–61). So, Art can operate on human fancy to the point of making it believe a statue can move. In fact, Leontes is by now "transported," as Paulina notes. To all effects, he is enraptured. "Let be, let be!" he cries, "Would that I were dead but that methinks already—/ What was he that did make it?" (5.3.62–64). Leontes, who apparently knows nothing of Giulio Romano, would like to learn something about him. But he is more interested in the actual piece of work. He observes, now, that "the fixture of her eye has motion in't," adding, "as we are mocked with art" (5.3.67–68). What is the meaning of "as" in that sentence? Does it imply a strict causal relationship, or is it a mere statement of fact? Does Leontes believe he detects motion in those eyes because he is deceived by art? The phrase is of course a topos, but the meaning of topoi depends on the context within which they are inserted. And at the core of this scene there lies, as we shall soon see in greater detail, epistemological doubt. As a matter of fact, when Paulina shows herself ready to draw the curtain, Leontes declares himself ready to abandon "settled senses" and embrace the present "madness." Once more, he thinks he sees "air" coming from "her"—no longer a stone, but a person. "What fine chisel / Could ever yet cut breath?" (5.3.78–79), he asks, this time doubting that art can imitate life to its very essence, and suddenly agreeing with the third Gentleman, who in the previous scene had said that if Giulio Romano "could put breath into his work," he would "beguile Nature of her custom" (5.2. 97–98). When Leontes finally proclaims he will kiss the statue, we find ourselves beyond art. We are, indeed, back with nascent, or renascent, life.

Paulina stops him. No, "the ruddiness upon her lip is wet: / You'll mar it if you kiss it" (5.3.81–82). Then, she once more proposes to draw the curtain. Leontes begs, "No, not these twenty years" (5.3.84). She asks him, at this crucial point, to either leave the "chapel" or "resolve for more amazement," for, even though she thinks he might consider her "assisted by wicked powers," she will make the statue move, descend, and take his hand. When the king shows himself open to any miracle, Paulina announces her claim. She expects Leontes to have *faith*: "it is required you do awake your faith" (5.3.94–95). At the same time she warns everyone to stand still: those who think hers is "unlawful business" must leave. The suspicion of magic pervades this section of the scene.

Finally, Paulina utters her solemn command, invoking music that it might awake the statue, strike her. "'Tis time"—this is the time, the *kairós*, the instant. May the stone cease to be stone, descend, approach, "strike all that look upon with marvel" (5.3.100). "Come," she orders, "I'll fill your grave up. Stir; nay, come away. / Bequeath to death your numbness, for from him / Dear life redeems you" (5.3.100–103). The tomb, precisely like Jesus's after three days, is by now empty. Life redeems from death and its torpor. Every gesture of the statue, Paulina says, will be as "holy" as her own "spell" is "lawful."

And Hermione moves, descends. "O, she's warm," Leontes exclaims, "If this be magic, let it be an art / Lawful as eating" (5.3.109–111). What an odd Easter morning this is, in which a sculpted image returns to life. It is a rebirth that looks very much like a renaissance, a new flourishing of culture and art. Hermione, now hangs about Leontes's neck, forgives, suffers, and rejoices with him. Polixenes asks Paulina to make her speak and reveal where she has lived or how she escaped death. Human questions, of course, that would like to penetrate the mystery or reduce everything to fiction. Paulina answers them with a paradox: "That she is living, / Were it but told you, should be hooted at / Like an old tale: but it appears she lives, / Though yet she speak not" (5.3.117–120). An "old tale," like those Lear wanted to exchange with Cordelia in jail: A winter's tale. Yet the paradox lies in the fact that what would normally look like a tale is supported by the material evidence, the "phenomenon," what appears: "but it appears she lives."

To call this an old tale, then, is not quite appropriate. Paulina shows Hermione her found Perdita. And Hermione finally speaks. She invokes the gods' grace on her daughter's head, asks her for the details of her being saved, her living, her being found. As far as she herself is concerned, she simply states that, in the hope of embracing her daughter again, she has "preserved" herself to see the "issue." Preserved in death, we ask, with an intact body? Or preserved in life, as Leontes seems to suspect when, a minute later, he asks Paulina *how*: "for I saw her, / As I thought, dead; and have in vain said many / A prayer upon her grave" (5.3.140–142). In sum, what is more plausible, an old tale or a statue that returns to life? For this is the alternative Shakespeare asks us to believe—in either of two *fictions*: that of life, which has miraculously preserved itself through time and adversities, and that of art which, in its verisimilitude, gives life back. To make one and only thing of the two, maintaining that Hermione never died and never was a statue and that she returns to life because Paulina wants to stage a sensational trick to prompt Leontes's repentance, is reasonable. It is *too reasonable* for a play that offers no answer—and for life, and death, that offer no explanation.

Furthermore, if, using Coleridge's "suspension of disbelief," we can believe that a statue imitates a real person perfectly—if we can believe in the mystery and miracle of art—then, Shakespeare seems to suggest, we can also believe in the resurrection of the dead, the mystery and miracle preached by Christianity and without which, as Paul says, "our preaching is vain, and your faith is also vain" (is it totally by chance that "Paulina" is the female of "Paul"?). Shakespeare seems to announce that all that is necessary to *faith* is a *suspension of disbelief*. This would indeed be sensational Good News, which would complement, and bring up to date, squarely into modernity, the New Testament and Dantean proclamation according to which "faith is the substance of things hoped for, the evidence of things not seen."

Thus, as in John's scenes as interpreted by Augustine and Gregory, we have first anagnorisis, then *pistis*, faith. Marina, Thaisa, Imogen, Perdita, Hermione—these Gospels preach, in the feminine gender and, therefore, in a declination that appears more revolutionary than the Gospels themselves, the resurrection of the *flesh*, not in the other world, but here and now, in a world that is ours and simultaneously new, in a time that is human yet delayed (the sixteen years of Perdita and Hermione, Marina's entire life). In the Nicene Creed, common to all Christians, this is called the *vita venturi saeculi*, the life of the world to come. And these Gospels announce such a resurrection on the basis of human ties, of the apparently most banal and daily, but in fact deepest love, that between husband and wife, between fathers, or mothers, and daughters.

However, let us try to use Aristotelian logic and Scholastic reason. If I were to formulate the problem that faces us at the end of the *Winter's Tale* in logical terms, I would put it in the following way. Four positions are possible. First, the whole business is a mere fiction. Hermione has always been alive, and at this point she just resumes her life at Court, joining Leontes and Perdita again after sixteen years. She herself says she has "preserved" herself. Second, Paulina's performance is a work of magic—be it white or black—and indeed she is worried her spectators might consider it such. Third, it all revolves about the mystery of art, a *perfect* imitation of reality. The whole *Winter's Tale* discusses this problem, and in this scene itself the miracle of artistic mimesis is constantly underlined. Fourth, the fundamental question is the resurrection of the flesh, and in fact Paulina herself announces, "I'll fill your grave up."

All these positions are legitimate, regardless of the fact that skeptical modernity will almost unhesitatingly choose between the first—possibly the majority view—and the third, entirely neglecting the second and the fourth. *Sed ad primum dicendum quod* Leontes maintains he had seen Hermione dead and prayed on her tomb. Furthermore, why should

Shakespeare have invented such an elaborate scene as this, which is not strictly necessary to the plot's denouement? He could have brought it off with a Pericles-Marina or Pericles-Thaisa scene, without using a statue and the music Paulina employs to strike Hermione back to life and, thus, without entering the tricky field of art. *Ad secundum dicendum quod* Paulina repeatedly states she is not "assisted by wicked powers" and hers is not "unlawful business." *Ad tertium dicendum quod* no art is a *perfect* imitation of reality, to the point for instance of making a statue breathe ("what fine chisel," Leontes asks quite rightly, "could ever yet cut breath?"). Before a work of art we do indeed recognize, as Aristotle puts it, that "this is that," but we are always aware that "that" is a fiction, an imitation. Finally, *ad quartum dicendum quod* one cannot, strictly speaking, talk of resurrection of the flesh, because what comes back to life is a statue, not the dead (and presumably, after sixteen years, putrefied, unless "preserved" intact) body of Hermione.

Respondeo dicendum quod the objections to the four positions would be sufficient to destroy, from a rational point of view, each of them. Yet Shakespeare's text keeps all the four intact because it answers each with the other three. In other words, the text considers the four positions *not separable* from each other. Because the mystery of life (of staying alive in spite of the tragedies one has gone through, and of the death—be it apparent or not—one has experienced), the mystery of magic, that of art, and that of resurrection are *the same*. What is important, the *Winter's Tale* seems to imply, is that we awake our "faith," that we suspend our disbelief in *all* senses of the word—in sum that we keep ourselves open to *all four mysteries*. It is not much, but it is that small amount a work of literature can do to help us return to life. It is for this reason, and after scenes such as this, that we can agree with Euripides's Helen: "There is something divine in recognition."

Notes

1. The text of Euripides's Helen is R. Kannicht's *Helene* (Heidelberg, 1969), with extensive commentary; the translation (often changed for greater fidelity to the original) P. Vellacott's in the Penguin edition (Harmondsworth, 1984). A useful commentary by A.M. Dale is available in Euripides, *Helen* (Oxford: Clarendon Press, 1967).
2. I use three words for "recognition": "recognition," "agnition" (the classical English word, derived from the Latin "agnitio"), and the Greek "anagnorisis."
3. The edition of the *Poetics* I use here is Aristotele, *Poetica*, a.c. C. Gallavotti for the Greek text; Aristotle, *Poetics*, trans. G.F. Else. See also G.F. Else, *Aristotle's Poetics: The Argument*.
4. See V. Goldschmidt, *Temps physique et temps tragique chez Aristote*, 294–97; R. Dupont-Roc et J. Lallot, éds., Aristote, *La Poétique*, 270–77.
5. On recognition I refer the reader back to the following: F. Kermode, "Recognition and Deception" in his *The Art of Telling*, 92–113; G. Wunberg, *Wiedererkennen*; D. Culbertson, *The Poetics of Revelation: Recognition and the Narrative Tradition*; T. Cave, *Recognitions: A Study in Poetics*; P.F. Kennedy and M. Lawrence, eds., *Recognition: The Poetics of Narrative: Interdisciplinary Studies on Anagnorisis*.
6. See N. Zemon Davis, *The Return of Martin Guerre*.
7. The Hades scene dominates the matinée; there is another explicit reference at page 528.
8. P. Ricoeur's *The Course of Recognition* offers a full survey and bibliographical details for this.
9. See *The Oresteia of Aeschylus* translated by Robert Lowell.
10. On recognition scenes inspired by reasoning (*syllogismos*: Electra plays and Shakespeare's *Hamlet*) and on those which combine perfection and the theme of annihilation, see P. Boitani, *The Genius to Improve an Invention*. On biblical (Old and New Testament) scenes, and on Mann's *Joseph and his brothers*, see P. Boitani, *The Bible and its Rewritings*. On recognition scenes in medieval romance and in Dante, see P. Boitani, *The Tragic and the Sublime in Medieval Literature*. On those that go from Sophocles to Tolstoy and then Shakespeare's in his romance plays, see P. Boitani, *Prima lezione sulla letteratura*.
11. I will, however, note here that a medieval play entitled *The Passion of Christ*, where many passages from Euripides's *Bacchae* are employed, used to be attributed to no less a Father than Gregory of Nazianuz.
12. See English translation of "Freud and the Future" in Mann's *Essays of Three Decades*.

13. Mark's original text ended at 16, 8. See Frank Kermode, *The Genesis of Secrecy.*
14. See also Peter Lombard, *Sententiae* III, 145–49.
15. The situation is different in *The Tempest*, where recognition plays a smaller role than in Shakespeare's other romance plays, and for which one would have to talk of "discovery" and revelation rather than anagnorisis proper.
16. I have discussed recognition in *Pericles* and *Cymbeline* respectively in *The Bible and its Rewritings, cit.*, and in the introduction to my edition and translation of *Cymbeline* (Milan: Garzanti, 1994), and, more fully, in *Il Vangelo secondo Shakespeare.*

Works Cited

Aeschylus. *The Oresteia of Aeschylus.* Trans. Robert Lowell. New York: Farrar, Straus and Giroux, 1978. Print.

Aristotle. *Poetica.* a.c. Carlo Gallavotti. Milano: Valla-Mondadori, 1974. Print.

———. *Poetics.* Trans. G.F. Else. Ann Arbor: University of Michigan Press, 1967. Print.

———. *La Poétique.* Eds. R. Dupont-Roc and J. Lallot. Paris: Seuil, 1980. Print.

———. *Problems* 19. Ed. and Trans. W.S. Hett and H. Rackham. Loeb Classical Library. 1953–1957. Cambridge, MA: Harvard University Press, 1970. Print.

Augustine. *Sermones* 145. A. Madrid: BAC, 1983. Print.

The Bible. Authorized King James Version. Oxford: Oxford University Press, 1997. Print.

Biblia Hebraica Stuttgartensia. Eds. K. Elliger and W. Rudolph. 4th ed. Stuttgart: Deutsche Bibelgesellschaft, 1980. Print.

Boitani, Piero. *The Bible and its Rewritings.* Oxford: Oxford University Press, 1999. Print.

———. *The Genius to Improve an Invention: Literary Transitions.* Notre Dame, IN: University of Notre Dame Press, 2002. Print.

———. *Il Vangelo secondo Shakespeare.* Bologna: Il Mulino, 2009. Print.

———. *Prima lezione sulla letteratura.* Roma-Bari: Laterza, 2007. Print.

———. *The Tragic and the Sublime in Medieval Literature.* Cambridge: Cambridge University Press, 1989. Print.

Botterwerk, G.J. *Theologisches Wörterbuch zum Alten Testament.* Zürich: Artemis, 1973. Print.

Cave, Terence. *Recognitions: A Study in Poetics.* Oxford: Clarendon Press, 1988. Print.

Chrysostom, John. *In Hebrew* 21, 2. *Patrologia Graeca.* 63, 151. Print.

Culbertson, Diana. *The Poetics of Revelation: Recognition and the Narrative Tradition.* Macon, GA: Mercer University Press, 1989. Print.

Eco, Umberto. "Edmond Dantès e la scoperta della conoscenza." *La Repubblica*, 1 February 2008. Print.

——. "L'agnizione: appunti per una tipologia del riconoscimento." *Il superuomo di massa*. Milano: Bompiani, 2001. 19–26. Print.

Else, Gerald F. *Aristotle's Poetics: The Argument*. Leiden, NL: E.J. Brill, 1957. Print.

Euripides. *Helene*. Ed. R. Kannicht. 2 vols. Heidelberg: Carl Winter Universitäts-verlag, 1969. Print. tr. *Helen*. 1956. Trans. P. Vellacott. Harmondsworth, UK: Penguin, 1984. Print.

Goldschmidt, Victor. *Temps physique et temps tragique chez Aristote*. Paris: Vrin, 1982. Print.

Gregory the Great. *Hom. In Evangelia*. II. 26. *Patrologia Latina*. Print.

Joyce, James. *Ulysses*. 1922. Ed. H.W. Gabler. New York: Random House, 1986. Print.

Kennedy, Philip F., and Marilyn Lawrence. *Recognition: The Poetics of Narrative: Interdisciplinary Studies on Anagnorisis*. New York: Peter Lang, 2009. Print.

Kermode, Frank. *The Art of Telling*. Cambridge, MA: Harvard University Press, 1983. Print.

——. *The Genesis of Secrecy*. Cambridge, MA: Harvard University Press, 1979. Print.

Lombard, Peter. *Sententiae* III, Dist. 23–24. Vol. 2. Grottaferrata: Editiones Collegii S. Bonaventurae ad Claras Aquas, 1971–81. Print.

Mann, Thomas. *Essays of Three Decades*. Trans. H.T. Lowe-Porter. New York: A.A. Knopf, 1947. Print.

——. *Joseph und seine Brüder*. 1943. Vol. 4. Frankfurt: Fischer, 1983; tr. *Joseph and His Brothers*. 1943. Trans. H.T. Lowe-Porter. Harmondsworth, UK: Penguin, 1978. Print.

Novum Testamentum Graece. Eds. E. and E. Nestle, B. and K. Aland, J. Karavidopoulos, C.M. Martini, and B.M. Metzger. 4th ed. Stuttgart: Deutsche Bibelgesellschaft, 1993. Print.

Proust, Marcel. *À la recherche du temps perdu*. Vol. 4. Paris: Gallimard, 1989. Print.

Ricoeur, Paul. *The Course of Recognition*. Trans. David Pellauer. Cambridge, MA: Harvard University Press, 2005. Print.

Septuaginta. Ed. A Rahlfs. Stuttgart: Deutsche Bibelgesellschaft, 1935. Print.

Shakespeare, William. *The Complete Works*. Eds. J. Jowett, W. Montgomery, G. Taylor, and S. Wells. 2nd ed. Oxford: Clarendon Press, 2005. Print.

Wunberg, G. *Wiedererkennen*. Tübingen: Narr, 1983. Print.

Zemon Davis, Natalie. *The Return of Martin Guerre*. Cambridge, MA: Harvard University Press, 1983. Print.

2

RECOGNITION AND IDENTITY IN EURIPIDES'S *ION*

NAOMI A. WEISS

THE MOTIF OF RECOGNITION is one that recurs throughout Greek tragedy.[1] Aeschylus, Sophocles, and Euripides, the three dominant tragedians of fifth-century Athens, all employed this motif, often in the form of a series of tokens that reveal the presence of one family member to another. Probably the best examples of their use of and interest in the process of recognition are their three different versions of essentially the same scene from the Electra story, in which she realizes that her brother Orestes, whom she has not seen since he was a baby, has returned to Argos.[2] Euripides particularly liked to play with and question the stages of the recognition process, as demonstrated by his famous parody of this scene as it was presented in Aeschylus's *Choephoroi*. The same tokens of a lock of hair, a footprint, and a piece of cloth, which persuade Electra that Orestes is present in Aeschylus's tragedy (*Cho.* 170–211), are pointed out to her by the old man in Euripides's play, but she ridicules the validity of each, and thus indirectly ridicules Aeschylus's use of this old dramatic technique too.[3] The increasing comedy of each logical rejection makes a mockery of the Aeschylean passage, demonstrating "a different construction of the realities of recognition" (Goldhill 247); but this scene mocks the mocker too, since for all her logic and scorn Electra is mistaken, as Orestes has in fact arrived in Argos. For full dramatic and comical effect here Euripides relies on the familiarity of at least the "competent" members of the audience with the Aeschylean scene.[4] The *Helen* similarly exemplifies not just Euripides's playful manipulation of the recognition motif but also his reliance on its popularity for the success of his own parody: Helen fails to recognize her husband, Menelaus, just when an audience so primed in the use of such scenes would be expecting her to do so (541–65). When she does then recognize Menelaus, he shrinks from her, believing she is a spectre rather than the "real" Helen (557–96).[5]

In the *Ion* Euripides also exploits the motif of recognition, though not simply through parody. The main recognition scene is particularly poignant and effective, as it is between a mother and son, separated since his birth up until the moment they meet on stage. It is also the climax of several near-recognitions between them, which have augmented their immediate and mutually sympathetic bond but not led them to realize their actual relationship. Finally, it is a "true" recognition after the "false" one in a parody of a recognition scene between Ion and his stepfather (517–62).

Recognition in this play is *psychologically* significant too, as it is an important part of the process of therapeutic change that is sparked by the meeting of the two main characters, Ion and Kreousa. This involves not only their mutual recognition as son and mother but also their *self-recognition*, enabling both at last to reach full maturity as, respectively, young man and matron. With such recognition comes the creation—or recreation—of identity, a sense for each (but particularly for Ion) of who they are, where they come from, and what place they have in the world. Their final recognition (both mutual and self) can occur only through a process of therapeutic change, involving the restructure of memory and identity. Repetition is crucial to this process, as we can see if we view the development of these two main characters in the light of Freud's notion of repetition compulsion ("Beyond the Pleasure Principle," 1920), as well as other patterns of behaviour concerning childhood development examined by both Freud and his successors.[6] Elsewhere I have discussed the similarities between Euripides's *Ion* and Freud's discussion in "Beyond the Pleasure Principle" more fully;[7] here I focus on the ways in which the reading of the one through the other can illuminate the processes of recognition at work in the play.

The *Ion* begins with a prologue (1–236) given by the god Hermes, who tells us that Kreousa, queen of Athens, was raped by Apollo and secretly gave birth to a son, whom she abandoned to die. Upon Apollo's instructions, however, Hermes rescued the baby and took him to Apollo's temple at Delphi, where he was reared by the priestess in ignorance of his true parentage. We learn that the boy will be reunited with his mother and called Ion (literally "the one coming/going") by Xuthus, Kreousa's husband and king of Athens. After finishing this prologue, Hermes exits and we see Ion, now a teenager, working in the temple at Delphi, sweeping the floor and shooing birds away. Kreousa then enters, as she has come to the oracle with her non-Athenian husband, Xuthus, to see if she will have any children from him. She and Ion meet and exchange their respective histories; they learn that one is childless and the other parentless (particularly motherless). The location of Delphi reminds Kreousa of her rape by Apollo, which she relates as the experience of a "friend." Despite questioning it suspiciously, Ion accepts her account.

Kreousa's departure is followed by the arrival of Xuthus, who has been told by the oracle that the first person he meets upon leaving the temple is his son. He encounters Ion and embraces him as a son, although, in a comical twist, Xuthus seems more like a lecherous old man pursuing an attractive youth than a father discovering his son. After much hesitation and many questions regarding the possible circumstances of his birth, Ion eventually accepts Xuthus as his father but wonders about the identity of his mother. He also predicts what sorts of problems now await him in Athens as an illegitimate son of a non-Athenian king. After Ion and Xuthus have left the stage, Kreousa enters again, this time with her old tutor. She is distressed upon learning through the chorus that Xuthus has accepted Ion as his son, and finally reveals how she was raped by Apollo and abandoned her baby. She does this first in the form of a monody (solo song), then by responding to the old man's questions. He urges her to take revenge on Apollo for behaving in this way, and so they plot to kill Ion using poison and leave the stage.

The events that follow are described by a messenger who tells us that the banquet held in honour of Ion was interrupted by a murder attempt (instead of Ion, a dove dies after drinking the poisoned wine). The old man has been caught and has betrayed Kreousa, whom Ion is now pursuing. Ion tries to kill Kreousa in revenge for her attempt on him, but she retreats to the temple for asylum. A fierce dialogue ensues and an impasse threatens the drama's progress. At this point, however, Apollo's priestess enters and shows Ion the basket in which he was originally found as a baby. Kreousa recognizes it and realizes that the young man is in fact her son. Ion is at first suspicious but gradually believes Kreousa as she correctly describes each item contained within the basket. He joyfully accepts her as his mother, though he does not seem fully convinced until the appearance of the goddess Athena, who confirms their relationship and praises Apollo. Athena tells Kreousa to keep quiet about the fact that she is Ion's biological mother so that Xuthus can continue to believe he is the father. Mother and son prepare to leave for Athens, where Ion will be king.

Repetition and duplication clearly abound in the *Ion*: within the play itself there are two recognition scenes, two consultations of the Delphic oracle, and two murder attempts. A sense of repetition is also present in the play's broader background of myth and the characters' own pasts. The original abandonment of Ion by his mother, his removal from Athens in the hands of Hermes, and his final restoration there following the reunion at the play's end recall the separation from and return to Attic land previously undergone by his ancestors, Kekrops, Erichonios, and Erechtheus.[8] The reception of Ion as a son by Xuthus and finally by Kreousa symbolically marks his "rebirth" as he enters manhood, whilst the queen's attempt on his life re-enacts her abandonment of him as a baby; this action is also relived through the repeated accounts of her rape by Apollo (10–27,

336–58, 879–922, 936–65, 1474–99). Such repetitions of past events, both mythical and personal, cause them to merge with the dramatic present. As in all tragedy, such a blend of the mythical story and its individual treatment by the dramatist prompts a particular type of recognition on the part of the audience. On the one hand, the Athenian spectator would recognize the characters on stage, being reminded, along with the characters themselves, of their ancestry, which was so tied to Athens' own. The spectator was also likely to know at least in general terms the Ion myth. On the other hand, such recognition only goes so far, as the audience is not yet aware of the characters' personal reaction to their past and the precise representation of the myth by Euripides. Consequently, the audience undergoes a kind of recognition process at the same time as the characters do: as the latter learn and have affirmed their own and each other's identity, so the audience recognizes these relationships according to its prior awareness of the Ion story. For this play, as for other tragedies, such a combination of novelty and recognition must have been a crucial element of the theatrical experience.[9]

Kreousa in particular dwells on past events and myth, recollecting them not only through her action but also in speech, as in her monody and descriptions of her ancestors' actions (839–922, 260–82, 987–1003). An "ancient memory" (μνήμη παλαιά, 250) preoccupies her mind and so also her speech from the moment she first comes onstage; and with this preoccupation the emphasis of the drama also turns backward, focusing on the moment when she abandoned her child all those years ago.[10] Ion, in contrast, initially seems to be concerned only with the present, his daily activity of caring for Apollo's temple, through which he views his past and future too: "I will labour on the tasks which I have always done since childhood" (102–03).[11] Such narrow vision begins to broaden, however, almost as soon as he encounters Kreousa: his curiosity in her ancestry is met by hers in his, so that in answering her questions he talks of his childhood and the unknown circumstances of his birth (258–329). Some sort of recognition between these two characters—as well as that of the place itself for Kreousa—prompts each to dwell upon not just their past but also their respective identities and positions in life. Kreousa is clearly well versed in hers, being able to answer all questions with ease, whereas Ion seems for the first time to reflect on who he is: with the emergence of the past comes a sense both of identity and of his lack of one. Recognition, the past, and identity are already interlinked, and not merely for the characters themselves: recognition of their foundation myth in the drama is also significant for the Athenian audience, whose own identity stems from that of their ancestor Ion.[12]

Repetitions of and preoccupation with the past in the *Ion* are strikingly similar to Freud's description of the "compulsion to repeat" in "Beyond the Pleasure Principle": following a past trauma, a patient "is obliged to *repeat* the repressed material as a contemporary experience instead of...*remembering* it as something belonging to the past" (18, emphasis original).[13] This phenomenon can be likened to the interference of past traumatic events in the present of Euripides's play, but more specifically to the behaviour of both Ion and Kreousa, particularly in the light of the case with which Freud introduces the concept of repetition compulsion: a young patient, who was very attached to his mother, used to throw objects away whilst making a sound that seemed to represent the German word "*fort*" ("gone"). Freud sees this action as a manifestation of the child's suppressed impulse to revenge himself on his mother for occasionally leaving him. The boy was able to gain a sense of control over the unpleasant experience of abandonment by repeating it and so transforming that originally passive situation into one in which he was the active agent, rejecting his mother himself (Freud, *Beyond* 14–17).[14] Such behaviour is like that of Ion, who responds to his own abandonment by his mother (which Kreousa's murder attempt symbolically re-enacts) by rejecting her in turn, becoming the active partner in their relationship by pursuing her into the temple.[15] His action strengthens our impression that, on some level at least, he is aware that Kreousa is in fact his mother, even though he does not fully realize their relationship until their recognition scene.[16] Ion's envelopment in the present and corresponding opposition to the emergence of the past (he asks Kreousa "not to prompt me to grieve over what had been forgotten" [361])[17] are also like the resistance of Freud's analysand towards attempts to transform his unconscious repetition into conscious memory of the original trauma (*Introductory Lectures* 331–33).[18] However, from the moment when he meets Kreousa and the process of recognition is sparked, Ion becomes increasingly preoccupied with the past. Such concern is particularly striking in the next recognition scene, in which he interrogates Xuthus in order to learn about the circumstances of his birth (540–61). Ion's concern for his *mother's* identity here highlights the great irony that Xuthus is not in fact his father and that this "recognition" scene is a false one.

Kreousa's great preoccupation with the past, with both her ancestry and above all her encounter with Apollo and abandonment of her child, is even more similar to Freud's cases of repetition compulsion, as well as to those of fixation to traumas: patients could be so "fixated" to a particular moment of their past that they would be "alienated from the present and the future" (*Introductory Lectures* 313). Kreousa is likewise embedded in the past, to the point where she hardly notices Ion when she first comes onstage (instead she admits that "I turned my mind there, though being here" [251])[19] and then fails to perceive any of the (many) signs indicating that the boy might be her son before the priestess finally produces the clear evidence of the basket in which she originally abandoned him.[20] Instead of interacting fully with the present, Kreousa repeats threefold her past experience with Apollo, seemingly unable to release herself from that "ancient memory." The vividness with which she describes it in her monody, with a rather aesthetically exaggerated concentration on colours (the golden light, Apollo's golden hair, the saffron petals), indicates quite how much this past has become her present (Weiss 42). Prior to the time of the dramatic action Kreousa has remained silent about this experience; although she is fixated to the past during the play itself, her increasingly open repetitions of it (first in the guise of her "friend," then to the old man, and finally to Ion himself) suggest that this memory is gradually being freed from repression. Through such repetitions, she also becomes an increasingly active agent again, just like Freud's analysand (Weiss 44;

Zacharia 97). This process is mirrored by the emergence of her past into the *play*'s consciousness too, beginning with Hermes's brief account of the affair and Ion's abandonment. For Kreousa, of course, such openness can only go so far: Xuthus must remain ignorant of the fact that she is Ion's mother, so she must keep silent once again.[21]

Through the repetitions of her past traumatic experience Kreousa seems to undergo a kind of therapeutic process, which culminates in her reunion with Ion. In the final recognition scene she fully acknowledges her own part in Ion's abandonment, equating this past action with her recent murder attempt: "tied down in fear, my son, I threw away your life. I killed you unwillingly" (1497–99).[22] Her "therapy" is therefore completed along with full recognition of not only her son, but also herself: through steadily editing her self-representations through this series of repetitions, Kreousa finally becomes reconciled to her own action. Only now can she emerge from her preoccupation with the past and perceive the signs indicating that Ion is her son; only now can she face the future, as she is ready to return to Athens with him ("O child, let us go home," 1616).[23]

Recognition and self-recognition also coincide with Kreousa's realization of her identity in the present.[24] By being reunited with her son she completes her maturation from maiden to mother, which her abandonment of Ion and subsequent childlessness with Xuthus previously prevented. The repetitions involved in her therapeutic progress through the course of the play are like those which in psychoanalysis can help promote the resumption of a previously arrested "maturational drive-representative" (Cohen 424).[25] By recalling so vividly in her monody her experience as a maiden, when she was seized by Apollo as she gathered flowers, Kreousa indicates that she has not yet freed herself from that status: rather, she is continuously regressing to this earlier stage of her development. Kreousa's lack of a baby for whom she might care has prevented her from completing the transition from maidenhood to motherhood: she laments how "I did not give you a mother's nurture with milk from my breast, nor washing with my hands" (1492–93).[26] She is therefore unable to recognize her son both because she is preoccupied with her past experience as a maiden to the exclusion of the present reality before her, and also because Ion is the manifestation of her matronly status, which she has not yet recognized in herself. With Ion "reborn" and her whole experience worked through again, Kreousa can finally acknowledge her son and proceed to the status of matron, as her age befits her.

In a sense, the drama itself grants Kreousa access to this crucial aspect of her identity. The Kreousa whom the Athenian audience would immediately recognize on stage would be the one whose glorious lineage is relayed early on in the play. The Kreousa whose identity as a maiden or matron is ambiguous is the one constructed by Euripides for and within his drama. The common motif of the recognition scene establishes for the characters within the play the identities that the audience have already recognized, but also forms the climax of those characters' *psychological* portrayal, making them more than merely mythical entities and allowing them to fulfill their self-identity at the same time as both the other characters and the external audience realize their particular status. Just as Euripides likes to play with and manipulate the recognition motif, both in this tragedy and in others, so he plays with the audience's own recognition of his characters and of their relationship to one another. Each representation of Kreousa's union with Apollo demonstrates a possible identity that Euripides could construct for her, although in each we also recognize the Kreousa of the Ion myth. The tragedian's particular presentation of this version of the known myth also brings about a concrete and imaginary specificity for the play itself, as a drama that is recognized as being both within this mythical tradition and Euripides's own creation, as well as (now) part of the audience's own experience in the theatre.

Although Kreousa undergoes a sort of maturation from maiden to matron, it is Ion's development that is most obvious in the play: his naive, boyish outlook in the opening scene matures into a critical, worldly intelligence.[27] The emergence of his critical capacity is concurrent with his exposure to questions regarding his birth, first when he probes Kreousa regarding the experience of her "friend" (not yet realizing its relation to himself or her), then in his interrogation of Xuthus. Soon he fully comprehends the dangers of a political life in Athens (585–620),[28] and by the time of the final recognition scene with Kreousa he demonstrates a keen sense of worldly wisdom by mentioning the tendency of young girls to claim divine parentage for their illegitimate children (1520–48). Repetition enables him, as it does Kreousa, to resume a previously arrested stage of maturation, so that he can progress from child to adult. His symbolic rebirth allows those stages of his development which were originally deficient to be now rectified: Xuthus performs "those sacrifices which we did not make at your birth" (653; cf. 1127),[29] whilst Ion's bond with Kreousa is finally re-established following a repeat of his original abandonment. Just as Kreousa's lack of a baby to care for hindered her from completing the transition from maidenhood to motherhood, so the emphasis that Ion places on his lack of maternal care suggests that this lack has caused a developmental scar in him too: "For at the time when I ought to have been coddled in my mother's arms and taken some delight in life, I was wrenched away from a mother's most loving care" (1375–77; cf. 319).[30] Once mother and son have been reunited, Ion, no longer solely concerned with a stagnant present, is able to leave Delphi, the place of his childhood, and embark upon an adult, political life in Athens.

Ion's understanding and misunderstanding of the outer world around him, sparked by that initial encounter with Kreousa, are therefore concurrent with his gradual recognition and misrecognition of other characters in the play. As well as beginning to recognize characters and situations around him, Ion also starts to show signs of *self*-recognition and identity. With his exposure to the world beyond his previously narrow vision comes his acquisition of identity, which is crucial for his development into adulthood. Maturation involves the development of what Richard Lazarus calls an "ego-identity," an attainment of "not merely self-concepts but concepts about the self in the world, including roles, commitments, relationships, and a set of niches or places in that world in which to function" (346). However, it is Ion's parentage that assumes a central place in his self-concept:[31] being ignorant of his parents' identity at the start of the play, he cannot give an account of who he is beyond saying, "I am called the god's slave, and I am" (309).[32] His understanding of his position in the world also depends on his heritage, as upon his encounter with his false father, Xuthus; Ion accepts his name and wonders about his political status and relationship with his "stepmother."[33] Following the recognition scene with Kreousa, he finally leaves for Athens, where his position is assured: Athena bids him, "Sit upon the ancient throne" (1618).[34] The significance of parentage for Ion, however, also demonstrates the limits of applying Freudian theory to every aspect of the drama, since Freud claims that domination of the pleasure principle ends once a child achieves complete psychical detachment from his parents (*Five Lectures* 48; *Introductory Lectures* 380). Anna Freud likewise emphasizes the importance of autonomy and individuation from parents in adolescence (*The Ego* 262–75).[35]

Above all, maternal contact facilitates Ion's awareness of his own identity, from the initial prompt to wonder about his own origins to his final reunion with Kreousa when he realizes his glorious lineage.[36] Kreousa also in a sense gains a stable identity through this reunion, as she completes the transition from maiden to matron, while the status of her house is also secured as a result of having an heir.[37] For all her knowledge of her ancestry, she is unable to come to terms fully with herself until she has recognized her *son*: only then can she, like Ion, position herself properly in the world around her. Mother and son each help the other in recovering their identities and simultaneously coming to terms with their past.[38] From the moment they first meet, their mutual empathy encourages Ion to identify Kreousa with his lost mother and she him with her lost son. This initial meeting and, for Kreousa, Delphi itself, spark off a process of therapeutic change and a corresponding recreation of identity that reach fulfillment in the play's closing scene. In sympathizing with one another, they also unknowingly begin to repair their mother-child relationship: Melanie Klein emphasizes how such mutual identification contributes to the process of "making reparation" (311–18).

The process of recognition undergone by Kreousa and Ion is therefore not just a sudden climax of the recognition scene at the play's end. Instead, it is an extended process lasting almost the entire length of the drama, beginning with the initial meeting of mother and son, and playing a key role in the course of "therapy" that they both experience. Euripides is clearly not merely interested in the *motif* of recognition, which could simply constitute a scene or two of the drama; nor is he just concerned with recognition in dramatic terms, playing with his audience's prior knowledge of the story he is presenting. Rather, what takes centre stage in the *Ion* is his exploration of recognition as a psychological experience and, more than anything else, a very human one.

Author's Note

Thanks are due to Armand D'Angour and Mark Griffith for their helpful advice while I was writing various versions of this article. All Greek quotations are taken from Diggle's 1981 edition of the *Ion*; all translations are my own.

Notes

1. On recognition and recognition scenes elsewhere in Greek literature, see, for example, Murnaghan on the *Odyssey*.
2. Aeschylus, *Choephoroi*, 167–234; Sophocles, *Electra*, 1221–24; Euripides, *Electra* 508–79. See Davies, Boitani, *The Genius*, 1–25, and Gallagher on recognition scenes in Electra plays.
3. In Euripides's *Electra* her arguments are that a man's hair would be unlikely to match that of a girl, especially given their respective activities (527–31); a female's feet probably would not be as big as those of her brother (535–37); and finally that the cloak cannot be the same as that which he wore as a child upon leaving Argos, "unless his robes grew together with his body" (544).
4. On the question of the "competency" of the audiences of Classical Greek drama, see Revermann. We should not simply assume that they were universally sophisticated, but could nonetheless expect a degree of shared competence as a result of frequent exposure to and participation in the theatre at Athens.
5. In Greek tragedy generally (though the *Ion* is another notable exception), it is the newly arrived, usually male "stranger" who recognizes his wife or sister before she does him. Euripides characteristically upturns this convention in the *Helen*, with mutual misrecognition followed by one-sided true recognition on the part of Helen

rather than Menelaus. See also Boitani, *The Bible*, 130–45 on the recognition scene in this play.

6. Pedrick also examines recognition in the *Ion* in the light of Freudian psychoanalysis, particularly emphasizing the significance of fire at moments of recognition in both Euripides's play and in Freud's case of The Wolf Man (see "From the History of an Infantile Neurosis," 154–84).

7. See Weiss.

8. See Zacharia on the basic mythemes operating in the play (67–68). Kekrops was buried in the Athenian soil whence he was born; Athena raised Erichthonios from the ground; Erechtheus was consumed by a chasm into the earth.

9. And indeed for theatre in general, as De Marinis points out: "the fragile balance is kept between the pleasure of discovery, the unexpected, and the unusual, on the one hand, and the pleasure of recognition, *déjà vu*, and the anticipated on the other" (112). On the degrees to which the Athenian audience might have engaged with drama on an inter-textual (or inter-performative) and mythological level, see Revermann.

10. Through her ancestry Kreousa is also most closely related to the play's various mythical figures, see Wolff, 182. This connection may heighten the sense of her detachment from the largely human present.

11. ἡμεῖς δέ, πόνους οὓς ἐκ παιδὸς / μοχθοῦμεν ἀεί. See Lee, "Shifts of Mood," 87. The position of the Greek for "always" (ἀεί) in line 103 cleverly also allows the meaning, "I will always work on the tasks which I have done since childhood," thereby emphasizing how completely settled Ion is within this environment.

12. Pedrick emphasizes the fear that the audience would therefore feel at the multiple identities created for Ion (and in turn for Athens) through the course of the play by the repeated but varying accounts of his original abandonment (57–103). An authoritative account of the city's foundation is eventually provided by means of a *deus ex machina*, Athena, who prevents the multiplicity of versions from spiralling out of control.

13. See also S. Freud, "Remembering," 150.

14. See also A. Freud, *The Ego*, 111–14.

15. Rustin and Rustin suggest that "the form of his revenge is to inflict on her what his baby self had felt exposed to at the time of his abandonment" (62). The anger demonstrated by Ion's murder attempt could also be seen as an important part of his "recovery" from a sense of maternal bereavement, which he has felt so keenly—and ironically—since his encounter with Kreousa. See Holmes on the

significance of such expression of anger (91–92), as emphasized by Bowlby in *Attachment and Loss: Volume II*.

16. Such unrealized awareness is indicated by his sympathy for Kreousa upon their first meeting and particularly by his reaction to the experience of her "friend," who is of course the queen herself: he likens their respective sorrows, saying "this misfortune is in accord with my own suffering" (359).

17. ἃ μή μ᾽ ἐπ᾽ οἶκτον ἔξαγ᾽ οὐ ᾽λελήσμεθα.

18. See also S. Freud, "Beyond the Pleasure Principle," 20–21. For Freud, the unconscious is the repository of what is repressed from conscious thought, of instinctual desires, needs and psychic actions. For his division of mental processes into conscious, preconscious and unconscious, see S. Freud, *An Outline* 34–35.

19. ἐκεῖσε τὸν νοῦν ἔσχον ἐνθάδ᾽ οὖσά περ.

20. See Lee, "Shifts of Mood," 91 on Kreousa's lack of recognition here, even when Ion himself approaches the truth at verse 357, suggesting that Apollo might have saved the child of her "friend" by rearing him in secret.

21. Athena instructs her now to "be silent about the fact that the boy is your son" (νῦν οὖν σιώπα παῖς ὅδ᾽ ὡς πέφυκε σός, 1601).

22. ἐν φόβωι, τέκνον, / καταδεθεῖσα σὰν ἀπέβαλον ψυχάν. Of course, these words also highlight Ion's *survival*, which is an important part of his heroic identity for the Greek audience—and is the opposite fate to that suffered by most babies abandoned in real life, see Pedrick, 35–51.

23. ὦ τέκνον, στείχωμεν οἴκους.

24. On the link between recognition and self-recognition in tragedy, see Bennett, 110–18.

25. See also Lipin, 399–405.

26. γάλακτι δ᾽ οὐκ ἐπέσχον οὐδὲ μαστῶι / τροφεῖα ματρὸς οὐδὲ λουτρὰ χειροῖν….

27. On Ion's development, see de Graft Hanson. His maturation could be viewed in terms of the pleasure stage succeeding from the reality stage of mental development, see Weiss, 46–49.

28. On this political speech as evidence of Ion's maturity, see Lee, *Euripides: Ion*, 225.

29. θῦσαί θ᾽ ἅ σου πρὶν γενέθλι᾽ οὐκ ἐθύσαμεν.

30. χρόνον γὰρ ὅν μ᾽ ἐχρῆν ἐν ἀγκάλαις / μητρὸς τρυφῆσαι καί τι τερφθῆναι βίου / ἀπεστερήθην φιλτάτης μητρὸς τροφῆς. Parental rejection or abandonment commonly results in developmental abnormalities (Lipin 400). Bowlby also emphasizes maternal love in infancy as a key factor in the emergence of a healthy ego. Novick and Novick describe how masochistic patients have often suffered from disturbance in the "infant-mother transactional system"; this leaves them "exclusively and anxiously

31. tied to their mothers" (315). The absence of a maternal bond has similarly left Ion, though not masochistic, certainly preoccupied with his mother's identity and his relation to her.
31. See Forehand, 175–78.
32. τοῦ θεοῦ καλοῦμαι δοῦλος, εἰμί τ.'
33. Ion's heritage is of course also crucial for the identity of Athens, see Pedrick, 57–103.
34. ἐς θρόνους δ' ἵζου παλαιούς.
35. See also Blos, 75–128.
36. According to Bowlby's Attachment Theory, consistent *maternal* contact is particularly important for such awareness of oneself and one's relationship with others to develop: as Holmes explains, "from maternal consistency comes a sense of history...from maternal holding comes the ability to hold one's self in one's own mind: the capacity for self-reflection, to conceive of oneself and others as having minds" (117). Upon contact with Kreousa, Ion not only gains increasing understanding of and interest in his own standing within the world, but also appreciates more and more the attitudes of others (his "stepmother" Kreousa, the Athenian citizens) towards himself.
37. Kreousa and her house therefore also seem to have been "reborn" in some way (Loraux 186–87).
38. Pedrick explores the interesting parallels between this mutual recovery process and the relationship between Freud as analyst and the Wolfman as analysand, showing how, through the gradual discovery of the primal scene, Freud constructs identities for himself as well as for his patient (see especially 59–103).

Works Cited

Aeschylus. *Septem Quae Supersunt Tragoedias*. Ed. Denys Page. Oxford: Oxford University Press, 1973. Print.

Bennett, Simon. "Recognition in Greek Tragedy: Psychoanalysis on Aristotelian Perspectives." *Freud and Forbidden Knowledge*. Ed. Peter Rudnytsky and Ellen Spitz. New York: New York University Press, 1994. 109–27. Print.

Blos, Peter. *On Adolescence: A Psychoanalytic Interpretation*. New York: The Free Press of Glencoe, 1962. Print.

Boitani, Piero. *The Bible and its Rewritings*. Oxford: Oxford University Press, 1999. Print.

———. *The Genius to Improve an Invention: Literary Transitions*. Notre Dame, IN: University of Notre Dame Press, 2002. Print.

Bowlby, John. *Attachment and Loss*. 3 vols. London: Hogarth, 1969–1980. Print.

Cohen, Jonathan. "Structural Consequences of Psychic Trauma: A New Look at *Beyond the Pleasure Principle.*" *International Journal of Psychoanalysis* 61 (1980): 421–32. Print.

Davies, Malcolm. "Euripides' *Electra*: the Recognition Scene Again." *The Classical Quarterly* 48 (1998): 389–403. Print.

De Marinis, Marco. "Dramaturgy of the Spectator." *The Drama Review* 31.2 (1987): 100–14. Print.

Edgcumbe, Rose. *Anna Freud: A View of Development, Disturbance and Therapeutic Techniques.* London: Routledge, 2000. Print.

Euripides. *Fabulae.* Ed. James Diggle. Vol. 2. Oxford: Oxford University Press, 1981. Print.

———. *Helen.* Ed. William Allan. Cambridge: Cambridge University Press, 2008. Print.

Forehand, Walter E. "Truth and Reality in Euripides' *Ion.*" *Ramus* 8 (1979): 174–87. Print.

Freud, Anna. "Adolescence." *Psychoanalytic Study of the Child* 13 (1958): 255–78. Print.

———. *The Ego and Mechanisms of Defence.* New York: International Universities Press, 1936. Print.

Freud, Sigmund. "Beyond the Pleasure Principle." *Standard Edition* 18. London: Hogarth Press, 1920. 7–64. Print.

———. "Five Lectures on Psycho-Analysis." *Standard Edition* 11. London: Hogarth Press, 1910. 9–58. Print.

———. "From the History of an Infantile Neurosis." *Standard Edition* 17. London: Hogarth Press, 1918. 7–122. Print.

———. "Introductory Lectures on Psychoanalysis: Part III." *Standard Edition* 16. London: Hogarth Press, 1917. 243–464. Print.

———. *An Outline of Psychoanalysis.* Ed. James Strachey. New York: Norton, 1949. Print.

———. "Remembering, Repeating and Working-through." *Standard Edition* 12. London: Hogarth Press, 1914. 145–56. Print.

Gallagher, Robert. "Making the Stronger Argument the Weaker: Euripides, *Electra* 518–441." *The Classical Quarterly* 53.2 (2003): 401–15. Print.

Goldhill, Simon. *Reading Greek Tragedy.* Cambridge: Cambridge University Press, 1986. Print.

Hanson, Joseph O. de Graft. "Euripides' *Ion*: Tragic Awakening and Disillusionment." *Museum Africum* 4 (1975): 27–42. Print.

Hoffer, Stanley E. "Violence, Culture, and the Workings of Ideology in Euripides' *Ion.*" *Classical Antiquity* 15 (1996): 289–318. Print.

Holmes, Jeremy. *John Bowlby and Attachment Theory.* London: Routledge, 1993. Print.

Huys, Mark. *The Tale of the Hero Who Was Exposed at Birth in Euripidean Tragedy: A Study of Motifs.* Leuven, BE: Leuven University Press, 1995. Print.

Klein, Melanie. "Love, Guilt and Reparation." *Love, Guilt and Reparation and Other Works 1921–1945*. London: Vintage, 1998. 306–43. Print.

Lazarus, Richard. *Emotion and Adaptation*. Oxford: Oxford University Press, 1991. Print.

Lear, Jonathan. *Love and its Place in Nature: A Philosophical Interpretation of Freudian Psychoanalysis*. New York: Farrar, Straus and Giroux, 1990. Print.

Lee, Kevin H. "Shifts of Mood and Concepts of Time in Euripides' *Ion*." *Tragedy and the Tragic*. Ed. Michael Silk. Oxford: Oxford University Press, 1996. 85–109. Print.

———. *Euripides:* Ion. Warminster, UK: Aris and Philips, 1997. Print.

Lipin, Theodore. "The Repetition Compulsion and 'Maturational' Drive-Representatives." *International Journal of Pyschoanalysis* 44 (1963): 389–406. Print.

Loraux, Nicole. "Kreousa the Autochthon: A Study of Euripides' *Ion*." *Nothing to Do with Dionysus? Athenian Drama in its Social Context*. Ed. John Winkler and Froma I. Zeitlin. Princeton, NJ: Princeton University Press, 1990. 168–206. Print.

Murnaghan, Sheila. *Disguise and Recognition in the* Odyssey. Princeton, NJ: Princeton University Press, 1987. Print.

Novick, Jack, and Kerry Kelly Novick. "Some Comments on Masochism and the Delusion of Omnipotence from a Developmental Perspective." *Journal of the American Psychoanalytic Association* 39.2 (1991): 307–31. Print.

Pedrick, Victoria. *Euripides, Freud, and the Romance of Belonging*. Baltimore, MD: Johns Hopkins University Press, 2007. Print.

Revermann, Martin. "The Competence of Theatre Audiences in Fifth and Fourth-Century Athens." *Journal of Hellenic Studies* 126 (2006): 99–124. Print.

Rustin, Margaret, and Michael Rustin. *Mirror to Nature: Drama, Psychoanalysis and Society*. London: Karnac, 2002. Print.

Weiss, Naomi. "A Psychoanalytical Reading of Euripides' *Ion*: Repetition, Development, and Identity." *Bulletin of the Institute of Classical Studies* 51 (2008): 39–50. Print.

Wolff, Christian. "The Design and Myth in Euripides' *Ion*." *Harvard Studies in Classical Philology* 69 (1965): 169–94. Print.

Zacharia, Katerina. *Converging Truths: Euripides'* Ion *and the Athenian Quest for Self Definition*. Leiden, NL: E.J. Brill, 2003. Print.

Zeitlin, Froma I. "Mysteries of Identity and Designs of the Self in Euripides' *Ion*." *Proceedings of the Cambridge Philological Society* 35 (1989): 144–97. Print.

3

ETHICAL EPIPHANY IN THE STORY OF JUDAH AND TAMAR

RACHEL ADELMAN

THE SCENE OF RECOGNITION in the story of Judah and Tamar (Genesis 38) serves as the keystone to the overarching narrative of Joseph and his brothers. The problem of generational continuity/discontinuity forms the main theme. As Esther Marie Menn claims, with regard to the Book of Genesis as a whole, "the central issue driving the biblical narrative consists of the transition from one generation of males to the next" (Menn 15).[1] In fact, Nahmanides aptly called Genesis "The Book of Genealogies" [*Sefer Toledot*] since it recounts the expansion of the "families of man" [*toledot Adam*], and the stories of Abraham and his chosen descendants' election to a covenantal relationship with God.[2] The story of Judah and Tamar proves to be no exception. Bracketed by the stories of Joseph's sale into slavery (Gen. 37) and his escapades in the House of Potiphar (Gen. 39), the chapter seems to disrupt the longer saga of Joseph and his brothers.[3] Rather than understanding it as an interruption, I adjure the reader to draw the threads of the narratives together, as this story begins the process of mending the seam rent by the brothers when they sold Joseph into slavery.[4]

The frame narrative begins with Joseph: "This is the lineage of Jacob [*toledot Ya'akov*]. Joseph, being seventeen years old, was shepherding the flock with his brothers" (Gen. 37.2).[5] Instead of a genealogy, the narrative sets us up for a rupture in continuity by presenting a glaring lacuna; the other brothers seem to be excluded from "the lineage of Jacob." Only, Joseph is named! Perhaps the gap anticipates the breach in Jacob's genealogy caused by Joseph's immaturity. Or the verse alludes to Jacob's myopic focus on his favoured son ("Now Jacob loved Joseph best of all" [Gen. 37.3]), leading to the near-fratricide, the sale into slavery, the deception with the bloodied cloak, and the collective descent down into Egypt during the famine. By underscoring the significance of rupture in continuity and its eventual resolution, the Judah and Tamar story plays a critical role. Judah's daughter-in-law, Tamar, not only reasserts the possibility of lineage for him, when thwarted procreation and bereavement prevail, but also enables him to play a pivotal role in bringing about the reunion between father and son in the larger drama. The pivotal points in both the Joseph and the Judah dramas are punctuated by the key expression "please recognize [*haker na*]" (Gen. 37.32, 38.25).[6] But where the first, accompanied by the bloodied cloak, marks a deception, the latter prompts the acknowledgement of responsibility, true ethical recognition. Drawing extensively upon Midrash, I follow Robert Alter, who suggests that this creative form of rabbinic exegesis engages the reader in a sensitive literary reading, pointing to the parallel plots, shared props, and word play (Alter 10–11). In addition, I will draw on Aristotle's theory of recognition and Levinas's ethics of substitution in order to reframe the rabbinic understanding in literary and philosophical terms.[7]

Aristotle, in his *Poetics*, claimed that the best of the complex plot structures in Greek tragedy entail a moment of recognition, *anagnorisis* in Greek—literally "the recovery of lost knowledge." In this narrative paradigm, the hero undergoes a "change from ignorance to knowledge, leading to friendship or to enmity, and involving matters which bear on prosperity or adversity" (Aristotle ch. 11, 52a 31f). The tension hinges on moments of dramatic irony in which the ignorance of the players is set in stark relief. In the complex plot, the resolution often entails the use of signs or tokens that prompt the revelation of identity, accompanied by a reversal of expectations, *peripeteia*. In Sophocles's play *Oedipus Rex*, for example, the messenger, who comes to relieve Oedipus of his anxiety about the oracle by heralding the death of his supposed father, the King of Corinth, effects the opposite by recounting the origins of his true birth and the source of the scars in his pierced ankles. The consequences that inevitably follow the scene of recognition are disastrous in Greek tragedy. Oedipus, upon realizing the identity of his wife, the one who bore his own children in the "field of double sowing" (Sophocles 1257), gashes out his eyes in moral horror; Jocasta takes her own life. The scene of recognition entails an initial *mis-*recognition, a masking, a deceit, or an obscuring of identity—and once the truth is bared, calamity strikes with the unravelling of ineluctable fate. Both the Greek term, anagnorisis, and the English, *re-*cognition, suggest a *re-*turn in thought, a "going back" (as the Greek prefix *ana* connotes), perceiving the past anew through the prism of the present truth.

Recognition in the Hebrew Bible draws on similar elements as those in Greek tragedy—misrecognition, the use of tokens or signs, revelation of identity and reversal—but the narrative leads to an altogether different kind of denouement. Rather than hinging on the plot where the elements of recognition and reversal, in Aristotle's terms, ensue from the preceding events "with probability or necessity" (Aristotle ch. 11, 52a 31f), the shift in the biblical narrative entails a transformation of character, based on a critical *choice* the player makes. Unlike Greek tragedy, there is no assumption that ineluctable fate must take its toll. Rather, the unfolding of the plot is left up to the characters' moral development; it entails an ethical epiphany, what Paul Ricoeur called "recognizing responsibility" (70), which allows for a positive resolution.[8] With this in mind, I will argue that the encounter with Tamar is critical to Judah's character development, enabling him to play a pivotal role in transforming the course of events from a potentially tragic to a redemptive end.

Verbal Cues (Part 1): The Descent

Genesis 38 opens with a movement of descent: "And it came to pass at that time, that Judah went down [*va-yered Yehuda*] from his brothers, and turned in to a certain Adullamite, whose name was Hirah" (Gen. 38.1). The verb "go down" [*yered*] is echoed again in the opening of the next chapter: "When Joseph was taken down [*hurad*] to Egypt, a certain Egyptian, Potiphar, a courtier of Pharaoh and his chief steward, bought him from the Ishmaelites who had brought him down [*horiduhu*] there" (Gen. 39.1). This later verse marks a "resumptive repetition," reasserting what we were told at the end of chapter 37. Commenting on the parallels between the passages, *Genesis Rabbah* poses the question: why does the chapter about Judah and Tamar interrupt the two stories about Joseph—the sale into slavery and the attempted seduction by the wife of Potiphar? "R. Le'azar said: so as to connect a descent with a descent [Joseph's with Judah's]. R. Yohanan said: in order to connect 'please recognize [*haker na*]' (Gen. 37.32) to the same expression, 'please recognize [*haker na*]' (Gen. 38.25). R. Samuel bar Nahman said: so as to connect the story of Tamar to the story of the wife of Potiphar" (*Gen. Rab.* 85.1; Theodor and Albeck 1080–81).[9] Three parallels between the two plots are listed: a descent, an act of recognition, and a seduction. According to the Midrash, the lives of the two brothers are inextricably bound together, represented by the verb "go down," understood as a descent into exile or assimilation. Judah, however, goes willingly: "Judah went down [*va-yered Yehuda*]," into a self-imposed exile among the Canaanites, while Joseph went unwillingly; he "was brought down to Egypt [*ve-Yosef hurad mitzrayma*]" and sold into slavery (Zakovitch and Shinan 1). According to another Midrash on the opening verse, "And Joseph went down from his brothers" (Gen. 38.1), the brothers *all* disbanded, fearing that if they were found together their crime would surface—for when all ten are together, "the debt is bound to be exacted" (*Gen. Rab.* 85.5; Theodor and Albeck 1033). And, in fact, the next time we hear of the assembly of these ten brothers (before the supposed viceroy of Egypt) trouble begins, memories surface, the collective conscience trembles (Gen. 42.21–22). But, at this point, they reject the pangs of conscience, which their presence for each other would inevitably stir. So the edict, which the old patriarch had uttered, "Joseph is torn, torn apart [*tarof toraf Yosef*]" (Gen. 37.33), rends a seam through the whole family. In disbanding, "going down," they deny conscience, shun the possibility of recognition.

Judah then attempts to mend that seam by occupying himself with marriage and procreation, the project of establishing a lineage (*toledot*) for himself. As the Midrash amusingly comments, "while the tribes were occupied with the sale of Joseph, Jacob with sack cloth and fasting, Judah with taking a wife, the Holy One, blessed be He, was creating the light of the messianic king" (*Gen. Rab.* 85.1; Theodor and Albeck 1080). Accenting the irony, the Midrash points out that precisely through Judah's attempts to establish continuity (*toledot*)—thwarted by his sons and realigned through Tamar's deception—the seed for the messianic succession is planted. Initially, however, Judah marries a Canaanite woman (clearly a discredited choice for the descendants of Abraham, Isaac, and Jacob).[10] He soon fathers three sons and marries the first-born off to Tamar, who, while named (in contrast to Judah's own wife), is of unknown stock. All goes awry when the sons fail to co-operate with the project of procreation. The first son, Er, dies by divine decree for he "did evil in the eyes of the Lord" (Gen. 38.7). The second, Onan, unwilling to conceive a child by Tamar in the name of his deceased brother, spills seed and he too is expunged. Judah, then, casting blame on Tamar as a real femme fatale, sends her back to her father in widow's garb with the false promise to give her to Shelah when he grows up, for "he thought that he [the third son] too may die like his brothers" (Gen. 38.11).[11] Sending her away marks the first stage in a series of ethically dubious acts, what Meir Sternberg calls "deceptions and counterdeceptions" (165). Tamar lives the life of a grass widow in her father's house. Years go by; Judah's Canaanite wife dies, the time of mourning passes, and the season of sheep shearing arrives.[12]

> *And Tamar was told, "Your father-in-law is coming up to Timnah for the sheepshearing." So she took off her widow's garb, covered her face with a veil,*

> and, wrapping herself up, sat down at the entrance to Enaim [Petah 'Enaim], which is on the road to Timnah; for she saw that Shelah was grown up, yet she had not been given to him as wife. When Judah saw her, he took her for a harlot; for she had covered her face. So he turned aside to her by the road and said, "Here, let me come into you"—for he did not know that she was his daughter-in-law.
>
> "What," she asked, "will you pay for coming into me?"
>
> He replied, "I will send a kid from my flock."
>
> But she said, "Only if you leave a pledge ['eravon] until you have sent it." And he said, "What pledge [mah ha-'eravon] shall I give you?"
>
> She replied, "Your signet and cord, and the staff in your hand." So he gave them to her and came into her, and she conceived by him. Then she went on her way. She took off her veil and again put on her widow's garb.
>
> (Gen. 38.13–19)

One cannot underestimate the risk Tamar assumes in taking the project of procreation into her own hands. If found pregnant, as a woman bound by promise to another man, according to the laws of levirate marriage, her illicit relations would be considered on par with adultery.[13] The severity of the consequences are later confirmed when Judah, upon discovering she is pregnant (supposedly by harlotry), orders that she be taken out and burned (Gen. 38.24).[14] Moreover, sexual relations between daughter and father-in-law are strictly forbidden according to laws of incest (Lev. 18.10).[15] Not only does Tamar break all social and legal norms, but she risks her life in doing so—the deception and seduction initiated out of extreme desperation.

This scene takes place at the entrance to Enaim [*Petah 'Enaim*], perhaps at a crossroads,[16] marked by a spring or well.[17] Later Hirah will refer to the place as Enaim by the road (Gen. 38.21). The name *Petah 'Enaim*, literally the "opening of the eyes," is fraught with irony for this is the place of deception, a veiling of sight. Yet, on another level, the term connotes a double irony; for eventually there will be a revelation of Judah and Tamar's true selves, in the *re*-cognition of what took place there.

The disguise, masking, and concealment all allow the deeper truth to eventually emerge. Tamar's actions are marked by four strong verbs in succession in verse 14: "Then she shed her widow's garb [*va-tasar*], covered her face with a veil [*va-takhas*], and wrapped herself up [*va-titalaf*], and sat [*va-teshev*], at the entrance to Enaim." Before the recognition comes the deception; before "*haker na*" can be spoken, there is an initial *mis*-recognition. Great emphasis is placed on his *not knowing*: "And Judah took her for a harlot for she had covered her face" (Gen. 38.15), and "he did not know that she was his daughter-in-law" (Gen. 38.16). The biblical narrative contains all the critical ingredients of anagnorisis (*re*-cognition): concealment or lack of recognition, an exchange of signs or tokens, and the transformation of relationship to either overt hostility or amiable resolution, through "the recovery of lost knowledge."

Clothing as "Cover Story"

The tokens, of course, are pivotal to the plot. At Enaim, in lieu of payment, Tamar demands a pledge or guarantee (*'eravon*)—Judah's "signet, cord and staff" (Gen. 38.18). Her demand is tantamount to asking for his car keys, driver's licence, and credit card, all marked indelibly with his identity. The promised payment—a kid (goat) (*gedi 'izim*) from the flock—evokes an association with the goat (*se'ir 'izim*) (Gen. 37.31), slaughtered to stain the ornamented tunic in lieu of Joseph's blood. Whereas the pledge here stands instead of the goat to *reveal* the truth, in the Joseph story, the goat's blood serves to *conceal* the truth as a cover story. In the Judah and Tamar episode, however, the promised goat is the catalyst for the *uncover story*, failing to fulfill its role as payment for services conferred. Following the sexual act (which, we are told, resulted in the much-sought conception), Tamar once again donned her widow's garb, with four emphatic verbs, the inverse of verse 14: "She arose [*va-takom*] and went on her way [*va-telekh*]. She took off her veil [*va-tasar*] and again put on her widow's garb [*va-tilbash*]" (Gen. 38.19). The scarf and widow's garb are symbolic counterpoints in negotiating the transition from harlot to widow, from a private, masked identity to a social role, from *mis*-recognition to public disclosure.

Joseph's ornamented tunic, likewise, seems to serve as a means of disclosure or recognition but, in fact, facilitates a *mis-recognition*; the blood-stained garment serves as the "cover story" for the sale of Joseph into slavery: "Then they took Joseph's tunic, slaughtered a kid, and dipped the tunic in the blood. They had the ornamented tunic taken to their father, and they said, 'We found this. Please recognize this [*haker na*]; is it your son's tunic or not?' He recognized it [*va-yakirah*], and said, 'My son's tunic! A savage beast devoured him! Joseph is torn, torn apart'" (Gen. 37.31–33). The tunic accounts for Joseph's absence and conjectured death. It diverts the grieving father from the truth about his beloved son's true fate—sold ignominiously into slavery in Egypt.

Similarly, in the story of Joseph's escapade with the wife of Potiphar, clothing serves as false testimony. The young man's garment is torn from him as he flees her lustful grasp. Potiphar's wife then uses the garment as her alibi, both with the servants and with her husband: "She kept his garment [*biggdo*] beside her, until his master came home. Then she told him the same story, saying, 'The Hebrew slave whom you brought into our house came to me to play with me; but when I screamed at the top of my voice, he left his garment [*biggdo*] with me and fled outside'" (Gen. 39.16–18). The Hebrew term referring to Joseph's garment, *begged*, is generic for clothing, yet also resonates with the word for betrayal, *biggud*. Clothing (*begged*) in the Joseph saga serves as betrayal (*biggud*), false testimony; the tunic and garment cover for heinous acts—the sale of Joseph into slavery and the married woman's attempted seduction of the handsome young Hebrew slave, whom she later frames with rape. Desdemona's handkerchief, in Shakespeare's *Othello*, is, similarly, used by Iago to rouse the moor's jealousy, the "green-eyed monster which doth mock the meat it feeds on" (3.3), instigating the tragic murder. In the two scenes in the Joseph story, the act of *mis*-recognition hinges on the leitmotif of clothing—a blood-stained tunic and a garment. In the case of Tamar, however, the signet, cord, and staff testify to truth and lead to *recognition*, by serving as a substitution, a pledge (*'eravon*) for the payment that is never received. It is this substitution that effects the reversal, Aristotle's peripeteia. Where one would expect the pledge to prompt payment, instead it impels the revelation of identity and brings about an ethical epiphany and confession from their owner. As the "private eye" at *Petah 'Enaim* ("opening of the eyes"), the tokens serve as testimony to the disguise and uncovering enacted there.

The Act of Recognition—*haker na*

When an attempt to pay the debt and reclaim the pledge is made, Judah's friend, Hirah, sets out to search for the harlot who sat at the entrance to Enaim. "He inquired of the people of that town, 'Where is the cult prostitute, the one at Enaim, by the road?' But they said, 'There has been no prostitute here'" (Gen. 38.21). Judah is then left with the goat, his tokens of identity unclaimed, and expresses anxiety that he may "become a laughingstock" if he were to pursue the matter further (Gen. 38.22). The turning point comes when he is told that his daughter-in-law is pregnant: "About three months later, Judah was told, 'Your daughter-in-law Tamar has played the harlot; in fact, she is with child by harlotry.' 'Bring her out,' said Judah, 'and let her be burned.' As she was being brought out, she sent [*shalha*] to her father-in-law, saying [*le'emor*]: 'I am pregnant by the man to whom these belong.' And then she said [*va-tomer*], 'Please discern/recognize [*haker na*] these, whose signet and cord and staff are these?' Judah recognized [*va-yaker*] them, and said, 'She is more in the right than I [*tzadka mimeni*], inasmuch as I did not give her to my son Shelah.' And he did not know her again" (Gen. 38.24–26). This scene marks the crisis in the drama, the moment of reversal, peripeteia in Aristotelian terms, where the tokens that *should have* been procured for payment, instead reveal the true identity of the protagonists. The scene signifies the best of the complex plots, according to the *Poetics*, wherein reversal and recognition coincide. The drama is heightened by irony (with the reader privy to knowledge withheld from the players themselves) and intensified by the element of surprise. But the course of events does not hinge on plot alone; for this scene is not dictated by the necessity or probability (as Aristotle would have it), but by a critical shift in moral consciousness on the part of Judah. Based on scant clues in the biblical text, the rabbinic sources amplify the degree of pivot, the about-face that Tamar demands of her father-in-law.

According to James Kugel, the rabbinic sages posit the presence of a court in this scene, made evident by the language of verdict, "take her out and let her be burned" (Gen. 38.24; Kugel, *Ladder* 180).[18] The judges, however, remain anonymous with an implied silent role in the biblical text, made significant in the Midrash. In the hearing, there are two stages to her defence: first, she *sends* the pledge (*shalha*), the signet, cord, and staff and then, she appeals (*va-tomer*) to Judah directly to examine them (*haker na*) or to recognize them. Tamar echoes the very words the brothers had addressed to their father, Jacob: "Please recognize this [*haker na*]; is it your son's tunic or not?" (Gen. 37.32). This phrase, according to the Midrash, is delivered *quid pro quo*: "The Holy One, blessed be He, said to Judah: you said 'please recognize [*haker na*]' to your father, by your life, Tamar will say 'please recognize [*haker na*]' to you" (*Gen. Rab.* 85.11; Theodor and Albeck 1045).[19] Upon hearing these words, a double entendre for Judah is implied. The Midrash conjectures a divine demand for a twofold *re*-cognition—to acknowledge the bereavement of his own father at the presentation of the bloodied cloak and to recognize his responsibility towards Tamar. He does so with respect to Tamar, in admitting that he had neglected her: "she is more righteous than I [*tzadka mimeni*] insofar as I did not give her to my son Shelah" (Gen. 38.26). With respect to his father, Judah revisits the scene of the deception, resonant through the words "*haker na*," since he is held most culpable, having initiated the idea of selling Joseph into slavery (Gen. 37.26–27). Later, he will enact a *reversal* of his previous role, when he stands as surety on behalf of Benjamin. I will address this role reversal later in the context of the discussion on the pledge and the role of guarantor.

Tamar's gesture, at that moment, allows Judah to either deny the identity of the tokens or, conversely, to claim them as his own, as it says: "she sent [*shalha*] to her father-in-law" (Gen. 38.25). Did she send a message or the tokens themselves? The biblical text is ambiguous. Furthermore, the words she relays are addressed in third person, "I am pregnant by the man to whom these belong," indicating that she does not confront him directly at this point. Only later does she address him face to face, according to the aggadic reading, after he had already acknowledged the signs in private. This is born out by the shift from third to second person, implied by the second part of her speech: "Please discern/recognize these" (Gen. 38.25). The Talmud enigmatically explains her action by drawing on a moral aphorism: "Better to cast oneself into a fiery furnace rather than put someone else to shame [*al yalbin penei havero be-rabim*, lit. "do not blanch the face of one's friend in public"].[20] Whence do we know this? From Tamar" (*b. Sotah* 10b).[21] That is, she *privately* sent him the tokens to spare him the shame, risking her life at the stake. In another version of this aggadic passage, we understand the significance of this aphorism from Tamar, "since she was set on fire [*mutzet*] yet still she did not shame him in public" (*b. Berakhot* 43b).[22] Is the Talmud being hyperbolically literal or is there a metaphorical dimension to the passage? If literal, this aggadic passage implies that Tamar already felt the scorching fire at her feet before Judah finally admitted to his fault. In being willing to risk death by fire rather than shame him publicly, the Midrash evokes a range of contrasting images—the blanching of the face in shame, or the rush of blood under the skin, substituted, in the virtual narrative, by the blistering of skin from the fiery furnace. According to the aphorism, it is "better to cast oneself into a fiery furnace rather than put someone else to shame"; the external burning takes ethical precedence over one internally generated.[23]

In exploring the symbolic dimension of the talmudic passage, I would like to draw on Levinas's reflections on the ethical imperative, conveyed by the term *hineni* ("here I am") in the Hebrew Bible. The French philosopher characterizes the ultimate ethical gesture as a "substitution": "the possibility of putting oneself in the place of the other, which refers to the transference from the 'by the other' into a 'for the other'" (Levinas, "Substitution" 107). In a relation of substitution, one may go so far as to give one's very life for the other. According to Levinas, the biblical expression "here I am" (*hineni*) functions as the quintessential verbal response of substitution: "answering for everything and everyone. Responsibility for the others has not been a return to oneself, but an exasperated contracting, which the limits of identity cannot retain...what can it be but a substitution of me for the others?" (Levinas, "Substitution"104). In the same essay, Levinas describes the ethics of responsibility in highly physical terms, in which, through responsibility, "as one assigned or elected from the outside, assigned as irreplaceable, the subject is accused in its skin, too tight for its skin...The irremissible guilt with regard to the neighbour is like a Nessus tunic my skin would be" (Levinas, "Substitution" 95, 99). The image of the mythical poisoned shirt is most telling. Hercules accidentally donned that "intolerable shirt of flame," daubed in the tainted blood of the centaur, Nessus, and was compelled, by the burning of his skin, to throw himself on the funeral pyre— "consumed by either fire or fire."[24] In Levinas's terms, it is the substitution of the *other*'s skin for one's own which demands the ultimate sacrifice, a "responsibility, for which I am summoned as someone irreplaceable...as being-in-one's-skin, having-the-other-in-one's-skin" ("Substitution" 104).

In a metonymic reading of the aggadic passage, Tamar's anticipation of Judah's burning skin compels her to sacrifice herself, substituting her own skin for his skin, on the funeral pyre—"to be redeemed from fire by fire" (Eliot IV 7). The self is bound in responsibility for the other through physical awareness of the other's pain. Levinas writes: "In the exposure to wounds and outrages, in the feeling proper to responsibility, the oneself is provoked as irreplaceable, as devoted to the others, without being able to resign, and thus as incarnated in order to offer itself, to suffer and to give" ("Substitution" 105). The talmudic passage lends us a graphic image of the ethical act of substitution, comparable to the Nessus tunic. It goes further insofar as Tamar *would have* thrown herself into the fiery furnace to save the other, Judah, from shame, from the burning skin of the face. It is this ultimate compassion, the transference of "by the other" into a "for the other," which makes Levinas's ethical imperative such a compelling means of understanding this aggadic passage. Tamar was saved from the funeral pyre because Judah responded to her sacrifice with a recognition of responsibility. Her gesture of "substitution" then becomes a model for Judah himself.

With this concept of an ethical epiphany in mind, I now return to the talmudic passage. Commenting on the parallel expressions of "please recognize [*haker na*]," the Talmud continues: "'*Na*' is nothing but the language of request. She said to him, 'Please, recognize the face of your Creator and do not cast your eyes away from me.' And Judah acknowledged, 'She is more righteous than I!'" (*b. Sotah* 10b). What does she mean by demanding recognition of the Creator? Is it a call to respond to one's conscience or to act on moral obligation? Or a request to acknowledge the role God played in the private spaces of the human encounter? The rabbinic sages suggest that a divine voice intervened to affirm Judah's paternity at this point—perhaps the "anonymous" judge at the implied court: "R. Jeremiah in the name of R. Samuel b. R. Isaac [said]: In three places God appeared: in the courtroom of Shem, in the courtroom of Samuel, and in the courtroom of Solomon. In the courtroom of Shem [as it says], 'And Judah acknowledged and said, "She is right...from me"' (Gen. 38.26). R. Jeremiah in the name of R. Samuel b. R. Isaac [said]: God said to them, 'You testify about what happened in public and I will testify to what happened in private'" (*Gen. Rab.* 85.12).[25] That is, Judah affirms Tamar's innocence, and God affirms Judah's paternity—"from me [*mimeni*]"; it was all part of a divine plot. The same exegetical move, splitting the phrase "she is more righteous...than I/from me [*tzadka...mimeni*]," is expressed in the Aramaic translation: "And Judah recognized them and said, 'She is right [*tzadka*]. She is pregnant *from me* [*mimeni*], on account of the fact that I did not give her to my son Shelah'" (*Tg. Onq.* on Gen. 38.26).[26] The Midrash, however, addresses the question of Judah's knowledge of his dubious fatherhood. Accordingly, God intercedes in the courtroom precisely where Judah's capacity for recognition is limited. The father can acknowledge the objects of the pledge (the signet, cord, and staff) as his own, but only the omniscient eye can affirm, unequivocally, the source of conception. As the passage in *Genesis Rabbah* notes, while Judah was consciously engaged in the project of procreation, seemingly doomed to failure, God was sowing the seeds of the messianic light in the private interstices of the face-to-face encounter, contrary to human knowledge and will (*Gen. Rab.* 85.1; Theodor and Albeck 1080–81).

The Pledge and the Role of Guarantor

What impact does this incident have upon the greater saga of Joseph and his brothers? The very next encounter with Judah in the biblical text entails the ethical act of "substitution," standing as surety for another, represented by the key term *'arev*, at the root of the same Hebrew word used for the pledge (*'eravon*) Tamar had exacted of Judah. It is two years into the seven years of famine, and Canaan has been sorely hit. The brothers have gone to Egypt for food and returned already once, with an edict from the alleged Egyptian viceroy not to return without their youngest brother, Benjamin. When hunger strikes again, Jacob refuses to comply, fearing he will be bereaved yet again of a beloved son (of the beloved wife) as he was with Joseph. Reuben fails to convince him. Judah, however, speaks up: "And Judah said to Israel his father, 'Send the lad with me, and we will arise and go, that we may live and not die, both we and you and also our little ones. I will be surety for him [*a'ervenu*]; of my hand you shall require him. If I do not bring him back to you and set him before you, then let me bear the blame for ever; for if we had not delayed, we would now have returned twice'" (NRSV, Gen. 43.8–10). The promise Judah makes here will determine the role he plays before the supposed Egyptian viceroy in Egypt, where he pleads to be taken as a slave instead of his brother, Benjamin, falsely accused of theft: "For your servant became surety [*'arev*] for the lad to my father, saying, 'If I do not bring him back to you, then I shall bear the blame in the sight of my father all my life.' Now therefore, let your servant, I pray you, remain instead of the lad as a slave to my lord; and let the lad go back with his brothers. For how can I go back to my father if the lad is not with me? I fear to see the evil that would come upon my father" (NRSV, Gen. 44.32–34). At this point Judah finally rectifies the tragedy he had brought upon his father, when (along with his brothers) he deceived Jacob with the bloodied cloak.

Having experienced the bereavement of his own two sons, he faces the imminence of yet a second loss to his father. In stepping in as guarantor at this point, he rises to the status of a true leader. The return of Jacob's two sons, Joseph and Benjamin, parallels the two sons (twins), which Judah gains "back" through Tamar. One of those twins, Perez, significantly becomes the father to the Davidic lineage.[27] With an interesting twist, the pledge Tamar had exacted of Judah serves as the means of showing him the principle of standing as surety for another. Just as the pledge (the signet, cord, and staff) disclosed Judah's paternal identity, so too Judah, as a human pledge for his brother, catalyzes the revelation of Joseph's identity and, ultimately, the reunion between father and son. Tamar risked her life in doing so; Judah rose to the ethical call and went on to act on the very same principle of "substitution," willing to throw himself "into the fiery furnace" to save the face of another in serving as surety for his brother.

The rabbis ask by what merit was Judah granted the kingship; for he was singled out as the progenitor of a lineage of kings (anticipated in Jacob's final blessing/prophecy to his son on his death bed, cf. Gen. 49.10).[28] The Tosefta answers: "because he acknowledged Tamar [*hodeh beTamar*]" (*T. Berakhot* 4.17).[29] The term *hodeh* may refer to the recognition of his sin and confession in neglecting her—*hodeh as hitvadeh* (confession)—when he declared, "she is more righteous than I" (Gen. 38.25). It could equally refer to his recognition of paternity through her, *hodeh* as a public declaration of debt or acknowledgement. The broadest understanding of the Hebrew verb *hodeh* is "to acknowledge" the source of truth (either through praise or confession). The term implies a re-evaluation of the past, expressed by both the English, *re*-cognition, and the Greek, *ana*-gnorisis ("the recovery of lost knowledge"). It is, in fact, imbedded in Judah's very name, *Yehuda* as Leah declared upon his birth: "'this time I will praise ['*odeh*] the Lord.' Therefore she named him Judah" (Gen. 29.35). Beyond the human dimension, the term *hodeh* implies the recognition of the role of the Ultimate Other—God's presence in the private interstices of the human encounter, what Levinas calls "an optical instrument to the divine" (*Difficile Liberté* 187).[30] In other words, the seeming "ontological absence" of God, is channelled through "ethical presence" on the human plane (Handelman, "Facing the Other" 276). According to the rabbinic sources, God acts through human interplay in plotting Judah and Tamar's union, in confirming the source of the conception, and in catching "the conscience of the king." But, on the surface level of the text, God is concealed in the crannies of the human conscience as it surfaces in the face-to-face encounter.

What is the role of this chapter within the overall theme in the Book of Genealogies (*Sefer Toledot*)? There are ten expressions of *toledot* in Genesis,[31] connoting "genealogy" or "lineage," as well as "story" or "history." Thus, "the Book of Genealogies" (*Sefer Toledot*, according to Nahmanides) is first and foremost a book of great stories and secondly about genealogies, families, continuity, and disrupted continuity. In the Book of Ruth, there is clearly a postscript to Genesis; Perez (Judah's son and, thus, Jacob's grandson) has his very own lineage (*toledot*), listing ten generations of his descendants that culminate in the birth of David, the founder of the kings of Judah (Ruth 4.18–22). The meaning of his name testifies not only to the manner of his birth (his hand thrust forth to claim the birth-right),[32] but also to the means by which the breach of continuity in the larger narrative was repaired. Perez, as a breach-birth, symbolizes the rupture in social and ethical norms initiated by his own mother, which led Judah to a higher ethical calling.

By ending with *toledot* Perez, the Book of Ruth provides a coda to Genesis—a resurrection and resolution of the problem that began with "This is the lineage of Jacob [*toledot Ya'akov*]: Joseph, being seventeen years old" (37.2). There are many parallels between the story of Judah and Tamar and the Book of Ruth,[33] but the central tension in both dramas hinges around the paradox of continuity/discontinuity. Only through the breach, can there be an ultimate resolution to the anxiety revolving around "the begats" of how to beget, procreate, and establish continuity in a fractured world of near-fratricide, bereavement, famine, exile, and the threat of assimilation. The story of Judah and Tamar is about the failings of one man and the courage of one woman, a story of rupture and repair, replete with expressions of outrageous neglect and meticulous sensitivity. While God seems absent in this biblical story (with only two brief punitive appearances), the midrashic narrative arouses our awareness of the divine in the ethical epiphany of the fragile face-to-face human encounter.

Author's Note

An earlier version of this paper was presented at the Centre for Comparative Literature's Conference on Recognition ("From Ignorance to Knowledge: Recognition from Antiquity to the Postmodern and Beyond") at the University of Toronto, April 2008. I want to thank Andrea Cooper for introducing me to Levinas's concept of "substitution" in reading the 'Aqedah (the binding of Isaac). I am also grateful to Avivah Zornberg for her comments on various drafts of this essay.

Transliteration of the Hebrew Bible

א alef ' or omitted; ב bet b or v; ג gimel g; ד dalet d; ה he h; ו vav v; ז zayin z; ח het h; ט tet t; י yod y; ך, כ kaf k or kh; ל lamed l; ם, מ mem m; ן, נ nun n; ס samekh s; ע ayin '; ף, פ pe p or f; ץ, צ tzade tz; ק qof q; ר resh r; ש sin s; שׁ shin sh; ת tav t or th.

Abbreviations, Rabbinic and Related Texts

b. = Babylonian Talmud

Gen. Rab. = Midrash Bereshit Rabbah, eds. J. Theodor and H. Albeck

M. = Mishnah, standard printed edition

Mek. = Mekhilta

Sifre Deut. = Sifre Devarim

T. = Tosefta

Tanhuma = Midrash Tanhuma-Yelammedenu

TanhumaB. = Midrash Tanhuma HaKadum ve'haYashan, ed. Buber

Tg. Ps.-J. = Targum-Pseudo-Jonathan (also known as the Targum Yerushalmi on the Torah)

Tg. Onq. = Targum Onqelos (standard printed edition)

Tg. Neof. = Targum Neofiti (based on The Aramaic Bible Targum, ed. and trans. McNamara)

y. = Palestinian Talmud (standard printed edition, Venice, 1523)

Notes

1. Menn refers to the insights of Steinberg, 41–50.
2. See Ramban's commentary to Genesis 5.1. (Nahmanides, medieval biblical exegete, known as the Ramban, Rabbbi Moshe Ben Nahman of Spain, circa thirteenth century.)
3. Among biblical scholars, there is a widespread consensus that the Judah and Tamar story was introduced into the Joseph narrative by a later redactional hand, without connection to its context (Speiser 299; Westermann 49; Brueggemann 307; Vawter 390; and Kugel, Appendix 1, 25–29). Given the scope of this work, I will not engage in a critique of this application of source criticism directly, but rather present a literary reading of the text as an integral whole with the assumption that its final redaction is intentional and artful. My concern is not with the Bible's composition, but with its canonical reception by both the rabbinic establishment and the modern reader.
4. Robert Alter pointed to various parallels between the Joseph and Judah stories, such as their respective "descents," the use of "*haker na*," "articles of attire" used for deception, the role of the goat (*seir 'izim*, which provided the blood to stain Joseph's tunic, and the *gedi 'izim*, promised to Tamar), and sexual seduction initiated by a woman (in the case of Judah, successfully, while in the case of Joseph, thwarted) (6–10). To this impressive list, Jon Levenson added the anxiety of losing another son (Judah's fear of losing Shelah; Jacob's fear of losing Benjamin) and the emergence of the younger son as leader of the kingdom—both Joseph and Judah become the progenitors of kings (157–62).
5. All translations of the Hebrew Bible that follow are my own unless otherwise indicated as New Revised Standard Version (NRSV).
6. The word *haker* (root: *nun.kaf.resh*) reverberates throughout the Joseph saga. Alison Joseph, in a paper delivered at the conference, "From Ignorance to Knowledge: Recognition from Antiquity to the Postmodern and Beyond" at the University of Toronto's Centre for Comparative Literature, April 2008, gave a fascinating analysis of the term as it plays itself out in the Joseph story. I have limited my analysis to Genesis 38 and the verbal echoes with the Joseph saga.
7. Menn, in an exhaustive study of post-biblical exegetical traditions on Genesis 38, convincingly argues that *Genesis Rabbah*, which forms the primary midrashic source for this study, "portrays the events of Genesis 38 as the means through which God brings to fulfillment his intentions to provide Israel with political leaders and eschatological redeemers" (349).

8. Other examples of this type of "ethical epiphany" are found in the confession of the brothers after selling Joseph into slavery (Gen. 42.21–22) and the story of King David's repentance when confronted by Nathan, the prophet following the adultery/murder (2 Sam. 11–12).
9. My translation of *Gen. Rab.* 85.1. All translations of the rabbinic materials are my own unless otherwise indicated.
10. See Gen. 24.4, 27.46–48.1, and the disapproval of wives of Esau, Gen. 28.8.
11. A similar assumption is made with regard to the "oft widowed bride, Sarai" in the apocryphal *Book of Tobit* (Tob. 3.7–17, 6.9–8.21); the woman is held culpable for the repeated deaths of her husbands. See Friedman, 23–61.
12. A time renowned for its drunken revelry, see 1 Sam. 25.2, 4, 7 and 2 Sam. 12.23.
13. The laws of levirate marriage are outlined in Deuteronomy 25.5–10. Sexual relations between daughter and father-in-law, however, are strictly forbidden according to the laws of incest (Lev. 18.15); the violation of this taboo constitutes a capital offence (Lev. 20.12). Given this incident occurs prior to the giving of the pentateuchal law, it could be that this quasi-levirate case extends the responsibility to the father-in-law. According to Nahum Sarna, levirate marriage predates pentateuchal legislation as recorded in various extrabiblical sources. The Hittite laws (14th–13th c. BCE), for example, state that if a married man dies, "his brother shall take his wife, then [if he dies] his father shall take her" (par. 193, qtd. in Sarna 266).
14. In rabbinic terms, Tamar would be considered "awaiting the levir [*shomeret yavam*]" and any relations outside that union would be considered adulterous, carrying with it the death penalty (See Lev. 20.10 and Deut. 22.22). See Sarna's comment on Gen. 38.24 (269). According to *Genesis Rabbah*, Judah's reaction is so severe because Tamar is identified as the daughter of a priest (Shem), and, according to the levitical laws (anachronistically applied), any daughter of a priest who defiles herself through harlotry must be burned (85.10; see also Lev. 21.9).
15. Ramban, in his commentary on Gen. 38.8, understands Tamar's act as an extension of the laws of levirate marriage [*yibbum*] to include not only the responsibility of the brother-in-law to raise seed in his brother's name for the sake of inheritance (see Deut. 25.5–7) but also the responsibility of the father-in-law. This interpretation is clearly *not* consonant with rabbinic law. Nevertheless, in Ramban's terms (drawing on early kabbalistic tradition), it is one of "the great secrets of the Torah," in which an act otherwise deemed a prohibition serves as a redemptive end.

16. The Aramaic *Targum Neofiti* and the Syriac *Peshitta*, in fact, omit the proper name of the place, designating it instead "at the crossroads" (*Pesh.* and *Tg. Neof.* on Gen. 38.24, 21; see the Latin Vulgate "*in bivio itineris*") (McNamara 175, note 10).
17. The term *'eyn* in Hebrew means spring, "the eye of the earth," so literally *Petah 'Enaim* means "entrance to two springs/eyes."
18. See *Jubilees* 41.28, *Gen. Rab.* 85.11, *TanhumaB*, ed. Buber, 1.187. See Kugel's very thorough analysis of this scene and the narrative expansions in Midrash and the Aramaic *Targum* (*The Ladder of Jacob* 169–85).
19. See also *Gen. Rab.* 85.11 (Theodor and Albeck 1045). Other midrashic sources point to this parallel as well: *Gen. Rab.* 85:1 (cited earlier); *b. Sotah* 10b, and *b. Berakhot* 43b.
20. The Hebrew expression, "*al yalbin penei havero be-rabim*" [lit. "do not blanch the face of one's friend in public"] seems to contradict the physiological phenomenon of shame, which usually entails the reddening of the face. A similar aphorism is found in *M. 'Avot* 3.11, attributed to Rabbi Elazar ha-Moda'i: "he who shames another [*ha-malbin penei havero*, lit. blanches the face of his friend] in public renounces the covenant of Abraham our forefather." However many manuscripts point to an alternative version of the aphorism: "he who *reddens* the face of another [*ha-ma'adim penei havero*]" (See S. Sharvit, 133).
21. Other midrashic parallels include: *Avot deRabbi Natan* B 38, *b. Ketubot* 67b, *b. Sotah* 10b. See also the parallel in the Testament of Judah 12.5–6: "Judah said: 'Not knowing what she had done, I wished to kill her but she privately sent me the pledges and put me to shame' [which Kugel argues should be emended: *did not put me to* shame]. And when she was taken out she sent word to her father-in-law, 'The man to whom these belong is the one by whom I am pregnant.' And she said, 'Recognize whose these are, the signet and the cord and the staff.' Then Judah recognized them" (Gen. 38.24–26). See the discussion in Kugel, *The Ladder of Jacob*, 180–82.
22. "Since she was set on fire" [punning on *mutzet*, "was taken out" in Gen. 38.25, as *mutzet*, "was set on fire"] (qtd. in Kugel, *The Ladder of Jacob* 182). The continuation of the talmudic passage makes the link between "the fiery furnace" and Tamar's burning at the stake even more explicit: "Judah who sanctified the heavenly Name in public [through confession] merited that the whole of his name should be called after the Name of the Holy One Blessed be He. When he confessed and said, 'She is more righteous than I,' A voice issued forth and said, 'You rescued Tamar and her two sons from the fire. By your life, I will rescue through your merit three of your descendants from the fire.' Who are they? Hananiah, Mishael and Azariah"

(*b. Sotah* 10b). Another passage in the Talmud states an opinion, in the name of R. Nahman b. Yitzhak, that "anyone who shames another in public [*ha-malbin penei havero be-rabim*, lit. "one who blanches the face of his friend in public"], it is as though he shed blood [*shofekh damim*]" (*b. Baba Metzia* 58b; see *Midrash ha-Gadol* and the *Yalkut Shimoni* on Gen. 38.25). *Not* shaming another is then tantamount to *not* committing bloodshed and is, therefore, a means of sanctifying the [divine] name—a willingness to be martyred rather than commit the three cardinal sins (murder, idolatry, and illicit sexual relations) under duress (*Kiddush Ha-Shem* in Hebrew). In the *Targum Neofiti*, as Menn points out, the central motif is the sanctification of the divine name (214–87). Both Tamar and Judah sanctify the name of God—she by not shaming him, he by sparing her death by fire— and therefore they merit "three just men in the Valley of Dura" as descendants, Hananiah, Mishael and Azariah, who become exemplars of martyrdom for the sake of "sanctifying the name" (*Kiddush Ha-Shem*). (See Dan. 1.6; 3.14–27; *b. Pesahim* 53b; *b. Sanhedrin* 93a; and *b. Sotah* 10b).

23. The overlapping images of burning in fire and burning in shame constitute a central motif in the *Targum Neofiti* (an ancient Aramaic paraphrastic translation of the Pentateuch). In response to Tamar's presentation of the tokens, "*Judah immediately stood upon his feet and said: 'I beg of you brothers, and men of my father's house, listen to me: It is better for me to burn in this world, with extinguishable fire, that I may not be burned in the world to come whose fire is inextinguishable. It is better for me to blush in this world that is a passing world, that I may not blush before my just fathers in the world to come*'" (*Tg. Neof.* on Gen. 38:25, McNamara 177, emphasis original).

24. T.S. Eliot alludes to the tunic of Nessus in "Little Gidding," the last section of the *Four Quartets*: "The only hope, or else despair/ Lies in the choice of pyre of pyre—/ To be redeemed from fire by fire./ Who then devised the torment? Love./ Love is the unfamiliar Name/ Behind the hands that wove/ The intolerable shirt of flame/ Which human power cannot remove./ We only live, only suspire/ Consumed by either fire or fire" (IV 5–14).

25. Based on Oxford MS 147, quoted in Kugel, *Ladder of Jacob* 183.

26. This splitting of the phrase is also found in the *Tg. Neof.* on Gen. 38.25 as well as the *T. Judah* 12.6. Though the actual divine utterance is missing in the latter, it is paraphrased by Judah, who refrains from killing Tamar when he realizes that what has happened "was from the Lord" (Menn 355).

27. See Gen. 38.29, 49.10; Ruth 4.18–22, and I Chron. 2.3–15.

28. In an alternative Midrash, the following speculations on Judah's merit as progenitor of the monarchy were made: "Was it because he had saved Joseph from murder in suggesting the sale into slavery (cf. Gen 37.26)? Or because he had acknowledged the righteousness of Tamar (cf. Gen. 38.26)? Or because he had served as guarantor for Benjamin (cf. 44.33)? In all three cases, one finds the 'guarantor,' *'arev* [that is Judah] is still liable to pay" (*Mekhilta deRabbi Yishmael, BeShallah* 5). See also *Sifre* Deut. 405, y. *Sotah* 1, 4).

29. The root of *hodeh*, *yud.dalet.heh.*, has a fairly broad semantic range: "to praise" (See Psalms 45.18, 49.19 and Job 40,14), also in Gen. 49.8 (a play on the name Yehuda), and Gen. 29.35 (as the etymology of Judah's name); "to thank in prayer" as in Nehemiah 11.17, 12.24, I Chron. 16.4, 23.30; and "to confess" (primarily in the *hitpa'el*) as in Lev. 5.5, 16.21, 26.40, Num. 5.7 and Dan. 9.20 (See Koehler, Baumgartner, and Stamm). In rabbinic literature, it takes on a formal, legalistic meaning as a declaration in court, acknowledging one's debt to another—*hoda'at ba'al din*, as in b. *Bavah Metziah* 3b (See Jastrow, 337).

30. Cited in Handelman, *Fragments of Redemption*, 270.

31. It begins with "*toledot ha-shamayim ve-ha-aretz*—such is the story of heaven and earth" (Gen. 2.4), and goes on to list the following nine genealogies: Adam (5.1), Noah (6.9), the sons of Noah (10.1), Shem (11.10), Terah (11.27), Ishmael (25.12), Isaac (25.19), Esau (36.1, 9) and Jacob (37.2). The *toledot* in Num. 3.1 (of Aaron and Moses) and Ruth 4.18 could be considered addenda to the previous genealogies—one with regard to the priesthood and the other with regard to the kingship (*toledot* Perez).

32. The midwife, in this case, names him: "'What a breach you have made for yourself [*mah paratzta*]!' So he was named Perez [*Peretz*]" (Gen. 38.29). The term connotes an outburst of water (See 2 Sam. 5.20, 1 Chron. 14.11), or, as in this case, to "burst forth from water" (i.e., the womb). It also suggests the making of a breach in a wall (See Amos 4.3; 1 Kg. 11.27; Neh. 6.1; Ps. 144.14; and Job 30.14); in the figurative sense, it implies the act of intercession—"to stand in the breach" (See Ezek. 13.5), but can also mean, conversely, an outburst of God's wrath (1 Sam. 68; 1 Chron. 13.11; Job 16.14; and Judges 21.15). See Brown, Drivers, and Briggs, *Lexicon*, entry 7877. Most telling, in terms of the role of leader, is the verse from Micah: "He who opens the breach [*ha-poretz*] will go up before them; they will break through [*partzu*] and pass the gate, going out by it. Their king will pass on before them, the Lord at their head" (Mic. 2.13). Tamar and Judah as progenitors of kings, figuratively, "open the breach" and "break through," so that "their king will pass on before" them (See Gen. Rab. 85.29).

33. For a thorough list of parallels see Zakovitch and Shinan, 26–28. See also Harold Fisch's insightful analysis in which he compares the stories of Lot and his daughters, Judah and Tamar, and Ruth in light of the theme of family continuity/discontinuity ("Ruth and the Structure of Covenant History" 425–37). He argues that the story of Ruth "redeems" the previous episodes by guaranteeing that social and familial relations are properly and legitimately observed. Similarly, Jacob Licht contends that the story of Ruth "endeavours to show how the apparently reprehensible female ancestor has been absorbed into the thoroughly respectable family of Boaz in a perfectly proper way and for irreproachable reasons" (125).

Works Cited

Alter, Robert. *The Art of Biblical Narrative*. New York: Basic Books, 1981. Print.

Aristotle. *Poetics*. Ed. and Trans. Stephen Halliwell. Cambridge, MA: Harvard University Press. 1995. Print.

Berlin, Adele, and James Kugel. "On the Bible as Literature." *Prooftexts* 2 (1982): 323–32. Print.

Biblia Hebraica Stuttgartensia. Eds. K. Elliger and W. Rudolph. 4th ed. Stuttgart: Deutsche Bibelgesellschaft, 1980. Print.

Brown, Francis, S.R. Driver, and Charles A. Briggs. *A Hebrew and English Lexicon of the Old Testament*. Oxford: Clarendon Press, 1966. Print.

Brueggemann, Walter. *Genesis: Interpretation: A Bible Commentary for Teaching and Preaching*. Atlanta, GA: John Knox Press, 1982. Print.

Eliot, Thomas Stearns. "Little Gidding." *The Complete Poems and Plays, 1909–1950*. New York: Harcourt, Brace and Company, 1952. Print.

Fisch, Harold. "Ruth and the Structure of Covenant History." *Vetus Testamentum* 32. 4 (1982): 425–37. Print.

Friedman, Mordechai A. "Tamar, A Symbol of Life: The 'Killer Wife' Superstition in the Bible and Jewish Tradition." *Association for Jewish Studies Review* 15 (1990): 23–61. Print.

Handelman, Susan. "Facing the Other: Levinas, Perelman, Rosenzweig." *Divine Aporia: Postmodern Conversations about the Other*. Ed. John C. Hawley. Cranbury, NJ: Associated University Presses; London: Bucknell University Press, 2000. 263–87. Print.

———. *Fragments of Redemption*. Bloomington: Indiana University Press, 1991. Print.

The Holy Bible: Containing the Old and New Testaments with the Apocryphal/Deuterocanonical Books (NRSV). New York: Collins, 1989. Print.

Jastrow, Marcus. *A Dictionary of the Targumim, the Talmud Bavli and Yerushalmi and the Midrashic Literature*. 2 vols. London: Judaica Press, 1903. Print.; rpt. New York: Judaica Press, 1992. Print.

Koehler, Ludwig, Walter Baumgartner, and Johann Jakob Stamm. *The Hebrew and Aramaic Lexicon of the Old Testament (HALOT)*. Leiden, NL: Brill, 1994–2001. CD-ROM edition.

Kugel, James. Appendix 1. "Apologetics and Bible Criticism Lite." *How to Read the Bible: A Guide to Scripture, Then and Now*. New York: Free Press, 2007. Available from http://jameskugel.com/read.php. Web.

———. *The Ladder of Jacob: Ancient Interpretations of the Biblical Story of Jacob and His Children*. Princeton, NJ: Princeton University Press, 2006. Print.

Levenson, Jon. *The Death and Resurrection of the Beloved Son*. New Haven, CT: Yale University Press, 1993. Print.

Levinas, Emmanuel. *Autrement qu'être ou au-delá de lessence*. La Haye: Martinus Nijhoff, 1974. Print.; tr. *Otherwise than Being or Beyond Essence*. Trans. Alphonoso Lingis. Pittsburgh, PA: Duquesne University Press, 1981. Print.

———. *Difficile Liberté*. 1st ed. Paris: Albin Michel, 1963. Print.

———. "Substitution." *The Levinas Reader*. Ed. Seán Hand. Oxford: Blackwell, 1989. 88–125. Print.

Licht, Jacob. *Storytelling in the Bible*. Jerusalem: Magnes Press, 1978. Print.

Mann, Thomas. *Joseph and His Brothers*. Trans. H.T. Lowe-Porter. Middlesex, UK: Penguin, 1978. Print.

McNamara, Martin, ed. and trans. *The Aramaic Bible Targum*. Vol. 2. Collegeville, MI: Liturgical Press, 1994. Print.

Mekhilta de-Rabbi Ishmael. Eds. H.S. Horovitz and I.A. Rabin. Frankfurt: Kauffman 1931; rpt. 2nd ed. Jerusalem: Bamberger & Wahrmann, 1960. (Hebrew); Trans. J. Lauterbach. 3 vols. Philadelphia, PA: Jewish Publication Society of America (JPS), 1933–35. Print.

Menn, Esther Marie. *Judah and Tamar (Genesis 38) in Ancient Jewish Exegesis: Studies in Literary Form and Hermeneutic*. Leiden, NL: E.J. Brill, 1997. Print.

Midrash Bereshit Rabba: Critical Edition with Notes and Commentary. Eds. J. Theodor and H. Albeck. 3 vols. Berlin, 1912–36. Print.; rpt. Midrash Bereshit Rabba: Critical Edition with Notes and Commentary. 5 vols. Jerusalem: Wahrmann, 1965. Print.

Midrash Tanhuma HaKadum ve'haYashan. Ed. S. Buber. Vienna, 1885. (Hebrew). Print.; Trans. J.T. Townsend. Midrash Tanhuma. 3 vols. Hoboken, NJ: Ktav Publishing House, 1989–2003. Print.

Midrash Tanhuma-Yelammedenu. 1st ed. Constantinople (Kushta), 1520–22. (Hebrew). Print. standard printed edition republished Jerusalem, 1971. Print. Trans. S.A. Berman. Hoboken, NJ: 2003. Print.

Ricoeur, Paul. *The Course of Recognition*. Trans. David Pellauer. Cambridge, MA: Harvard University Press, 2005. Print.

Sarna, Nahum. *The JPS Commentary on Genesis*. Philadelphia, PA: Jewish Publication Society, 1989. Print.

Shakespeare, William. *Othello*. Ed. Julie Hankey. New Haven, CT: Yale University Press, 2005. Print.

Sharvit, Shim'on. *Tractate Avoth Through the Ages*. Jerusalem: Bialik Institute, 2004. Print.

Sifre Devarim (Sifre on Deuteronomy). Eds. H.S. Horovitz and A. Finkelstein. Berlin: 1939; rpt. New York: The Jewish Theological Seminary of America, 1969. (Hebrew). Print.

Sophocles. "Oedipus the King." *Greek Tragedies*. Eds. David Grene and Richard Lattimore. 1st ed. Vol. I. Chicago: University of Chicago Press, 1942. Print.

Speiser, E.A. *Genesis*. Garden City, NY: Doubleday, 1964. Print.

Steinberg, Naomi. "The Genealogical Framework of the Family Stories in Genesis." *Semeia 46: Narrative Research on the Hebrew Bible*. Eds. Miri Amihai, George W. Coats, and Anne M. Solomon. Atlanta, GA: Society of Biblical Literature, 1989. 41–50. Print.

Sternberg, Meir. *The Poetics of Biblical Narrative*. Bloomington: Indiana University Press, 1987. Print.

Targum Onkelos to Genesis. Trans. with a critical introduction, apparatus, and notes Bernard Grossfield. Wilmington, DE: Michael Glazier, 1988. Print.

Targum-Pseudo-Jonathan. Ed. E.G. Clarke. Hoboken, NJ: Ktav Publishing House, 1984. (Hebrew). Print.

Tosefta. Ed. S. Lieberman. American Academy for Jewish Research: New York, 1950. (Hebrew). Print.; also TSK, Tosefta KePushta. Ed. S. Lieberman. 12 vols. New York: Hotsaat Mekhon Meir Leyb Rabinovits a. y. Bet ha-midrash le-rabanim sheba-Amerikah, 1955–1988. (Hebrew). Print.

Vawter, Bruce. *On Genesis: A New Reading*. Garden City, NY: Doubleday, 1977. Print.

Westermann, Claus. *Genesis 37–50: A Commentary*. Trans. John J. Scullion. Minneapolis, MN: Augsburg Publishing House, 1986. Print.

Zakovitch, Yair. *Ruth: Introduction and Commentary*. *[Miqra' le-Yisra'el]*. Tel Aviv and Jerusalem: Am Oved and Magnes Press, 1990. Print.

———. "The Threshing-Floor Scene in Ruth." *Shnaton: An Annual for Biblical and Ancient Near Eastern Studies* 3 (1978–79): 29–33. Print.

Zakovitch, Yair, and Avigdor Shinan. *Ma'aseh Yehuda ve-Tamar: Breshit 39 ba-Mikra, ba-targumim ha'atikim uva-sifrut ha-Yehudit.* Jerusalem: Mifale ha-mehkar shel ha-Makhon le-madae ha-Yahadut, 1992. Print.

4

BIBLICAL RECOGNITION

Separation From Bestiality and Incestuous Relationships as Resistance to Hellenization

HARRY FOX (LEBEIT YOREH)

ARISTOTLE IN HIS *POETICS* DISCUSSES plot and how the plot moves forward in a theatrical performance. He defines the element of recognition "as the very word implies, a change from ignorance to knowledge, and thus to either love or hate, in the personages marked for good or evil fortune" (Aristotle 1465; 1452a). The closest Hebrew word for this concept of discovery or recognition seems to be the root *n.kh.r.* The semantic range of this word used by just one scriptural translation project such as New Revised Standard Version of the Oxford Bible includes, in addition to recognize, discern; take notice; acknowledge; show; perceive; know; acquainted; point out; see. Verbs used in appositional phrases are mainly "to see" and "to know" while the opposite meaning is achieved by negation of the above list or by such a contrary word as "ignore." Hence, a future study of the notion of recognition/discovery in Scripture would require at the very least a study of the two verbs commonly used in apposition. One such example of recognition using the cognate root "to see" is Jacob wrestling with the angel (literally, the man): "And he recognized [literally saw] that he could not contend with him" (*Torah, Nevi'im, Ketuvim,*

Gen. 32.26),[1] in which the root *r..'h.* (to see) is used in describing the angel's self-recognition of his own limitations.

The most extensive discourse on Aristotle's concept of recognition is provided by Paul Ricoeur in a work entitled *The Course of Recognition*. Ricoeur asks how it is that in French the word for recognition contains also within it a sense of gratitude (x). To answer this question he develops the idea that recognition involves a course, a series of social links in which one begins with a sense of recognition as knowing or, to use Ricoeur's language, "grasping with one's mind objects as identification" (12, 23). The case brought above of Jacob and the angel refers to "ipseity" or "self-recognition." What follows is a study of some biblical verses in Scripture that involve an element of recognition. The reception history of these Scriptures is subsequently explored following Aristotelian *anagnorisis* and Ricoeur's phases of recognition and gift giving in order to examine bestiality and incestuous relationships in early human sexual history.

I

The biblical account of creation in Genesis provides us with an example of the first stage of recognition, that is, as identification and reads as follows: "And the Lord God said, 'It is not good that ha-Adam should be alone; I will make him/her an associate to match him/her.'[2] And out of the soil the Lord God formed every beast of the field, and every bird of the heavens: and brought them to ha-Adam to see what s/he[3] would call them: And whatever ha-Adam called every living creature that was its name. And ha-Adam gave names to all the cattle and to the birds of the air, and to every beast of the field: but for Adam[4] there was not found an associate to match him/her" (Gen. 2.18–20).[5] The first stage of recognition may further be related to Hegel's formulation of recognition (*Anerkennung*) and what Italo Testa sees as "natural recognition" an intrinsic pre-reflective mode of recognition as identification of others, or a first nature (343–44).[6] When the earthling ha-Adam is divided into two beings, s/he recognizes his/her soulmate, which leads to a second nature recognition that Testa after Hegel called "spiritual recognition." The so-called second nature can become reflexive and allow for self-reference and self-recognition,[7] which may lead to mutual recognition as outlined by Ricoeur.[8]

The second stage in the course of recognition, according to Ricoeur, is self-recognition (69–149). In his depiction of thematic continuity from Homer's to Aristotle's sense of recognition, Ricoeur uses the example of Ulysses in disguise who returns home to be recognized first by his faithful dog Argos, who dies from the excitement of his revelation (73–74) and hence does not betray Ulysses. In a sense, the dog's recognition allows Ulysses to recognize himself as one and the same person who left his home and family. Emmanuel Levinas tells the story of Bobby, a concentration camp dog, which was the only living creature there that treated Jews as human.[9] He also brings Homer's Ulysses as a comparative example. The inmates, reduced to slavery and maltreated as if subhuman, recognized in the dog's response their own continuing unrelinquishable grasp on their own humanity.

> But we called him Bobby, an exotic name, as one does with a cherished dog. He would appear at morning assembly and was waiting for us as we returned, jumping up and down and barking in delight. For him, there was no doubt that we were men. Perhaps the dog that recognized Ulysses beneath his disguise on his return from the Odyssey was a forebear of our own. But no, no! There, they were in Ithaca and the Fatherland. Here, we were nowhere. This dog was the last Kantian in Nazi Germany, without the brain needed to universalize maxims and drives. He was a descendent of the dogs of Egypt. And his friendly growling, his animal faith, was born from the silence of his forefathers on the banks of the Nile. (Levinas 153)

The process of self-recognition also becomes one of separation and distinction in which the named objects of one's universe—for example the living creatures named by Adam—are other than oneself. Therefore, self-recognition may also be a road to alienation. The formation of the "I" is in fact the cornerstone of Cartesian philosophy, which is so centred on recognition in the sense of *cogito*, "I think" as self-knowledge (Ricoeur 89–90).

Cognition, allows for the Socratic ideal of "Know thyself." Self-cognition, though, is not quite the same as recognition. It possesses a possibility of solipsism, being alone with one's objects, with one's toys: "but for ha-Adam there was not found an associate to match him/her" (Gen. 2.20).

This leads to Ricoeur's final course of recognition—mutual recognition. He explains this phase with a quotation from Jean-Jacques Rousseau's *Essay on the Origin of Language*: "As soon as one man was recognized by another as a sentient thinking Being similar to himself, the desire or need to communicate feelings and thoughts to him made the first man begin to look for ways to do so" (Ricoeur 150). So Adam's first speech act, as we shall soon see in detail, requires the creation and separation of Eve, a woman. He recognizes in her a true associate, which involves a sense of mutual recognition. This is best understood from the story of *The Bunyip of Berkeley's Creek* in which none recognize the bunyip until he comes upon another bunyip. Finding one's opposite as a moment of recognition is also the theme of the delightful story of the bunyip, who, when he asked the scientist what he looks like, is greeted with, "'Bunyips simply don't exist.' "In contrast to this grand failure of recognition comes the story's conclusion": 'What am I?' It murmured. 'What am I, what am I?' The bunyip jumped up in delight. 'You are bunyip!' He shouted. 'Am I? Am I really?' Asked the other bunyip; and then, 'What do I look like?' 'You look just like me,' said the bunyip happily. And he lent her his mirror to prove it." While reflecting upon moments of my own personal recognition, I recalled what I considered the *locus classicus* of such an event of recognition from my early schooling crystallized in one word, "*eureka!*" Recently David Perkins, in a work entitled *Archimedes' Bathtub*, alerts us to another facet of recognition that will inform our topic. His subtitle is, *The Art and Logic of Breakthrough Thinking*. Perkins describes *eureka* as follows: "Any breakthrough worth its salt is an exclamation. Most of us would probably say 'Aha!' but we might say 'Eureka!' *Eureka* is a word from ancient Greek meaning 'I have found it!' It's curious that a term more than two thousand years old should be in anyone's vocabulary today" (7).

Hebrew does not possess *eureka* as a Greek loan word. Contemporary Hebrew may use a translation of its meaning "I have found it" but the term lacks sufficient force to create an exclamation mark as its natural punctuation, other than perhaps for some absolutely amazing discovery. The best translation of *eureka* that I know is fairly recent and found in an illustrated work for children by Avner Katz entitled *...And Then the Tortoise Built Himself a Home*, which I have dealt with at some length elsewhere. In *...And Then the Tortoise Built Himself a Home*, the genius tortoise has a moment of recognition and a major breakthrough in which he uses the Hebrew word "*yesh!*" "I have it!" He shouted, "I have an idea!" The illustration depicts an exclamation mark above his head that has literally knocked the pipe he constantly puffed away at from his mouth and the cap right off his head. It is also the moment of his success after much trial and error. Lacking any clear linguistic markers for recognition in Hebrew, especially biblical Hebrew requires prodigious acts of memory of these texts to elicit instantiation of moments of recognition, clarity, breakthrough.[10]

The first such verse of recognition in Scripture belongs to Adam when in Genesis 2.23, following the verses cited above, he said, "This *is* now (*zot hapa'am*) bone of my bones, and flesh of my flesh! This one shall be called Woman, because this one was taken from Man."[11] Several ancient translators render the first two words *zot hapa'am* uttered by Adam in a variety of ways: the New Jewish Publication Society states, "This one at last" (The Jewish Bible, Gen. 2.23); and the Aramaic Targum attributed to Onkelos translates it as, *hada zimna* "This time" (*Torat Chaim* to Gen. 2.23). Taken out of context the statement may seem rather unremarkable until we realize that this occasion of recognition is also the first time Adam, now definitively gendered male, speaks. It also marks the beginning of biblical gender hierarchy as Adam (male) becomes the primary subject. Context is determinative.[12] The very next verse provides an etiology for heterosexuality, as well as a shift away from parental fealty towards spousal alliance. This serves to heighten and highlight the significance of the statement.

The twelfth-century Spanish exegete R. Abraham Ibn Ezra glosses the biblical text with, "I have found my associate, like myself for she was from himself" (*Torat Chaim* to Gen. 2.23). One may conclude this *eureka* moment with an exclamation mark. If the biblical recognition appears personal and comparative, it would seem to return to Genesis 2.20 ("and ha-Adam gave names to all the cattle and to the birds of the heavens and to every creature of the field but for ha-Adam there was not an associate to match him/her"), where the same phrase used by Ibn Ezra is found, namely that Adam had not found his associate.[13] Yet even Ibn Ezra cannot resist, against his more usual predilections for rationality, to introduce the mythic even if his intention is its dismissal.[14] Hence, he also recontextualizes the verse by saying, "And the matter of Lilith is homiletic" (*Torat Chaim* to Gen. 2.23). Herein is hinted that prior to the creation of the flesh-and-blood Eve, Adam had connections with the demoness Lilith or the first Eve: "And God created the human being [ha-Adam] in his image in the image of God he created him—male and female he created them. And God blessed them and God said to them: be fruitful and multiply and fill the earth and subdue it and rule over the fish of the sea and the birds of the heavens and all the creatures which crawl upon the earth" (Gen. 1.27–28).

Sexuality with Eve is heteronormative with the man on top, whereas with Lilith, the temptress, it is dangerous and deviant.

> When the Holy-One-blessed-be created primordial man (Adam) alone, He said: "It is not good for the primordial man (Adam) to be by himself." He created for him a woman from the earth like himself and called her Lilith. Immediately they began to quarrel with each other, she said: "I will not lie beneath [you]," and he said: "I will not lie beneath [you] but on top since you are worthy to [lie] beneath and I on top." She said to him: "We are both equal and we are both from the earth." And they would not listen to each other. Upon seeing him Lilith said the explicit name [of God] and fluttered in the atmosphere of the universe. Adam stood in prayer before his maker and said: "Master of the Universe, the woman you have given me ran away from me."

Immediately the Holy-One-blessed-be sent these three angels after her to bring her back. The Holy-One-blessed-be said to him: "If she wishes to return—it is well, and if not she will bring upon herself that a hundred of her children will die each day." They left her and went after her and caught up to her at the sea in powerful waters in which the Egyptians will [one day] drown and related to her the words of God yet she did not desire to return.
(Alpha-Beta of Ben Sira)[15]

The two biblical accounts of creation are seen as mutually contradictory: the first offers a radical egalitarianism, whereas the second establishes a hierarchy and, consequently, a patriarchy.[16] The resolution of the intense embarrassment is accomplished by the demonization of Lilith,[17] who is relegated to haunt Adam and Eve and their progeny in devilish form either as a temptress or abductor; she is responsible for the high infant mortality rate suffered in antiquity.[18] In particular, the moment of recognition in this second creation account becomes *This time* God got it right. Eve is recognized as the vital "mother of all living" whereas Lilith is relegated to the polar opposite as the deadly destroyer of all living.[19]

If this was not dramatic enough, other commentators provide yet other contexts, that is, other elements of recognition and breakthrough. Rashi the eleventh-century French exegete engages in a different sort of sexual anxiety. He comments: "*This time* teaches that Adam had sexual congress with all the cattle and animals and was not cooled off by them" (*Torat Chaim* to Gen. 2.23). In other words, Adam did not find bestiality or zoophilia entirely satisfactory, but recognized Eve as a suitable sexual partner. Rashi's comment is based on the classical talmudic sages: "R. Eleazar further stated: What is meant by Scripture, *This is now bone of my bones, and flesh of my flesh*? This teaches that Adam had intercourse with every beast and animal but found no satisfaction until he cohabited with Eve" (*bYevamot* 63a). This is a rather shocking resolution to the demonstrative "this" that implies another, a "that," because the Geonic ninth-century *Halakhot Gedolot* lists bestiality as the fifth and sixth transgressions of precepts, which is so severe that stoning is considered the punishment for transgressors (*Sefer Halakhot Gedolot* 8). This topic has received considerable attention in subsequent generations as recently discussed by Eric Lawee ("Rashi"; "Sepharad"). An interesting twist to Rashi's commentary is found in the thirteenth-century Provençal scholar R. David Kimchi. Concerning the etiology of Genesis 2.24, "Therefore shall a man leave his father and his mother," he claims that his predecessors are conflicted as to whether this is the continuation of Adam's speech or whether it belongs to Moses (*Torat Chaim* to Gen. 2.24). Today, we would say these words are the narrator's. Surprisingly after raising this critical matter, he settles for the classical sages who claim that they are the continuation of Adam's speech, and as it may, they then consider themselves to be divinely inspired. This highlights heteronormativity, which is then expanded to include a warning concerning incestuous prohibitions.[20] The phrase "and shall cleave [unto his wife]" is understood by Kimchi as "and not with a male which is not the way of cleaving of a man and a woman," and the following phrase "unto his wife" is mentioned "to exclude his neighbor's wife. *And they shall be one flesh*, those who are able to be one flesh with humans to exclude animals, beasts and birds who do not make one flesh with humans" (*Torat Chaim* to Gen. 2.24).[21] The verses of recognition become breakthrough statements of theology whose hidden subtexts include the Noahide prohibitions already largely in play from Adam onward, the Levitical incest laws including same-sex prohibitions, and bestiality as well as the Ten Commandments. Recognition has become inspired breakthrough thinking.

If this were not already enough, Rashi's grandson, Rashbam (*Torat Chaim* to Gen. 2.23), followed by many later exegetes, introduced a miraculous element: "bone of my bones verily but from now on it is not so but man comes from out of woman." Again this introduces the mythic, in which Athena may be birthed from the head of Zeus. Finally, Nachmanides, the thirteenth-century Spanish exegete, indicated that the words "this time" contain "a secret" (*Torat Chaim* to Gen. 2.23). From the mythic and miraculous we have come to the mysterious. And in the commentary of Recanati, "the word *zot* (this) hints to the Shekhinah" (*Torat Chaim* to Gen. 2.23). We have arrived herein to the very portals of the Godhead. Recanati reveals more of what he means on his comment to Genesis 29.13: "And when Laban heard the news of Jacob his sister's son, he ran to greet him, and embraced him and kissed him and brought him into his home." Recanati reads the verse eschatologically and in light of similar phraseology in Genesis 2.23. "His home" in the heavenly Jerusalem, for it is good for a human in his home. And this commentary is supported by Laban's statement: "'lo you are like my bones and flesh' (Gen. 29.14) as you said (Gen. 2.23) 'this time bone of my bones and flesh of my flesh' and the discerning will comprehend" (*Torat Chaim* to Gen. 2.24).

II

The mutual recognition of two subjects is a wonderful moment in the history of humankind, one given to countless repetitions. Nonetheless, the differentiations of an I, a self-recognition, as separate from others, creates also a desire to provide the moment of recognition with a mechanism of remembrance, recall, and perhaps one may say, reliability and ritual. Hence, with the active recognition one desires to give some token or gift of the self to the other. Alas, this generates an act of deconstruction as well. It is the gift that creates an asymmetry in the relationship. Ricoeur calls this a paradox of the gift, a disturbance in the mutuality of two subjects, because the gift is always an I to a you, a subject to an object (225). The process of objectification is a perilous byproduct of the desire to give personal expression to mutuality. As scholars of the gift have noted, the gift has an ability to create a lack in its wake. That "lack" can create a need to reciprocate, to rebalance the scales shaken by the weight of the gift, the profundity of obligation with which it burdens the recipient. Once given, the gift creates a struggle for recognition (Ricoeur 246). For Ricoeur, the gift is only given and received successfully if there continues to exist a sense of mutuality determined by gratitude (243). For gratitude and obligation to remain good, the giving must also be gratuitous or freely given to allow it to be freely received. This allows for the possibility that the mutuality of recognition be maintained.

In light of Ricoeur's analysis of gifts,[22] I would attempt a rereading of the forbidden fruit episode in Genesis chapter 3 now seen as a gift. By pretending there are no consequences to eating the fruit of knowledge, in our context one may say the fruit of discernment or of recognition between good and evil, the snake beguiled Eve into eating its fruit, which seems to be his gratuitous gift to her especially in light of affinities to the ancient Pandora (= all gifts) myth as first related by Hesiod.[23] The sages understood the beautiful implications of such a freely given gift and, hence, impute negative motivations to the snake that are not stated in Scripture. Noticing that the biblical text juxtaposes the nakedness of Adam and Eve (Gen. 2.25) with the nakedness and cunning of the snake (Gen. 3.1), they claim the snake is in lust after having seen Adam and Eve copulating in the garden as mentioned by Rashi (*Torat Chaim* to Gen. 2.25) on the basis of *Genesis Rabbah* (II. 18.6; 168–69).

The biblical narrative is exceptionally terse here; in Hebrew, it is little more than a series of verbs (eight words in total), Genesis 3.6: "She took of its fruit, and ate and gave also to her husband with her, and he ate." The speed of the actions propelling the plot forward is break-neck. Adam's action seems precipitous, spontaneous, as if he is totally unaware of its being calamitous, catastrophic. They seem entirely unreflective, and the gift with its potential of disruption is avoided by the apparently mutual recognition, by gratitude toward the gratuitous, a gift freely given and freely received.

The potential asymmetry created by these actions, ones that could have placed Adam and Eve on different sides of a yawning chasm, is avoided by a lack of discord or disloyalty in their actions. In a flawed universe, however, rupture is unavoidable. Poignantly enough the breakdown in communication of the freely conversant snake, Eve and Adam is with the source of life itself, God their creator (Gen. 3.14–19). All three are variously cursed in such a way that the moment of complete mutuality also becomes a far more fleeting experience of wholeness, oneness, and being in love. One must constantly struggle to re-achieve this condition of completeness.

Even the sages who slow down the proceedings by filling in the white gaps between the verbs of the canonical text cannot shake the wonderful strength of loyalty displayed in the simultaneous moment of grace and fall. Eve, having eaten of the fruit, having recognized her new situation, gave the fruit to all the animals of the garden, presumably to the snake as well, then she gave the fruit to Adam—essentially her recognition or insight was one that understood intuitively that divided we shall all fall but united we shall all live (*Torat Chaim* to Gen. 3.6).[24] God's choice is either to accept a fait accompli or destroy the entire universe just now so painstakingly completed. The seal of existence is kissed with sin and disobedience. Normative circumstances for humans and animals alike would be short and miserable. Yet, what saves humanity from dwelling constantly in the pit of despair and ultimately subverts the curses placed on us by God is our moments of recognition, which puncture the gloom with sparks of primordial light.

According to the rabbinic sages,[25] the verse Genesis 2.23 stands at the nexus of human sexual expression. It favours heterosexuality over bestiality (which is the context they understood for the recognition or discovery achieved by Adam in regard to Eve) and possibly by implication homosexuality as well, though it is important to note that this is by no means explicit and so may be an intended inference read into the text with prejudice. Yet, the biblical context is one in which Eve leads Adam to fall from grace, resulting in their banishment from the Garden of Eden (Gen. 3.22–24). Hence, heterosexuality also has its price and yields a friendship/hostility duality in the same relationship.

One more facet of recognition as developed by Christina Tarnopolsky requires exposition. This involves an alternate route, as it were, of a consequence of sin, namely the shame immediately felt by Adam and Eve (Gen. 3.7). This verse depicts Adam and Eve covering their nakedness in shame.[26] Tarnopolsky describes such a situation as "the moment of recognition within the occurrent experience of shame" (476). The next verse will be inextricably linked to one covering the nakedness of forbidden consanguinity (Lev. 18, 20), that is, sexual partners who transgressively lift their forbidden skirts or, put in the words of the Genesis context, their fig leaves (Gen. 3.7).

Adam and Eve's clothing is mentioned again at the end of the chapter (3.21), which has God make them leather garments. *Genesis Rabbah* 20.12 on this verse mentioned that "in the Torah of Rabbi Meir they found that [the verse] was written as *garments of light*" (I.196). These are the emperor's new clothes, visible to him and invisible to everyone else. In this case, the veil of nakedness and the consequent potential in human sexuality are always both normative and transgressive at the same time—leather and light vying with each other simultaneously.

III

The second set of verses we shall focus upon centre around Numbers 11.10: "And Moses heard the people weeping, according to their clans, each person at the entrance of his tent. The Lord was exceedingly angry and in the eyes of Moses it was evil." The immediate biblical antecedent seems to be the gluttonous cravings of the Israelites, which involves a moment of recognition: "And the riffraff in their midst felt gluttonous cravings; and the Israelites, once again wept and said: Who will feed us meat? We remember the fish that we used to eat freely in Egypt, the cucumbers, and the melons, and the leeks, and the onions, and the garlic. Now our spirits are shrivelled. There is nothing at all to look forward to but this manna to eat!" (Num. 11.4–6). The immediate scriptural context is a response of embarrassment in which the manna is described and praised (Num. 11.7–9).[27] The interpretation by the rabbinic sages both decontextualizes the verse in question and at the same time places it in a very different setting. They feel compelled to do so because the crying of the Israelites is mentioned twice (Num. 11.4, 10). So why is there an uproar on two occasions in nearby verses? If one verse is designated as a cry of hunger, then in accordance with rabbinic lore the record is freed up to comment on another situation. Because of the familial phrase, the complaint is attached to the incest lists of Leviticus 18 and 20.

Rashi (*Torat Chaim* to Num. 11.10), basing himself on the sages' comments, remarks on the verse as follows: "'weeping, according to their clans' each and every clan is gathered and weeping to proclaim their complaint publicly. And our sages said: 'according to their clans' concerning clan matters, on the consanguineous marriages disallowed them" (*bShabbat* 130a, *bYoma* 75a, *pTa'anit* 4.5, 68d, etc.). Rashi has summarized several talmudic texts and clearly designated these particular tears as complaint about incest taboos and not merely hunger, which now becomes solely the act of earlier crying (Num. 11.4). We may surmise that the topic is a sensitive one because Ibn Ezra emphasizes the public nature of the complaint as well as a large gathering together of the clans (*Torat Chaim* to Num. 11.10). There he uses a simile, "like when they cry over the dead," rather than attempt to guess what this particular complaint is about. Numbers 11.1 mentions God's anger as a fire burning among them and "consuming them that were in the outermost parts of the camp." The exegete remains somewhat contextual even though the *manna* description has interrupted the biblical narrative sequence. As such, a link is possible. Ibn Ezra in deference to the sages does not designate the crying to any specific complaint. The talmudic sages, however, are not so reticent. In their hermeneutics multiple readings are legitimate. They are governed by what could easily be construed as a postmodernist proclivity that "there are seventy facets to the Scriptures."[28] Hence, in *bYoma* 75a we read "'weeping, according to their clans' on clan matters that disallowed them to lie with each other, but for the one who said [the crying was because] of the fish, what is 'weeping, according to their clans?' This and that occurred [that is, they cry for both]." If the major theme were the incest lists of Leviticus 18 and 20, then the Israelites would have wept about scriptural edicts. Apparently, this is inconceivable for *pTa'anit* (4.5, 68d) since the Torah was accepted by them unconditionally.[29] Therefore, the sages, ever alert to the nuances of Scripture, placed emphasis on Moses's role in these verses. Specifically, they took notice of the fact that those complaints were directed at Moses: "And the people cried unto Moses" (Num. 11.2); "And Moses heard the people weeping" (Num. 11.10). Furthermore, Moses reacts by praying in the first instance (Num.11.2), and takes personal affront in the second: "and in the eyes of Moses it was evil" (Num. 11. 10). The sages then cause the text to swerve in a new direction. The people complained about an oral teaching in which Moses added to the scriptural strictures. Namely, the people complained "about six consanguineous marriages Moses disallowed them" (*pTa'anit* 4.5, 68d). These are not listed specifically in Scripture but disallow sexual relations such as with one's grandmother (and the list goes up three generations and down three generations). The people are said to cry over the additions made to the scriptural list as if the original list were not already restrictive enough. The talmudic text at *bShabbat* 130a has the scriptural text in Numbers 11.10 at the epicentre of the complaint about the incest laws. It sees these as strictures only reluctantly accepted by the people and sees the acceptance itself emanating from "strife." From this perspective, the originary strife is one in which "they still have strife over [marital] matters, as there is no [marital] contract that there is no haggling [over the financial issues];" the tannaitic midrash of the early third century provides explicit examples of what the people regretted: "'Moses heard the people weeping, according to their clans.' R. Nehorai would say this teaches that the Israelites were regretful when Moses said to them to separate from the consanguineous marriages and it teaches us that a man would marry his sister, or his father's sister or his mother's sister and when Moses told them to separate from the consanguineous marriages they were regretful" (*Siphré D'be Rav to Numbers, piska* 90; Horovitz 91).

The Israelites are weeping because they enjoyed all of the incest taboos listed in Leviticus 18 and 20, which would henceforth govern Israel, much like Adam enjoyed the beasts prior to the creation of Eve. This change from ignorance to knowledge has profound repercussions in the history of Western sexuality, a topic I have addressed elsewhere. Once again heterosexuality is privileged as normative. The result is that, even Adam, who had enjoyed (though apparently not to such an extent) sexual relations with the animals, was thereby obliquely censured.

IV

We have seen that on two significant occasions the rabbinic sages posited transgressive behaviour on the part of Adam and the Israelites involving sexual taboos—Adam transgressing norms of bestiality and the Israelites transgressing norms of incest. Indeed the transgressive acts are considered normative, perhaps even natural. For the incest laws, at least, the Israelites are asked not to behave in the manner of the surrounding nations (Lev. 18.3; 18.24–30; 20.23–24).

When we ask ourselves why it is that the sages cause the biblical text to swerve so far from its simple meaning to the point of what would seem to be extreme embarrassment and shame, we enter the realm of speculation. Nonetheless, the question is begging and hence so too must an answer be compelling. It would seem to me, at least, that the sages hereby provide a powerful answer to their imperialistic Greco-Roman overlords. We too were once like you, involved in every form of sexual and religious depravity. Our law, however, civilized us and though defeated by might, the righteous form of living is provided not by the imperial powers who regularly justified their conquests by such rhetoric but by our law as present in the (dual) Torah.

This theme is also found in the Passover Haggadah, which begins with the deprecation of Israel's ancestors as mere "idol worshipers" who, by the telling of the Exodus, have regained their lost freedom and received the rule of law in the form of the Torah. So too in the ancient Palestinian prayer rite the central moment of prayer included recitation of the Ten Commandments as representative of the Torah as a whole (*mTamid* 5.1).

Abbreviations

b = Babylonian Talmud

m = Mishnah

p = Palestinian Talmud

Notes

1. The reader should note that all translations from original Hebrew or Aramaic texts are my own unless specifically indicated.
2. I have deliberately chosen "associate," a gender-neutral word in place of King James Version (KJV) translation "help meet," which, though also gender-neutral, has a sense of subordination to it immediately identifying it with woman. My claim here is that woman does not exist neither before man in the three biblical creation accounts, nor man before woman. For this reason I have also used the alternate readings him/her in my translation.
3. One need not gender Adam male until the creation of Eve and the word *adam* retains non-generic features even afterward. See, for example, Genesis 5.1–5. The word *adam* is specifically used to include both males and females in rabbinic legal hermeneutics. Such is the case also in Modern Hebrew. Some versions have this as verse 25 others as verse 26.
4. Masoretic Text (MT) provides a *shewa* here and not a *qamatz* (which would indicate the presence of the definite article along with a preposition). It seems to me that the *shewa* cannot be original as the definite article is present before Adam in all references after the first reference in Genesis 1.26–27 (attributed to P) and Genesis 2.5–3.24. The only exceptions are the prepositional *lamed* "to" for *leAdam* here at Genesis 2.20 and at Genesis 3.17 and 3.21, and I would read those as well against MT with *qamatz*, thereby making them all possess the definite article. Reading against the vowelization of MT in this case has interpretive results. The name "Adam" for primordial man, in my opinion, does not exist before the separation of Eve (woman). This is why it is so readily provided with a definite article, something not required for the proper name of the person. Collins provides a totally traditional rendering of the creation of Adam texts by seeing the definite article as an anaphoric back reference to the unmarked man. While this comment is correct, it fails to recognize that two of the three creation accounts certainly do not see Adam as gendered despite the anaphoric reference (Gen. 1.28, 5.2). The fact that the Septuagint does not support the definite article at Genesis 2.20 is beside the point as its reading throughout is traditional patriarchal, hence also constructive

and interpretive as is the Masoretic reading. See C. John Collins's *Genesis 1–4: A Linguistic, Literary and Theological Commentary* (135–36nn84–85).

5. Recently R.S. Kawashima has challenged the non-gendered reading of the text first introduced by Phyllis Trible in *God and the Rhetoric of Sexuality* (80; cited in Kawashima 46n2) and in Phyllis A. Bird's *Missing Persons and Mistaken Identities* (182n24; cited in Kawashima 46n2). Kawashima divides scholarship into "feminist" and "biblical" claiming that biblical scholars, such as Alter and Boyarin, have rejected this rendering while Wenham and Seebass have ignored it (47nn4–5). In my opinion, both Alter and Boyarin have accepted the "feminist" reading but argue only at precisely what point Adam is to be gendered male. Those who ignore this rendering do so at their own peril and patriarchy is certainly not dead. Kawashima wishes to favour what he calls "philosophical realism," for which I ask the reader to reread the previous sentence. Nor is the assessment that the gender-neutral perspective has been abandoned correct. As indicated, it is not true for either Alter or Boyarin. As well, it is the adopted position of Mignon R. Jacobs, see *Gender, Power, and Persuasion: The Genesis Narratives and Contemporary Portraits* where the argument is brought that God in the text did not anticipate a female and so used a masculine reference to the being about to be created (*ezer kenegdo*), which I have translated as "associate" (Jacobs 33–42, esp. 35n35). T. Stordalen, *Echoes of Eden: Genesis 2–3 and Symbolism of the Eden Garden in Biblical Hebrew Literature*, despite believing that Adam is "certainly male" in Genesis 2–3 nonetheless uses gender-neutral language in translating Genesis 2.5 as "human being" because the "focus is on class" (222–27, esp. 222n36). Is it so certain that "class" contains only men? See further, Joseph Abraham, *Eve: Accused or Acquitted? An Analysis of Feminist Readings of the Creation Narrative Texts in Genesis 1–3* (esp. 56–65). Reliance on Trible and Bird continues unabated among biblical scholars as well, see, for example, Paul Niskanen, "The Poetics of Adam: The Creation of *ha'adam* in the Image of *'elohîm*" (417–36), who emphasizes that the definite article has created "More Trouble with Translation" (417–36, esp. 434–36). To conclude this lengthy excursus, Kawashima in his appeal to "philosophical realism" is calling in question feminist readings as ideologically motivated hence not partaking in what is called by Susan Haack, "The Ideal of Intellectual Integrity in Life and Literature" (359–37). Whereas natural law theorists have more often than not ended up with gender hierarchy, Cristina Traina in "Feminist Natural Law" argues that even in this bastion of patriarchal philosophy there may be room for another viewpoint (79–87). See further the exchange between James Barr and Johannes C. de Moor. De

Moor's response may be buttressed by many further considerations but I hope to return to this topic on another occasion.

6. For further consideration of Hegel's theory of recognition see Ricoeur's *Course of Recognition*, 17–21.
7. The failure of mutual recognition creates friction in the social sphere that may cause its breakdown through "divorce" or the imposition "hierarchy" including "patriarchy" or its postmodern social fragmentation. See Testa, 367–68, and see below on seeing the fruit of the garden as a gift with the potential for total disruption and I daresay violence.
8. See Ricoeur on Hegel, 171–86. The splitting of *ha-Adam*, the earthling into two entities creates the possibility of community (Aristotle's *polis*) where each human being is by nature also a *zoon politikon*, a political being. Hence, the changing order of humanity created a bioethical problem in natural law because disturbances and/or mistakes may intervene to prevent equality, especially if potential partners in the debate of what "should" be are systemically silenced as in the case of say "patriarchy." See Ludwig Siep, "Natural Law and Bioethics," 44–67, esp. 48–49. One resolution of these dilemmas from the perspective of Michael Walzer is offered by Jean-Pierre Wils, "'Does the Natural-Law Approach Have a Future?' A Hermeneutical Proposal: Nine Objections to Natural Law" (68–78).
9. On Levinas and recognition see also Ricoeur, 150–246, esp. 157–61.
10. See also Gen. 12.11, 22.12, 37.4, and 42.1 and 2 Samuel 5.1.
11. The first person to have understood the exclamation point of recognition in this verse using precisely these terms is George W. Ramsey, "Is Name-Giving an Act of Domination in Genesis 2.23 and Elsewhere?" (24–35, see 35n37). Ramsey avoids the dominant interpretation through comparative philology despite a traditional understanding of gender.
12. See, for example, Gen. 5.1–5 as opposed to Gen. 3.17. Gen. 5 refers to the male and female creatures as Adam. Gen. 3.17 is after the division of Adam into two beings, Adam and Eve.
13. See Jenny Wagner, *The Bunyip of Berkeley's Creek*, unpaginated. Concerning the significance of such interpersonal mutual recognition, see Arto Laitinen's "Interpersonal Recognition: Response to Value or a Precondition of Personhood?" (463–78).
14. This quotation of Ibn Ezra is not found in all editions. See the comments by Weiser, *Ibn Ezra al HaTorah* (24n93).
15. This is a translation of the Hebrew text taken from *Alpha-Beta of Ben Sira, Ozar Midrashim: Library of Two Hundred Minor Midrashim/ Ozar Midrashim* (47).

16. The second creation account belongs to J and is its beginning. It chiastically reflects its conclusion with the recognition of David as monarch over a united kingdom of Judah (gendered male) and Israel (gendered female) at 2 Sam 5.1. Just as David will rule over his kingdom, so too will Adam rule over Eve (Gen 3.16). For the full philological argument about the extent of J see Tzemah Yoreh's website http://www.biblecriticism.com.

17. See Harry Fox, Introduction to *Vixens Disturbing Vineyards: Embarrassment and Embracement of Scriptures—A Festschrift in Honor of Harry Fox* (5–11).

18. A similar process is involved in the demonization of Queen Sheba. See Lassner, *Demonizing the Queen of Sheba: Boundaries of Gender and Culture in Postbiblical Judaism and Medieval Islam.*

19. Lilith has been reclaimed by the Jewish feminist movement as a role model and inspiration for equality. See Joy Kogawa and Lillian Broen (2001) and the sources cited on page xxi as well as Gershom Scholem's article in *Encyclopaedia Judaica* (1972), "Lilith." Such reclamation is also evident in the use of "Lillith" as the title of a magazine that advocates feminism.

20. The issue deserves far more attention than may be provided here.

21. Kimchi bases himself on the talmudic sages but is apparently more explicit than they are in indicating that Adam was divinely inspired when he said this (since he had no human mother or father) (*Torat Chaim* I 55n42).

22. There is much recent discussion on gifts, especially whether they are ever freely given, that is, altruistic, or are always the expression of the selfish gene whose function is to place expectations or demands or claims against the recipient creating a degree of debt or indebtedness or obligation. Marcel Mauss discusses this (esp. 1, 42, 110–11n131) as does Jacques Derrida who is further discussed by Jean-Michel Rabaté and Michael Wetzel. The range of debate on altruism or selfishness is discussed by Thomas Nagel (esp. 7–12) and William Scott Green (esp. ix–xiv and bibliography cited on xiv) and Richard Dawkins.

23. For a thorough analysis of the Pandora myth and its resonance in the story of Adam and Eve both in the biblical account of creation and in rabbinic lore see Samuel Tobias Lachs (341–45), Pamela Norris's *The Story of Eve* (Ch. 4, "Curious Women: Eve, Pandora, and Psyche" 111–34), Anne Lapidus Lerner (102–05, 199n86), citing Daniel Boyarin, *Carnal Israel: Reading Sex in Talmudic Culture* (86–87). On Hesiod's two versions of the Pandora myth, akin in some ways to the Eve/Lilith doubling see Bronwen L.Wickkiser (557–76). Perhaps somewhat surprisingly, Eve whose depiction may have been influenced by the Pandora myth and to some extent is an amalgam of both of Hesiod's versions resembles the nameless more

statuesque version of the *Theogony*. Ḥava, an isomorphic form of Ḥaya meaning creature or birthgiver, seems nondescript and generic as she is called "the mother of all living creatures," a godlike epithet. Only in the sense of gift giving as outlined above is there any animation provided to her character which links it to the second Hesiodic depiction in *Works and Days*. There Pandora (all gifts of the gods) is named, animated, more human, lies, is deceptive and thievish in her character. These features, though not entirely absent in Eve, depict more the Eve of midrash who saved all from destruction by feeding the animals and Adam the forbidden fruit she has eaten. Alternatively, the demonic figure of Lilith is endowed with some of these features making her into a more dominant, persuasive character.

24. Rashi, Kimchi (Radak), and Ḥizkuni all base themselves on *Genesis Rabbah* 19.5 (I.174) where "she said to all the animals and beasts and birds, all listen to her and ate except for one fowl whose name is *hol*." As the continuation makes explicit, this is the myth of the Phoenix who lives a thousand years, is consumed by fire, and then is reborn from the remaining ashes.

25. See in particular Kimchi cited above who bases himself on *bSanhedrin* 58a.

26. See J. David Velleman (27–52). Though I found Velleman's account of the genesis of shame fascinating, he neglects the audience that the animals (all clothed with furs and feathers) and God (all seeing and discerning) may play on the notion of privacy or lack thereof. Even the snake, which may have been considered naked, sheds its skin periodically. It is also possible that they felt guilt having transgressed the law of the garden, what has been called the sin of disobedience. See Herant Katchadourian (201). Katchadourian juxtaposes this to a Pauline concept of original sin as developed by Augustine and Aquinas (207–12). Though original sin is not the dominant explanation in Judaism, it apparently does make its appearance both in Scriptures and later sources. See Tirzah Meacham (162–63). The bite of forbidden fruit is also a challenge to God's sovereignty. Once the dangerous breach of the sacred occurs, God maintains authority only by banishing Adam and Eve from the garden. Nonetheless, Adam and Eve are not immediately killed thus the text observes God's deconstruction. See Nick Mansfield (32).

27. See above note 17.

28. See *A Thesaurus of Sayings and Aphorisms* for a list of sources citing the phrase "*shev'im panim latorah*."

29. The topic of unconditionality in Judaism requires further elaboration. See note 19, Mansfield, 2–3.

Works Cited

Abraham, Joseph. *Eve: Accused or Acquitted? An Analysis of Feminist Readings of the Creation Narrative Texts in Genesis 1–3*. Carisle, UK: Paternoster Press, 2002. Print.

Alpha-Beta of Ben Sira. *Ozar Midrashim: Library of Two Hundred Minor Midrashim / Ozar Midrashim*. 1915. Ed. J.D. Eisenstein. Jerusalem: n.p., 1969. (Hebrew). Print.

Aristotle. *The Basic Works of Aristotle*. Ed. Richard McKeon. 24th ed. New York: Random House, 1941. Print.

A Thesaurus of Sayings and Aphorisms. (Mikhlol haMaamarim vehaPitgamim) Ed. Moshe Sabar. Vol. 3. Jerusalem: Mossad HaRav Kook, 1962. (Hebrew). Print.

Barr, James. "One Man, or all Humanity? A Question in the Anthropology of Genesis 1." *Recycling Biblical Figures*. Eds. Athalya Brenner and Jan Willem van Heuten. Leiderdrop, NL: Deo Publishing, 1999. 3–21. Print.

Bird, Phyllis A. *Missing Persons and Mistaken Identities*. Minneapolis, MN: Fortress Press, 1997. Print.

Boyarin, Daniel. *Carnal Israel: Reading Sex in Talmudic Culture*. Berkeley: University of California Press, 1995. Print.

Collins, C. John. *Genesis 1–4: A Linguistic, Literary, and Theological Commentary*. Phillipsburg, NJ: P & R Publishing, 2006. Print.

Dawkins, Richard. *The Selfish Gene*. 1976. Oxford: Oxford University Press, 2006. Print.

De Moor, Johannes C. "The First Human Being a Male? A Response to Professor Barr." *Recycling Biblical Figures*. Eds. Athalya Brenner and Jan Willem van Heuten. Leiderdrop, NL: Deo Publishing, 1999. 22–27. Print.

Derrida, Jacques. *Given Time: I, Counterfeit Money*. Trans. Peggy Kamuf. Chicago: University of Chicago Press, 1992. Print.

Fox, Harry. Introduction. *Vixens Disturbing Vineyards: Embarrassment and Embracement of Scriptures—A Festschrift in Honor of Harry Fox (leBeit Yoreh)*. Eds. Tzemah Yoreh, Aubrey Glazer, Justin Jaron Lewis, and Miryam Segal. Boston: Academics Press, 2010. 5–11. Print.

Green, William Scott. "Introduction: Altruism and the Study of Religion." *Altruism in World Religions*. Eds. Jacob Neusner and Bruce Chilton. Washington, DC: Georgetown University Press, 2005. Print.

Haack, Susan. "The Ideal of Intellectual Integrity in Life and Literature." *New Literary History* 36 (2005): 359–73. Print.

Ibn Ezra al HaTorah. Ed. Asher Weiser. Jerusalem: Mossad HaRav Kook, 1977. Print.

Jacobs, Mignon R. *Gender, Power, and Persuasion: The Genesis Narratives and Contemporary Portraits*. Grand Rapids, MI: Baker Academic, 2007. Print.

*The Jewish Bible: Tanakh: The Holy Scriptures—The New JPS Translation According to the Traditional Hebrew Text: Torah * Nevi'im * Kethuvim.* Philadelphia, PA: Jewish Publication Society, 2006. Print.

Katchadourian, Herant. *Guilt: The Bite of Conscience.* Stanford, CA: Stanford University Press, 2010. Print.

Katz, Avner. *...And Then the Tortoise Built Himself a Home.* Jerusalem: Keter, 1979. (Hebrew). Print.

Kawashima, Robert S. "A Revisionist Reading Revisited: On the Creation of Adam and Then Eve." *Vetus Testamentum* 56 (2006): 46–57. Print.

Kogawa, Joy. *A Song of Lilith.* Illus. Lillian Broca. Vancouver: Raincoast Books, 2001. Print.

Lachs, Samuel Tobias. "The Pandora-Eve Motif in Rabbinic Literature." *Harvard Theological Review* 67 (1974): 341–45. Print.

Laitinen, Arto. "Interpersonal Recognition: A Response to Value or a Precondition of Personhood?" *Inquiry* 45.4 (2002): 463–78. Print.

Lassner, Jacob. *Demonizing the Queen of Sheba: Boundaries of Gender and Culture in Postbiblical Judaism and Medieval Islam.* Chicago: University of Chicago Press, 1993. Print.

Lawee, Eric. "From Sepharad to Ashkenaz: Case Study in the Rashi Supercommentary Tradition." *AJS Review: The Journal of the Association for Jewish Studies* 30 (2006): 393–425. Print.

———. "The Reception of Rashi's Commentary on the Torah in Spain: The Case of Adam's Mating with the Animals." *The Jewish Quarterly Review* 97.1 (2007): 33–66. Print.

Lerner, Anne Lapidus. *Eternally Eve: Images of Eve in the Hebrew Bible, Midrash, and Modern Jewish Poetry.* Waltham, MA: Brandeis University Press, 2007. Print.

Levinas, Emmanuel. "The Name of a Dog, or Natural Right." *Difficult Freedom: Essays on Judaism.* Trans. Seán Hand. London: Athlone Press, 1990. 150–53. Print.

Mansfield, Nick. *The God Who Deconstructs Himself: Sovereignty and Subjectivity Between Freud, Bataille, and Derrida.* New York: Fordham University Press, 2010. Print.

Mauss, Marcel. *The Gift: The Form and Reason for Exchange in Archaic Societies.* Trans. W.D. Halls. New York: Norton, 1990. Print.

Meacham, Tirzah. "A Suggested Commentary for the Doubling of Days of Impurity and Purity for the Woman who Births a Daughter." *Shnaton: An Annual for Biblical and Ancient Near Eastern Studies* 11 (1997): 162–63. (Hebrew). Print.

Midrash Genesis Rabbah. Eds. J. Theodor and H. Albeck. 5 vols. Jerusalem: Wahrmann, 1965. (Hebrew). Print.

Nagel, Thomas. *The Possibility of Altruism*. 1970. Princeton, NJ: Princeton University Press, 1978. Print.

Niskanen, Paul. "The Poetics of Adam: The Creation of *ha'adam* in the Image of *'elohîm*." *Journal of Biblical Literature* 128.3 (2009): 417–36. Print.

Norris, Pamela. *The Story of Eve*. New York: New York University Press, 1999. Print.

Perkins, David. *Archimedes' Bathtub: The Art and Logic of Breakthrough Thinking*. New York: Norton, 2000. Print.

Rabaté, Jean-Michel, and Michael Wetzel, eds. *L'Ethique du don: Jaques Derrida et la pensée du don*. Paris: Métailié-Transition, 1992. Print.

Ramsey, George W. "Is Name-Giving an Act of Domination in Genesis 2:23 and Elsewhere?" *Catholic Biblical Quarterly* 50 (1988): 24–35. Print.

Ricoeur, Paul. *The Course of Recognition*. Trans. David Pellauer. Cambridge, MA: Harvard University Press, 2005. Print.

Scholem, Gershom. "Lilith." *Encyclopaedia Judaica*. Ed. Cecil Roth. Vol. 11. Jerusalem: Keter, 1972. Print.

Sefer Halakhot Gedolot. Attributed to Rabbi Simeon Qayara. Jerusalem: Makhon Or HaMizrah, 1992. Print.

Siep, Ludwig. "Natural Law and Bioethics." *Human Nature and Natural Law*. Eds. Lisa Sowle Cahill, Hill Haker, and Eloi Messi Metogo. London: SCM Press, 2010. 44–67. Print.

Siphré D'be Rav to Numbers. 1917. Ed. H.S. Horovitz. Jerusalem: Wahrmann Books, 1966. Print.

Stordalen, T. *Echoes of Eden: Genesis 2–3 and Symbolism of the Eden Garden in Biblical Hebrew Literature*. Leuven, BE: Peeters, 2000. Print.

Tarnopolsky, Christina. "Prudes, Perverts, and Tyrants: Plato and the Contemporary Politics of Shame." *Political Theory* 32.4 (2004): 468–94. Print.

Testa, Italo. "Second Nature and Recognition: Hegel and the Social Space." *Critical Horizons* 10.3 (2009): 341–70. Print.

Torah, Nevi'im, Ketuvim. Jerusalem: Koren Publishers, 1988. (Hebrew). Print.

Torat Chaim Pentateuch. Ed. Mordecai L. Katzenellenbogen. 7 vols. Jerusalem: Mossad HaRav Kook, 1986–1993. Print.

Traina, Cristina. "Feminist Natural Law." *Human Nature and Natural Law*. Eds. Lisa Sowle Cahill, Hill Haker, and Eloi Messi Metogo. London: SCM Press, 2010. 79–87. Print.

Trible, Phyllis. *God and the Rhetoric of Sexuality*. Philadelphia, PA: Fortress Press, 1978. Print.

Velleman, J. David. "The Genesis of Shame." *Philosophy and Public Affairs* 30.1 (2001): 27–52. Print.

Wagner, Jenny. *The Bunyip of Berkeley's Creek*. 1973. Ringwood, Victoria, AU: Puffin Books, 1975. Print.

Wickkiser, Bronwen L. "Hesiod and the Fabricated Woman: Poetry and Visual Art in the Theogony." *Mnemosyne* 63.4 (2010): 557–76. Print.

Wils, Jean-Pierre. "'Does the Natural-Law Approach Have a Future?' A Hermeneutical Proposal: Nine Objections to Natural Law." *Human Nature and Natural Law*. Eds. Lisa Sowle Cahill, Hill Haker, and Eloi Messi Metogo. London: SCM Press, 2010. 68–78. Print.

5

ENTER JOB, WITH FEAR AND TREMBLING

RHIANNON GRAYBILL

THE BOOK OF JOB is the story of an innocent man afflicted with great suffering. At the same time, it offers a sophisticated philosophical critique of the relationship between universal ethics and the individual. Job's speeches argue that the very notion of the world as governed by a universal ethical system that punishes the wicked and rewards the good is absurd—but also necessary. Though deeply critical of its justice, the text nevertheless insists on the necessity and inescapability of a universal ethical system. The Book of Job argues against the tantalizing possibility that ethics can be suspended in favour of subjective experience.

This philosophical critique is implicit in the narrative progression of the text. In making it explicit, I set the Book of Job against *Fear and Trembling*, Søren Kierkegaard's philosophical meditation on the biblical story of the sacrifice of Isaac. Kierkegaard argues that Abraham's willingness to kill his own son for God represents the suspension of his ethical obligations in favour of an absolute relationship with God, known as the "teleological suspension of the ethical," which I will describe in greater detail later. Job, too, is a man tested by God, and his trials share a number of features with Abraham's, among them failed speech, alienation, and violence. He also experiences a theophany—the manifestation of God to a human being—that further isolates him from ordinary social reality and privileges a radically individual relationship over all else.

Although Job the man is alienated from what Kierkegaard names the ethical realm, the Book of Job rejects the possibility of the teleological suspension of the ethical. Taken as a whole, Job's experience reinforces the very durability and inescapability of the ethical system. Here, the philosophy of the Book of Job resembles Jacques Derrida and his critique of Kierkegaard in *The Gift of Death*. Derrida argues that however absurd the choice—kill your son, or disobey your God—ethics cannot be suspended. Instead, paradox, absurdity, and suffering lie at the heart of all ethical action. Absurdity does not offer a movement beyond ethics—it is the foundation of ethics. The Book of Job likewise argues that ethics are both absurd and unsuspendable. What Derrida struggles to extract from Abraham and Kierkegaard is already present in Job.

Reading the Book of Job's narrative as philosophy and using it to challenge Kierkegaard—and to evoke Derrida—is at once a project of recognition and of misrecognition. Though the phrase "fear and trembling" appears in the Book of Job, in a speech by his friend Eliphaz, Job nowhere appears in *Fear and Trembling*, and only once in *The Gift of Death*. And yet as Derrida comments in the latter work, the most important biblical texts for Kierkegaard—and, we might say, for Derrida, too—are those that go unnamed in the text, that appear only through insinuation and allusion. Job haunts the margins of both texts, a figure of philosophical challenge and promise.

A Note on "Abraham" and "Job"

Before saying anything else, I want to make clear what I mean when I refer to "Abraham" and "Job." I am not here concerned with the biblical figure of Abraham, but rather with Abraham as Kierkegaard presents him in *Fear and Trembling*. The validity and fidelity of Kierkegaard's interpretation of the biblical character is a different issue, one that lies beyond my central concern. Instead, I am interested in Abraham as an exemplar of the teleological suspension of the ethical, and the relationship between this suspension and Job's experience of theophany.

Unlike Abraham, there is no Job in *Fear and Trembling*, though he does occasionally appear elsewhere in Kierkegaard's works. In *Repetition*, for example, Job's "ordeal" is acknowledged and praised, but he is explicitly denied the Abrahamic status of a "hero of the faith." However, Kierkegaard's body of work (much of it pseudonymous) resists consistency and cohesion, and as I will argue, his Joban references in *Repetition* and other works do not preclude reading another Job into the margins of *Fear and Trembling*. In fact, the very difficulties of reading Kierkegaard—the rejection of canonicity, the rhetorical slippage, the obsession with silence and unsaying—themselves set forth not just the possibility, but the imperative, to read Job into, and against, *Fear and Trembling*.

And this Job is not the wan Job of *Repetition*, but rather the righteous man of Uz as he appears in the Hebrew Bible. Unlike with Abraham, I do not read Job through layers of interpretive history and tradition, Kierkegaardian or otherwise. Instead, I have placed a modern philosophical creation—Kierkegaard's Abraham—against a powerful and untamed figure of antiquity—the Hebrew Bible's Job.[1]

The Task of Reading Kierkegaard

To set forth a more rigorous argument for the possibility and, indeed, the importance of reading Job with, and in, *Fear and Trembling*, I want to begin with the question of authorship and authority. To this point, I have referred to the author of *Fear and Trembling* and other works as Søren Kierkegaard. This is both true and untrue; for Kierkegaard writes under no fewer than eleven pseudonyms (Jegstrup 71). *Fear and Trembling* is attributed to a certain "Johannes de Silentio"; *Repetition*, published on the same day (October 7, 1843), is the work of "Constantin Constantius." This pseudonymous authorship is part of a broader critique of language and authority. As Elsebet Jegstrup writes, the "use of pseudonyms, subtexts, and other ironic approaches to writing render [Kierkegaard's] labyrinthine authorship an entanglement of textual difference embroiling the reader" (71).

The "entanglement of textual difference" does not end with the relationship between works. *Fear and Trembling*, even considered independently of the "Kierkegaardian" anti/canon, sets forth a radical critique of authority and totality. In the preface Kierkegaard/de Silentio[2] confides, "the present author is by no means a philosopher" and insists, "this is not the system; it has nothing to do with the system" (Kierkegaard 8). The form of the text enacts this critique. In place of a Hegelian system, he gives us prefaces, eulogies, retellings, repetitions, and parody interwoven with poetry. This rhetorical excess also plays itself out through a variety of modes of unspeaking, including allusion, aposiopesis, and metonymy.

The final, and most important, feature of Kierkegaard writing is its silences. Nowhere is its author more passionate or more eloquent than when he waxes lyrical on the silence of Abraham: "Speak he cannot; he speaks no human language. And even if he understood all the languages of the world, even if those he loved also understood them, he still could not speak—he speaks in a divine language, he speaks in tongues" (Kierkegaard 114). While he protests that he can never be, or hope to be, Abraham, Kierkegaard employs his own skilful rhetoric of unspeaking. His critique of the "system" takes the form not of a rigorously outlined philosophical argument but of series of poetic guerrilla attacks and pregnant silences. He is a particular master of the aposiopesis, the sudden silence that interrupts a sentence and leaves the reader/listener to fill in what is missing. Nowhere is his rhetoric more excessive then when he refuses to speak.

The Traces of Job

When Kierkegaard does write about Job, it is in other places—in his early religious discourses, and in *Repetition*. In the section of *Repetition* entitled "Letters from a Young Man," the young man, painfully separated from his beloved, frequently invokes Job. He begins one letter to Constantius, "Job! Job! O Job! Is that really all you said, those beautiful words: the Lord gave, and the Lord took away; blessed be the name of the Lord?" (Kierkegaard

197). This passage, from the prologue, is of particular importance to Kierkegaard, who also makes it the subject of a religious discourse. In the discourse, he suggests that Job's existential resignation is his great trait and his significance as a biblical figure (Bøggild 112–27). In *Repetition*, however, Kierkegaard/Constantius/the young man modifies this position. Instead, "Job's significance is that the disputes at the boundaries of the faith are fought out in him, that the colossal revolt of the wild and aggressive powers of passion is presented here" (Kierkegaard 210). While Abraham's testing is entirely individual, hidden from and incommunicable to the world, Job's ordeal becomes a very public record of the struggle of faith. As painful as this struggle is, it has a definite ending point. And this ending, unlike the knight of faith's slow passage up Mount Moriah, is happy; for Job receives what he has lost, double. According to Kierkegaard, Job also exemplifies the movement of repetition.

There is a problem with all of this: Kierkegaard flinches. In privileging the happy resolution of Job's story, he ignores the disturbing implications of the ordeal and the huge suffering Job endures. Such approach is no different than reading the binding of Isaac and privileging the moment Abraham stays his knife over all the events that precede it. This is not an illegitimate reading (it is, in fact, the alternate reading Emmanuel Levinas suggests in his critique of *Fear and Trembling*), but it is also not a Kierkegaardian one (Levinas 34–35). The spirit of *Fear and Trembling* demands another Job than the figure of *Repetition*.

The form of *Fear and Trembling* facilitates a different reading than the one Kierkegaard himself ultimately gives. The critique of authority, the rhetorical excess, and the significance of silence, all justify reading another Job than the Job of *Repetition* into its margins. *Fear and Trembling* is a text devoted to the question of what it means to be tried by God, but it ignores entirely the man tested by God *par excellence*. However, in a text obsessed with silence and aposiopesis, such refusal to speak is also meaningful. Kierkegaard's silence on Job within *Fear and Trembling* is a silence that speaks. It proclaims the impossibility of assimilating Job into the ethical and religious realms of the text. In so doing, it critiques the validity of the very system the text lays out (for Kierkegaard is nothing if not suspicious of the system.)

The title of Kierkegaard's work, *Fear and Trembling*, is a reference to Paul's letter to the Philippians. Paul writes, "Therefore, my beloved, just as you have always obeyed me, not just in my presence but even more so in my absence, work for your own salvation with fear and trembling" (Phil. 2.12).[3] However, "Fear and Trembling," φόβος καὶ τρόμος in the Greek, is not Paul's coinage, but a rhetorical figure in the Book of Job as well. In recounting his night vision (Job 4.12–21), Eliphaz tells his beleaguered friend, "A word was brought to me in stealth. My ear took a whisper from it. In a nightmare, among the visions of the night, when deep sleep falls upon me, fear and trembling[4] came upon me, and caused all of my bones to shake" (Job 4.12–14). Jacques Derrida comments on Kierkegaard's elliptical use of biblical texts and their complicated relationship to secrecy and unsaying. He draws attention to a passage almost at the end of *Fear and Trembling*, where Kierkegaard writes of Abraham's suffering, "And yet what did he achieve? He remained true to his love. But anyone who loves God needs no tears, no admiration; he forgets the suffering in the love. Indeed, so completely has he forgotten it that there would not be the slightest trace of his suffering left if God himself did not remember it, for *he sees in secret* and recognizes distress and counts tears and forgets nothing" (120, emphasis added in Derrida 81). For Derrida, the key to the passage—and indeed to much of *Fear and Trembling*—lies in the four-word, unmarked quotation from Matthew 6.4, where Jesus instructs his followers to give alms in secret, so that "your father who sees in secret will reward you." Secrecy and subtlety are everything. Derrida observes, "That text isn't cited; rather, like the 'kings and counselors' of 'Bartleby the Scrivener,' it is simply suggested, but this time without the quotation marks, thus being clearly brought to the attention of those who know their texts and have been brought up on the reading of the Gospels" (81). That which is most important is excluded, accessible only through allusion and inference. Job's importance to *Fear and Trembling* is signalled precisely by his elision.

In describing the ellipses in Kierkegaard, Derrida is alluding to his own rhetorical style as well. Like Kierkegaard, his rhetoric is excessive, and his relationship to Job is veiled. In *The Gift of Death*, his "genealogy of responsibility," and close reading of Kierkegaard, Job makes only a single appearance, in a reference to Herman Melville's "Bartleby the Scrivener." Melville's text, in turn, contains a single elliptical reference to the Book of Job, when the narrator imagines Bartleby, the doomed law clerk, sleeping "with kings and counselors" (131). The phrase comes from Job's speech in chapter 3, when he demands, "Why was I not dead from the womb?... / for now I would lie down and I would be quiet, I would sleep and then I would have rest / with kings and counselors of the earth" (Job 3.11–14). Despite the references to Job, Derrida refuses the "tempting and obvious comparison" in favour of Abraham (74). Bartleby, but not Job, returns several pages later, in the passage quoted above. Yet this is the very passage where Derrida claims that what is important "isn't cited...it is simply suggested." This is precisely the function of Job for Derrida's text, and in Kierkegaard's that precedes it. In these two texts about secrets, silence, and the paradoxes of ethics, Job is an unmentionable, unforgettable presence. The remainder of this chapter traces out the biblical Job who is at once excluded and unforgettable.

Job Between Agamemnon and Abraham

Kierkegaard insists, again and again, that there is "no one like Abraham," that faith such as his is so rare as to be impossible. Though Job is never mentioned in *Fear and Trembling*, in *Repetition* Kierkegaard states plainly that the man from Uz, however great his merits, is not a "hero of faith," as Abraham is (207–13). Yet Job does not fit neatly into the other categories (particularly that of tragic hero) that Kierkegaard sets forth in *Fear and Trembling*. I want to refine my previous comments on the exclusion of Job from *Fear and Trembling* to suggest that Job is excluded not because he lacks faith, but because he upsets the careful balance between the knight of faith and the tragic hero that Kierkegaard works so hard to construct. Job comes to us from an ambivalent space between the tragic and the religious and something else entirely. Job also helps re-inscribe the original horror in the text, a horror that Kierkegaard intended but that later interpretation all too often leaches out.

Even with its critique of the Hegelian system, *Fear and Trembling* is not without a certain systematics of its own. In two famous phrases, Kierkegaard describes faith as a "movement of the absurd" that stages a "teleological suspension of the ethical" (54, 101). Both concepts speak to the broader distinction between the ethical and the religious that underlies the text. Kierkegaard begins by defining the ethical as the universal, which "applies to everyone," "at all times," and "rests immanent in itself" (54). However, everything changes with Abraham—the willingness of the father of the faith to sacrifice Isaac is an abomination from the viewpoint of the ethical because it violates the ethical command not to kill your son. Kierkegaard writes, "either Abraham was a murderer every minute or we stand before a paradox that is higher than all mediations" (66). Faith "is namely this paradox that the single individual is higher than the universal" (55). Faith remains, however, exterior to ethics. It belongs not to the ethical but to the religious realm.

In drawing out the difference between the ethical and the religious, Kierkegaard sets Abraham against another great man who places his child on the altar and raises the sacrificial knife: Agamemnon. To appease the gods and insure fair weather, Agamemnon sacrifices his daughter Iphigenia. While Abraham's sacrifice suspends the ethical, Agamemnon's fulfills an ethical obligation, to his troops and to his countrymen. That this obligation (to community) is in conflict with another ethical obligation (to child) renders the situation tragic. This is also the case with another of Kierkegaard's examples, Jephthah, who vows to Yahweh that, if he is victorious over the Ammonites, he will make a burnt offering of "whatever comes forth from the doors of my house to meet me when I return in peace" (Judges 11.31). When his only daughter rushes to greet him, dancing and playing the timbrels, he is forced to offer her up to fulfill his oath. His obligation to keep his word—necessary to the existence of ethical society—conflicts with his obligation to guard the life of his own child. According to Kierkegaard, Jephthah and Agamemnon are both tragic heroes who have experienced painful events arising from conflicting ethical obligations.

Job, another great man who loses his beloved children to divine caprice, has likewise been read as a tragic hero. Richard Sewall, for example, calls him "the towering tragic figure of antiquity" and the "universal symbol for the western imagination of the mystery of undeserved suffering" (21). Sewall's claims and the relationship of Job to Oedipus, Prometheus, and the other greats of Greek tragedy is a subject of much lively debate. However, I am less interested in whether Job functions as a classical tragic hero than with his relationship to the Kierkegaardian tragic. As with Abraham, the Agamemnon of *Fear and Trembling* represents a philosophical stance more than a particular literary or textual antecedent. And that which he represents is not Joban. Kierkegaard writes, "The tragic hero is still within the ethical. He allows an expression of the ethical to have its τέλος in a higher expression of the ethical...[but] here there can be no question of a teleological suspension of the ethical itself" (59). But Job, like Abraham, has no τέλος in the ethical realm. Nowhere is this more apparent than in the difference between tragic speech and Joban speech, between Agamemnon's lament and Job's incessant complaint.

Language and the Alienation from the Ethical

In drawing forth the difference between ethical and religious experience, Kierkegaard emphasizes the differing role of language in each realm. Language sustains the ethical by mediating between individuals. As Kierkegaard writes, "The relief provided by speaking is that it translates me into the universal" (45). This is the great consolation of the tragic hero—Agamemnon can speak of his suffering, his love of Iphigenia, his distress at her fate, and in this speaking can find a certain consolation. Such relief through speech is precisely what Abraham is denied.

Kierkegaard writes, "Abraham *cannot* speak, because he cannot say that which would explain everything (that is, so it is understandable): that it is an ordeal such that, please note, the ethical is the temptation" (114–15, emphasis original).

This failure of language links Abraham's ordeal to Job's suffering. At a first glance, the two men use language very differently. While Abraham speaks minimally, Job speaks constantly, to his friends, to his wife, to himself, and to God. He complains of his afflictions and insists upon his innocence. He insists, "As for me, I will not restrain my mouth; I will speak of the distress of my spirit, and I will complain in the bitterness of my soul" (7.11). But Job's discourse, for all its surplus of words, is fundamentally different from the speech of the tragic hero. His words do not make his experience comprehensible to others—in Kierkegaardian terms, they do not translate him into the universal. As an appeal for his friends to recognize his suffering, his speech fails. His protests are constant precisely because his protest receives no satisfactory answer. In 16.6, he claims, "If I speak, my pain is not assuaged, and if I desist, it does not leave me."[5] A few chapters later, Job complains, "I cry 'Violence!' and am not answered; I cry out for help, but there is no justice" (19.7).

Job's speeches (and his complaints of unfair treatment in particular) are often read as a critique of normative theology. Such normative theology is represented by his friends, who insist that suffering is God's just punishment for the wicked. Eliphaz, for example, tells Job, "Recall for me! Who ever perished innocent?" (Job 4.7), and Bildad insists, "Indeed, God will not reject a blameless man, nor will he deliver him into the hands of the wicked" (Job 8.20). Job's friends assume the universal applicability and validity of moral principles. Cast in Kierkegaardian terms, they represent the universal, ethical realm. Fittingly, they turn to language to offer comfort, assimilating his curses and absurd demands for justice to the paradigms of the ethical. Job's inability to communicate his complaint to them, despite his unending speech, signals his exclusion from this same ethical realm. As such, his speech represents a use of language not unlike Abraham's ironic unspeaking in *Fear and Trembling*. Though Job utters words upon words, like Abraham he "*cannot* speak, because he cannot say that which would explain everything" (Kierkegaard 115, emphasis original). Language, the great mediator of the universal, requires two parties, one to speak and one to listen. This is what Job and Abraham both lack.

Violence

The move outside the ethical realm entails violence, which further links the experiences of the biblical Job and of Kierkegaard's Abraham. Job complains repeatedly of the violence he has suffered and continues to suffer. The biblical account begins with the destruction of his property, the death of his children, and the affliction of his flesh. His first words after seven days of silence are a curse on the day of his birth. Though his friends move to console him, he soon perceives violence in their words as well, for they refuse to acknowledge the injustice of his suffering. In chapter 19, for example, Job laments, "All the men of my circle abhor me; those I love have turned against me" (19.19) and asks a few verses later, "Why do you pursue me like God, and are not sated with my flesh?" (19.22). Worse still is the divine violence Job perceives and decries. In chapter 6.4, Job moans, "The arrows of Shaddai are in me; my spirit drinks its poison; the terrors of God are arraigned against me."

According to Kierkegaard, such violence is always part of the teleological suspension of the ethical. Abraham, after all, becomes a knight of faith only because he is willing to murder his own son. From the perspective of the ethical, he is and remains a murderer. Kierkegaard never forgets, nor lets us forget, this violence. "Either Abraham was a murderer every minute or we stand before a paradox that is higher than all mediations," he writes (Kierkegaard 66). The teleological suspension of the ethical is not neat philosophical slight of hand so much as a necessary paradox in the face of an absurd, dreadful command. It makes possible a perspective beyond the ethical—that of religious subjectivity. But the ethical remains violently opposed to such a movement beyond it, and Job and Abraham alike participate in this violence—one as its victim, the other as its agent.

Theophany

And then, after close to forty chapters of debate, of Job's ceaseless complaint and his friends' counter-argument, God speaks. From a whirlwind, God demands, "Who is this who darkens counsel, with words but without understanding? Gird your loins like a man! I will ask and you will inform me" (Job 38.2–3). A lengthy description of the power and beauty of creation follows. The meaning of this theophany and the degree to which God addresses Job's complaint are subject to much interpretive debate. I do not intend to give an extensive overview of the arguments here, only to chart out a few major directions.[6]

The first and most important interpretive question is this: does God answer Job's complaint? While most scholars endeavour to answer in the affirmative, a significant contingent insists that the speech fails. According to this interpretive tendency, Yahweh is either powerless to address the evil of the world, or intentionally permits it to flourish. David Wolfers, for example, writes of the theophany, "There broods the novel, truly anthropomorphic personality of God, irascible, vain, resentful at having been drawn from His proper preoccupations," and concludes, "The universe is fundamentally cruel, and randomly so" (223, 222).

Other readers are less willing to accept a capricious or impotent God, and look instead for resolution and meaning in the theophany. Where this meaning is found is a difficult and much-debated matter, however. God's words never directly answer Job's complaint. While Job raises his voice to complain of injustice, God speaks of the mysteries of mountain goat birthing and the wonder of Leviathan and Behemoth. Drawing on the excess of creation rhetoric, some scholars argue that creation's beauty and multiplicity offers itself as an answer. Robert Gordis, for example, writes, "The vivid and joyous description of nature is not an end in itself: it underscores the insight that nature is not merely a mystery, but is also a miracle, a cosmos, a thing of beauty. From this flows a basic conclusion at which the poet has arrived: just as there is order and harmony in the natural world, though imperfectly grasped by man, so there is order and meaning in the moral sphere, though often incomprehensible to man"

(133). Where Wolfers sees a cruel and random universe, Gordis finds "a miracle" and "a thing of beauty." The text itself is richly ambiguous—is the nature that Yahweh praises the earthly representation of an ordered moral sphere, or the mere effect of a random and amoral universe? A third interpretive track, confronted with such interpretive difficulty, argues instead that the general event of theophany, not the particular content of God's speech, holds the answer to Job's complaint. Albion King, for instance, writes, "At the moment of collapse and crisis, religious faith presents man with 'the vision of God which makes further dialectic unnecessary'" (104).[7] The appearance of God is enough. In his essays on the Bible, Martin Buber offers a similar formulation, writing, "God offers Himself to the sufferer who, in the depth of his despair, keeps to God with his refractory complaint; He offers himself as an answer" (196).

Like Buber and King, my reading emphasizes the theophanic *event* over the particular content of the divine speech. Where I break with this interpretation, however, is his portrayal of the theophany as a moment situated within an ongoing relationship between the sufferer and God. Instead, I propose reading Job's theophany as a teleological suspension of the ethical. Rather than evaluating Job against the twin figures of the tragic hero and the knight of faith—a categorization that Job resists— I want to approach the theophany through Kierkegaard's analysis of the teleological suspension of the ethical.

According to Kierkegaard, the teleological suspension of the ethical does not merely preclude language and harbour violence. It also ushers in religious existence, one that privileges the individual's absolute relationship to God over the absolute relationship to the universal realm of ethics. In accepting God's call to kill his son, Abraham sheds the universal and enters an absolute relationship with the singular divine. Kierkegaard's reading speaks only to Abraham's suspension of the ethical in order to enter an absolute relationship with God. As Derrida's critique of Kierkegaard makes clear, however, Abraham's action is predicated on another action—God's command. God's call to Abraham stages the absolute relation to the individual no less than Abraham's decision to answer this call. Following Derrida, I want to think of the absolute relationship not as a vector from human being to God, but from God to human being.

God speaks to Job, too, in another scene of absolute address to a single individual. His words do not answer Job's incessant complaint about the injustice of suffering, any more than God's appearance to Abraham gives a reason for the command to kill his son. Nor does the content of what God says to Job matter so much as the fact of his address. God is not actually curious, for example, where Job was when the mountain goats were created, to take but one of his many questions. What matters instead is the form of his utterance: the series of questions mark God's speech as a *summons*. Like the call to Abraham, the address formulates Job as a subject by calling him to account.

At the same time, this summons is marked by what Derrida calls "an absolute dissymmetry" (91). He writes, "there is no face-to-face exchange between God and myself...God looks at me and I don't see him and it is on the basis of this gaze that singles me out that my responsibility comes into being" (91). God speaks to Job from a whirlwind, unseen, for this absolute relationship is not one of exchange. The distance between God and Job is not eased, even in God's speech.

Though the divine address formulates Job as a subject, it also does not challenge the status of the ethical realm. Job is a subject, but he is a subject *in* the ethical realm—not the religious. Although Job is temporarily alienated from the ethical, this is not a permanent and teleological suspension. The theophany, the scene of absolute relation to the individual, rejects Job's demands that his subjective experience be elevated above the universal. Instead, God leaves the ethical, and the normative theology of the friends, intact. The conclusion of the story—having "repented unto dust and ashes," Job receives back everything he has lost, double, likewise confirms the ethical system of the friends—the good are rewarded, the wicked are punished—and not Job's criticisms thereof. Even God's reproach to the friends is in line with their theology of punishment and reward because it stresses the virtue of the righteous man, Job.

The Subject and *The Gift of Death*

To theorize this divine address, and the text's refusal of the teleological suspension of the ethical, I want to draw further on *The Gift of Death*. In that work, Derrida complicates the categories of ethical and religious that Kierkegaard outlines in *Fear and Trembling*. Derrida's central argument is that the teleological suspension of the ethical is no suspension at all, but rather the underlying structure of all ethical obligation. Ethical action for Derrida, therefore, is always violent, paradoxical, and at the expense of another. According to Derrida, the fact that *God* commands Abraham to sacrifice Isaac does not grant him ethical absolution. Instead, like every ethical subject, Abraham is called to choose between conflicting ethical obligations—to serve God, and to love and preserve the life of his son. Derrida writes, "I cannot respond to the call, the request, the obligation, or even the love of another without sacrificing the other other, the other others" (68, 71). Abraham's situation is not so different from Agamemnon's, after all. The sacrifice of Isaac represents not the suspension of ethics, as Kierkegaard claims, but rather the very structure of ethical obligation. This is what Derrida calls "the paradox constituting the concept of duty and absolute responsibility" (66).

Derrida argues that the "suspension of the ethical" is not its suspension so much as its actualization—every ethical action comes at the expense of something else, through the suspension of another ethical obligation. He writes, "The account of Isaac's sacrifice can be read as a narrative development of the paradox constituting the concept of duty and absolute responsibility" (Derrida 66). The Book of Job makes a similar argument with its narrative structure. Job ceases his attack on the normative ethics of his friends—an ethics that the book as a whole seems to extol—only in the moment of theophany, when this same ethical realm is suspended. The conclusion to the story, in which Job receives everything he has lost back again, double, likewise illustrates the simultaneous excess and absurdity of the summons to ethical subjectivity. Here, that summons takes the form of God's singular, terrifying address from the whirlwind.

Job's Response

Though Derrida begins with Kierkegaard, his conclusions about the meaning of the sacrifice of Isaac are different. According to Derrida, Abraham is constituted as a subject by an absolute summons that excludes *a priori* the possibility of perfect justice. Abraham represents not the suspension of the ethical, but rather the paradigmatic ethical subject. *Every* ethical subject is summoned to impossible and contradictory ethical action. But what Derrida struggles to extract from Kierkegaard is already implicitly present in the Book of Job.

For Job is no Abraham. Confronted by God, summoned outside of the realm of ethics but still oppressed by it, Job does something even Abraham does not dare to do: He talks back. In the midst of the theophany, Job responds to God—twice. First, he describes himself as "of small account" (40.3), and professes he will speak no more (40.5). His second speech reasserts his lack of knowledge—"therefore I have uttered what I did not understand" (41.3) and ends with "I recant[8] and repent in dust and ashes" (42.6). Job does not engage God in dialogue or propose a shared ground between himself and the divine other. Nor does he seek to assimilate the ethical, represented by his friends, into the religious absolute. Still, however pathetic or even unintelligible Job's words, his very attempt to speak is shocking. He speaks back across the terrifying asymmetry that is the summons to subjectivity.

In doing so, he transforms the scene of address into one of recognition. Job acknowledges God's words and communicates this acknowledgement through speech. Language, the stuff of Kierkegaard's universal, breaks into the teleological suspension of the ethical. The scene of absolute address becomes, for a moment, a space of mediation and communication, of recognition between speaking subjects. And yet Job's response remains, fundamentally, a denial of communicability and of knowledge: "I have uttered what I do not understand, things too wonderful for me, which I know not" (42.3). The great recognition of the scene is one of the *failures* of language. While Abraham suggests this with his silence, Job bears testimony through speech.

By refusing silence, Job also refuses the mantle of the knight of faith and becomes something else entirely. Derrida's subject endeavours to act ethically even as she knows full well that pure ethical action is impossible, that the condition of possibility for the single ethical act is also the condition of impossibility for total ethical action. She also knows, however, that suspending or otherwise avoiding the ethical is impossible. Unlike Kierkegaard's Abraham, the biblical Job gives voice to human incomprehension in the face of the insoluble paradox of how to act ethically in a world where total ethical action is impossible. He concedes that his demand for the teleological suspension of the ethical—figured in the dialogues as a demand for a trial, an avenger, or a stone-etched record of his suffering—is ignorant and wrong. And yet he also says that he cannot understand the ethical that God's theophany so forcefully reinstates. Language, previously the marker of his alienation from the ethical, exposes the absurdity and violence of that same ethical.

The Book of Job does not "anticipate" Derrida or Kierkegaard, any more than Derrida repeats Job. Instead, both the postmodern philosopher and the ancient book challenge the possibility of finding relief in the suspension of the ethical, even as they take up Kierkegaard's suspicion of universal ethics as a necessary and sufficient state in and of itself. Derrida draws his critique of the universal—and of the radical subjectivity Kierkegaard poses as its alternative—from the tragic history of the twentieth century. The Book of Job instead invents the *story* of a man sorely tested by God, a man whose radical and individual complaints reveal the failure of the universal without allowing for an alternative mode of subjectivity. In the end, Job is forced to accept the ethical realm.

From the far side of modernity, the Book of Job presents a potent critique of the radical subjectivity that Kierkegaard advances as an alternative to universal ethics. To Derrida, the great value of the story of the sacrifice of Isaac is that it lays bare the economy of sacrifice that underlies all ethical decisions. While Abraham's nearly wordless ordeal exposes the sacrifices that ethics always requires, Job's response to God in the space of theophany registers his protest at the injustice upon which the universal is built. In God's speech, the ethical realm is left intact; the movement beyond its borders is marked as alienating, violent, and unspeakable; and yet, Job's voice still lodges its complaint. The replacement of his lost children and possessions is twofold: both an affirmation of the normative theology of the friends and recognition of its absurdity, and the absurdity of every ethical call. The philosophical system that Kierkegaard builds on Abraham's sacrifice is negated in the Book of Job, which at once decries the absurdity of universal ethical systems that condemn innocents like Job to suffer, and insists upon the impossibility of escape or transcendence.

In *Fear and Trembling*, the teleological suspension of the ethical is a frightening proposition, but also a seductive one. Kierkegaard suggests an escape from the totality—and frequently tyranny—of universal ethics and offers in its place a new understanding of subjective existence that embraces paradox. The Book of Job shares in Kierkegaard's skepticism toward the universal ethical system, highlighting the suffering that such a system permits, and even inflicts, upon the individual. But ultimately, the Book of Job resists the movement beyond ethics. The teleological suspension on the ethical is ultimately impossible. The ethical endures, through all absurdity.

Notes

1. The Book of Job consists of a prose frame narrative (chapters 1–2 and 41.7–17) and a series of poetic dialogues (3–41.6). The former contains the bet between God and Satan and Job's consequent affliction, while the latter describes the restitution of his fortune and the chastisement of his friends. The dialogues contain Job's speeches (3, 6–7, 9–10, 12–14, 16–17, 19, 21, 23–24, 26–27, 29–31, 40.3–5, 42.1–6); the responses of his friends Eliphaz the Temanite (4–5, 15, 22), Bildad the Shuhite (8, 18, 25), and Zophar the Naamathite (11, 20); the "Hymn to Wisdom" in 28; the speeches of Elihu, another intercessor (32–37); and Yahweh's response (39–41). The compositional relationship between the two parts of the book is complicated, though they are generally accepted as the work of different authors. In addition, the authorship of the Hymn to Wisdom and Elihu's speeches is frequently argued

to be different than that of the remainder of the dialogues. (On compositional issues, see Pope, xv–lxxxiv).

This research, while acknowledging the fraught compositional history of the text and the multiplicity of its authors, accepts the final text as a whole, redacted with intention and skill. With this in mind, the Job discussed here is the Job who emerges when the frame narrative and the dialogues are read together. He is neither the blameless man of the prologues who humbly acquiesces to suffering nor the furious, death-craving plaintiff of the dialogues, but rather a combination of the two. The productive tension between these two versions of the hero complicates not just the character of Job but the implicit philosophical positions of the book as a whole. This chapter traces those complicated positions.

2. For simplicity, I will continue to refer to the author of *Fear and Trembling* as "Søren Kierkegaard," though with an awareness of the ambiguous status of authorship and authority.

3. All translations from the Bible, both Hebrew and Greek, are my own.

4. In the Hebrew פַּחַד קְרָאַנִי וּרְעָדָה, "fear and trembling came upon me" (or in Hebrew word order, "Fear came upon me, and trembling"). The Septuagint translates φρίκη δέ μοι συνήντησεν καὶ τρόμος. τρόμος, "trembling," is the same word that Paul uses in Philippians; φρίκη, "shivering," including in religious awe," is closer in meaning to τρόμος and more somatic in its range of meanings than φόβος, "fear," in the Pauline passage. My interest is not in the degree to which the Pauline passage quotes, or deviates from, Eliphaz's words in Job, but rather in tracking the permutations of a rhetorical figure backward to Job and forward to Kierkegaard and Derrida. On a grammatical note, the Hebrew phrase is technically a hendiadys, defined by Waltke and O'Connor in *An Introduction to Biblical Hebrew Syntax* as "the juxtaposition of two nouns with a single referent, with or without the conjunction," as in English "assault and battery" (4.4.1b, 70). Some scholars choose to represent this single referent by translating the two words as a phrase, yielding, for example, "a fearful dread came upon me." However, translating the two terms as separate nouns preserves the Hebrew syntax without placing unnecessary demands upon the English.

5. Reading מַה as negative, not interrogative. On the question of translation, see Pope, 123.

6. For such an overview, see, for example, Leo G. Perdue, *Wisdom in Revolt: Metaphorical Theology in the Book of Job*, and Yair Hoffmann, *A Blemished Reflection: The Book of Job in Context*.

7. The internal quotation comes from King's personal correspondence with Dr. Lynn Harold Hough (King 104).
8. Hebrew אֶמְאַס. The Septuagint translates ἥγημαι δὲ ἐμαυτὸν, adding a reflexive pronoun as the object of the verb ("I despise myself"). However, as Pope argues, the Hebrew root is not used for self-loathing. Furthermore, the verbal root has an implicit object—the earlier words or attitudes that are now rejected (Pope 349).

Works Cited

Biblia Hebraica Stuttgartensia. Eds. K. Elliger and W. Rudolph. 5th ed. Stuttgart: Deutsche Bibelgesellschaft, 1997. Print.

Bøggild, Jacob. "Revocated Trials: On the Indirect Communication in Two of Kierkegaard's Early Religious Discourses." *The New Kierkegaard*. Ed. Elsebet Jegstrup. Bloomington: Indiana University Press, 2004. 112–27. Print.

Buber, Martin. *On the Bible: Eighteen Studies*. Ed. Nahum Norbert Glatzer. New York: Schoken Books, 1982. Print.

Derrida, Jacques. *The Gift of Death*. Trans. David Wills. Chicago: University of Chicago Press, 1995. Print.

Girard, René. *Job the Victim of His People*. Trans. Yvonne Freccero. Stanford, CA: Stanford University Press, 1987. Print.

Gordis, Robert. *The Book of God and Man: A Study of Job*. Chicago: University of Chicago Press, 1965. Print.

Hoffmann, Yair. *A Blemished Perfection: The Book of Job in Context*. Sheffield, UK: Sheffield Academic Press, 1996. Print.

Jegstrup, Elsebet. "A Rose by Any Other Name." *The New Kierkegaard*. Ed. Elsebet Jegstrup. Bloomington: Indiana University Press, 2004. 71–87. Print.

Kierkegaard, Søren. *Fear and Trembling/Repetition*. Ed. Howard V. Hong. Trans. Howard V. Hong and Edna H.R. Hong. Princeton, NJ: Princeton University Press, 1983. Print.

King, Albion Roy. *The Problem of Evil: Christian Concepts and the Book of Job*. New York: Ronald Press, 1952. Print.

Levinas, Emmanuel. "Existence and Ethics." *Kierkegaard: A Critical Reader*. Eds. Jonathan Reé and Jane Chamberlain. Oxford: Blackwell, 1998. 26–38. Print.

Novum Testamentum Graece. Eds. E. and E. Nestle, B. and K. Aland, J. Karavidopoulos, C.M. Martini, and B.M. Metzger. 4th ed. Stuttgart: Deutsche Bibelgesellschaft, 1993. Print.

Perdue, Leo G. *Wisdom in Revolt: Metaphorical Theology in the Book of Job*. Sheffield, UK: Almond Press, 1991. Print.

Pope, Marvin H. *The Anchor Bible: Job*. 3rd ed. Garden City, NY: Doubleday, 1973. Print.

Schleifer, Ronald, and Robert Markley. "Editors' Introduction: Writing Without Authority and the Reading of Kierkegaard." *Kierkegaard and Literature: Irony, Repetition, and Criticism*. Ed. R. Schleifer and R. Markley. Norman: University of Oklahoma Press, 1984. 3–22. Print.

Septuaginta. Ed. Alfred Rahlfs. Stuttgart: Deutsche Bibelgesellschaft, 2004. Print.

Sewall, Richard B. *The Vision of Tragedy*. New Haven, CT: Yale University Press, 1959. Print.

Waltke, Bruce K., and M. O'Connor. *An Introduction to Biblical Hebrew Syntax*. Winona Lake, IN: Eisenbrauns, 1990. Print.

Wolfers, David. *Deep Things Out of Darkness: The Book of Job: Essays and a New English Translation*. Grand Rapids, MI: Williams B. Eerdmans, 1995. Print.

6

THOMAS AQUINAS ON CHRISTIAN RECOGNITION

The Case of Mary Magdalene

KEVIN FREDERICK VAUGHAN

MUCH WORK HAS BEEN DONE recently on the concept of recognition in the fields of philosophy and comparative literature. The names of eminent scholars such as Piero Boitani and the late Paul Ricoeur come to mind.[1] With the hopes of supplementing the work done in these disciplines, the following chapter will explore the concept of recognition in the context of Christian theology, and for this purpose, fully focus on the thirteenth-century Christian theologian Thomas Aquinas.

The concept does not figure prominently in Thomas's corpus, as any search of Roberto Busa's *Index Thomisticus* will prove.[2] The concept occurs only thirty times in the *Summa theologiae*, and a paltry three times in the *Summa Contra Gentiles*. As Paul Ricoeur observed in his last book, up until his own work at least, the history of Western philosophy has lacked a systematic treatment of the concept, and Thomas proves no exception. Instead, we find the concept scattered loosely throughout his corpus in various contexts. But this does not mean that the concept was without significance to Thomas. Indeed there is one case, at least, where Thomas places recognition at the very heart of Christian life itself. In his comments on the appearance of the risen Jesus to Mary Magdalene in his *Commentary on the Gospel of St. John*, Thomas takes the opportunity to offer one of the longest treatments on recognition found in his corpus. The intention of this article is to demonstrate, through Thomas's comments on this scene from John's Gospel, how Mary Magdalene emerges as a model for the recognition proper to Christian life, a recognition perfected by the supernatural gift of faith. Faith, Thomas shows us, transforms recognition, allowing it to serve the Christian life rather than hinder it. In recognizing her risen Lord, Mary illustrates the transformation of recognition, a transformation that occurs in the life of justified believers.

The scene between Mary Magdalene and the risen Jesus takes place in Chapter 20, verses 1 through 18 of John's Gospel, in which the Evangelist recounts the first appearances of the newly resurrected Jesus to his disciples.[3] Mary finds herself before the empty tomb, alone and in tears over what she fears is the theft of her Lord's body. Peering into the tomb, she sees two angels in white sitting where Jesus's body had been laid. They ask her, "Woman, why are you weeping?" She responds, "Because they have taken away my Lord, and I do not know where they have laid him." At this point, she turns around and sees Jesus standing before her, but she does not recognize him. He asks her, "Woman, why are you weeping? Whom do you seek?" Mary, thinking him the gardener, asks him, "Sir, if you have carried him away, tell me where you have laid him, and I will take him away." At this point, Jesus says her name, "Mary." And upon hearing her name she recognizes him, and calls him "Rabboni," meaning Teacher. The scene between the two ends with Jesus prohibiting her from touching him, and sending her off to tell the other disciples that he is returning to his Father, which she immediately does.

Thomas understands this scene as describing the process by which Mary comes to have a vision of the risen Christ, a vision in which recognition plays a key role. Thomas understands this process as an ordered one, the principal stages of which are found in the text. He describes this process for us along two distinct levels of meaning: the literal level, which deals with it as it took place in the heart of the historical Mary, and the mystical, which deals with how what happened to Mary represents what happens in the hearts of all believers by the grace of justification. The mystical meaning is built on the literal, and so, as we learn on one level how recognition serves Mary's vision of the risen Jesus, we learn on the other how recognition serves the life of the justified believer. For Thomas, reading the Gospel was not just a reading of past events but an occasion to draw lessons applicable to his day and to the Christian life in general. It is not unusual for Thomas to find symbolic meanings in the Gospel that transcend the historical or literal sense of the text. In fact, Thomas sees in Mary a symbol of the Christian life, and so, to understand Mary better is to understand better how to live as a Christian. Following this order, then, I will first attempt to articulate Thomas's portrait of Mary as it appears in his *Commentary on the Gospel of St. John*, and then proceed to a discussion of how she represents the place of recognition in the Christian life as a whole.

Thomas's discussion of the appearance of the risen Jesus to Mary Magdalene occurs in Chapter 20, Lecture 3, of the *Commentary*.[4] Thomas's literal interpretation requires some interpretation of its own. Those familiar with Thomas's great *Summae* are often put off by the rather loose and hasty style of his biblical commentaries, due in large part, no doubt, to the fact that most of them were written reports of lectures given during the course of his tenure as a *magister sacrae paginae*. Among theologians, it was a well-established custom by the end of the twelfth century to make written records, *reportationes* as they were called, as the chief means of preserving university courses and sermons (Weijers 361). In Thomas's case, the task was assigned to one or more of his trusted secretaries, on whose tireless efforts much of his productivity relied. His *Commentary on the Gospel of St. John* is a *reportatio* of a course delivered at Saint-Jacques, the Dominican *studium generale* in Paris, sometime between 1270 and 1272, and recorded by one of his most trusted secretaries and fellow Dominican, Reginald of Piperno. Although it was the custom for a *reportatio* to be edited later by the master, it is doubtful whether Thomas did so for the

Commentary on St. John, and so, we cannot demand from it the tightness of expression that marks some of his other works.[5]

The chief aid to following the argument of the *Commentary* is the *divisio textus*, the detailed divisions Thomas makes throughout the *Commentary*. The *divisio textus* was a scholastic technique for outlining the argument of a text by breaking it down into its various parts. The scholastic division of the text was made according to a principal theme, usually stated at the outset of the *divisio textus* (Boyle 276). The theme provided the concept under which the entire text could be considered. All of the features of the text, its words and passages, are related back to this one idea. In the theme, then, can be found the "conceptual unity" of the divisions, "a unifying idea in the light of which the whole can be seen and, still more important, each part can be understood" (Boyle 277). It appears that these divisions were not understood to be definitive, evident from the willingness amongst scholastics to apply different divisions to the same texts. Instead, as John F. Boyle has pointed out, they appear to have an illuminative quality, for a text that was considered to be rich in meaning and ultimately inexhaustible in profundity (Boyle 279).

The first task, then, in understanding any discussion in Thomas's *Commentary* is to grasp the principal theme in which he placed it. Identifying the principal theme is the easiest part of the task of reading Thomas's *Commentary*; for it is most often clearly stated in the divisions. The divisions, however, do not spare the reader the further effort of pulling together the various elements of the discussion, or from explaining how they serve the theme and are in turn illuminated by it. This effort of relating the parts to the whole is the challenge in understanding Thomas's interpretation of Mary Magdalene. But, lest any be discouraged by such effort, Thomas himself reminds us that difficulties should not deter eager minds from study, but instead egg them on all the more.[6] It is with this encouragement, then, that I will attempt to articulate the structure of Thomas's discussion on Mary, and highlight the function of recognition within it.

The Principal Theme: The Vision of Christ

According to the *divisio textus*, the principal theme of the scene between Mary and the risen Jesus is how Mary came to have a "vision of Christ" (*visio Christi*).[7] Anything Thomas has to say about recognition, then, will be understood in relation to this vision. That this vision involves more than just recognition is evident from the divisions Thomas makes of the scene. The scene is divided into two principal parts. In the first, John tells us how Mary saw Jesus; while in the second, he shows us how she came to know him. It is clear that merely seeing Jesus will not be sufficient for knowing him, and that the conditions required for the vision of Christ will not be the same for a simple recognition of him. In fact, as we will see, recognition will have to be transformed in order to have a place within the vision of Christ.

The Conditions for the Vision of Christ

Thomas divides this division into two parts: the first on Mary's seeing Christ; the second on what Christ said to her. Thomas begins his comments on the first division with a comparison of Mary to the angels. It was while speaking with the angels that Mary turned around to see Jesus. Following Chrysostom, Thomas deems it necessary to explain why Mary turned around before allowing the angels to answer her earlier question, lest it be interpreted as a sign of disrespect on Mary's part. Thomas explains that Mary turned around when she saw the angels, who rose out of respect when they saw Jesus. According to Thomas, Mary did not know it was Jesus because he did not appear glorious to her, as he did to the angels. Thomas then draws a moral lesson from Mary's turning, saying, "We see from this that if anyone desires to see Christ, they must turn round to him: 'Return to me, says the Lord of hosts, and I will return to you' (Zechariah 1.3)" (2504).

In clarifying what might seem an inconsequential detail of the scene, Thomas outlines the conditions for a vision of Christ, one concerning the object seen, the other concerning the means of seeing it. What the angels see and what Mary does not is the glory of Christ. Christ's glory is understood here in terms of his glorified body, which manifests the glory of his beatified soul (*Summa theologiae* III Q54 a2corpus). To have a vision of Christ is to see Christ in the glory of his risen body, as the angels did. But if Mary is to see Christ's glory, it must be in a human and not angelic way. The means by which Mary can see Christ's glory is given to us in the moral lesson tacked on to the end of the discussion. Thomas says that if any wish to see Christ, they must do so by turning to him, just as it says in the Book of Zechariah: "Return to me, says the Lord of hosts, and I will return to you." Thomas goes on to explain that this turning is done out of love, as the Book of Wisdom reminds us: "She (Wisdom) hastens to make herself known to those who desire her" (2505). As a human being, then, Mary is not privileged with the constant vision of divine glory as the angels are. Instead, Mary requires a kind of preparation if she is to know divine things, in particular, a preparation of the will. Mary must turn herself (*convertatur*) to Jesus in love of him. And so, however Mary comes to recognize Jesus, it will be by her own effort.

But there is another condition for a vision of Christ, one which is revealed in a question Thomas raises. Thomas asks, "Why didn't Mary recognize Christ, since he was the same person as before?" (2506). This question is all the more acute when asked in light of what Thomas says about Mary in the previous lecture. In Lecture 2 of this chapter, Thomas devotes much energy to describing the intensity of Mary's love for Jesus. It was her "burning affection," her "unwavering love," her "desire for heavenly things," that fuelled her "earnest search for Christ" and brought her before the empty tomb. How could someone who loved Jesus so passionately not see his glory, when it is love that enables one to do so?

Thomas offers two explanations for this: "either because she did not believe that the one she had seen dead had risen, or else her eyes were held so that she would not recognize him, like the two disciples on their way to Emmaus (Lk. 24.16)" (2506). Thomas provides little guidance in understanding these two explanations. He neither elaborates on them, nor gives us any indication as to which is to be preferred. As is often the case in the *Commentary*, the reader is left to find unity and coherence on his/

her own. Efforts are rewarded, however, if these explanations are viewed in light of previous discussions in the *Commentary*. It appears that these explanations are not unrelated; but are both centred on Mary's lack of faith. Looking to Thomas's earlier comments on Mary Magdalene in the *Commentary*, we see that the first explanation is indeed true. Thomas makes it very clear that Mary did not believe in the resurrection by the time she reached the tomb. He tells us that "the angels knew that Mary was uncertain about the resurrection" (C20 L2 2501). Thomas understands this lack of faith as universal for Christ's disciples, and that they only came to believe in the resurrection through the tutelage of the risen Jesus himself and the Paraclete, that is, the Holy Spirit, sent to them to teach them all things, as John tells us in 14.26 (*Commentary* C14 L6 1938–60). This lack of faith in the resurrection could be an obstacle to the love required for the vision of Christ, since, as Thomas tells us in the *Summa theologiae*, we love something only insofar as we know it (II–II Q4 a7corpus). If Mary did not believe in the resurrection, then she would not have been able to love Christ as risen.

The second explanation says that Jesus did not want to be known, just as he did not want to be known by the disciples on the road to Emmaus, as recounted in Luke's Gospel. The only commentary we have of Thomas on Luke is from the *Catena Aurea*, a running commentary on the four Gospels, heavily sourced by Thomas for his *Commentary on St. John*. According to the *Catena*, it is this same lack of faith that caused Jesus to withhold recognition from the disciples on the road to Emmaus. According to Thomas, the disciples suffered from a lack of faith in the resurrection and needed, therefore, to be brought to this faith by Jesus himself. Jesus does so by enflaming their hearts with the "love of God," thereby increasing their "heavenly desire" (*Catena* in Luc. C24 L3). It appears then that the two explanations concern the same problem of a lack of faith, but from different perspectives—that of Mary and that of the risen Jesus. Mary cannot generate the love requisite to come to a vision of Christ because she lacks the necessary faith, while the risen Jesus suspends her recognition of him because he did not want to be recognized until she was prepared to do so by the gift of faith. With Thomas's explanations of why Mary did not recognize Jesus when she saw him, we have the final condition for a true vision of Christ—namely, the gift of faith. For Mary to see Jesus in his glory, she must turn herself towards him in love, a love aided by the supernatural gift of faith.

Spiritual Instruction

The second part of the first division is devoted to what Christ said to Mary. Here we see how the conditions for the vision of Christ, which were introduced to us in the first part of this division, are met by the skilful pedagogy of Christ himself. Christ's response to Mary's lack of faith is the same as to that of the disciples on the road to Emmaus. Jesus prepares Mary by way of a spiritual instruction. This instruction is like no other, since it prepares Mary for the reception of a supernatural gift. Christ has to dispose her heart for receiving it, by enflaming the love she already possesses for him.

External Lessons

We discover that Christ's teaching occurs on two levels: the external and the internal. The external teaching is conducted through the questions Jesus poses to Mary. These questions, according to Thomas, are carefully crafted to draw out her love for him, thus fulfilling one of the conditions for seeing Christ's glory. Thomas understands Jesus's question, "Woman, why are you weeping?" as a pedagogical tactic to get Mary to speak about who she is looking for; "for when she spoke of the one she was seeking, her love burned more intensely" (2508). But Mary's love for Jesus is demonstrated most of all by what Thomas calls her "marvelous courage" (*mirabilis audacia*), evident in her offer to retrieve her Lord's body herself, if she should be told where he lay. Thomas interprets this offer as a sign of love because it indicates a hope for the impossible. Thomas considers Mary in her offer as overestimating her physical strength, and so sees it as a sign of love by being a sign of the hope that love engenders, a hope for all things, to paraphrase 1 Cor. 13.7. And so, it is only after having drawn out Mary's love for him that Jesus causes Mary to recognize him by mentioning her name. Mary's love for Jesus, then, is rewarded with vision of him. The external teaching of Christ shows how the first condition of coming to a vision of Christ was met. Jesus skilfully coaxes Mary into turning her heart towards him out of love for him.

Internal Lessons

The internal instruction demonstrates how the second condition is satisfied. Thomas shows us that the external teaching is inspired by an internal one. It turns out that, simultaneous to his asking her questions, Jesus helps Mary to progress in her love by infusing her with his own love. Thomas says, "he planted the seeds of virtue in her heart by the strength of his love" (2510). Here, as with the disciples on the road to Emmaus, Jesus encourages her love as only he could do, that is, by moving her from within. Thomas explains elsewhere in the *Commentary* that Jesus is the only teacher who teaches internally (C13 L3 1775), since only God has the power to put things into the heart by moving the will from within (C13 L1 1742). Mary's courage, perhaps, is *mirabilis* for this reason too, namely, that it is moved by the *mirabilis* inspiration of grace. This is consistent with Thomas's teaching on grace (*Summa theologiae* I–II Q112 a2corpus). Grace works on the heart or will directly, turning the person from within to assent to the gifts of grace given by God. Thomas insists that there is no coercion involved, as the will is turned from within and so remains the principle of its own act. To be moved by grace is to move yourself freely by God's grace. The agency of both God and the individual is preserved in the movement of grace. Christ's internal instruction is in fact the explanation for how Mary overcame her lack of faith. As we have already observed, since Mary lacked faith in the resurrection, she could not love the risen Jesus by her own power; for, according to Thomas, "the will has no inclination for anything except in so far as it is apprehended by the intellect" (*Summa theologiae* II–II Q4 a7corpus). The only other love that could move her heart towards God and without coercion is the one that issues from the object of faith itself, Jesus Christ, the Incarnate Word.

By inspiring Mary with his own love, Jesus moves her heart internally to assent to his resurrection.

Having identified the principal theme of the discussion as the vision of Christ, having discovered the conditions for such a vision, and having observed its coming about in Mary, we can now understand the nature of Mary's recognition according to Thomas. It appears that Mary's recognition is one that has been transformed by the grace of faith, so as to elevate it for the vision of Christ. The implication throughout Thomas's interpretation is that, without divine illumination, Mary's recognition would have hindered her vision of the risen Jesus. In fact, later in the same lecture, Thomas hints that this would indeed have been the case. Following Augustine, Thomas explains that Jesus did not allow Mary to touch him in order to teach her not to limit her faith to what she now believes of him. Mary, then, is at risk of cutting herself off from a deeper faith by restricting herself to what she already knows. Jesus had to prepare her for a deeper knowledge, one that was open to the glory of the resurrection, so as to prevent her former familiarity with him from closing her off from his newly resurrected state. It is out of love for her, then, that Mary is kept from recognizing Jesus prematurely, before her heart could be opened up to a more perfect faith.

Recognition and Justification

Thomas's comments on Mary's recognition of Jesus provide evidence that Mary serves as a model for all Christians. Thomas uses the occasion of Mary's recognition of the risen Jesus to make two points about the grace of justification, both of which concern Jesus calling Mary by name. First, Thomas states that Jesus called Mary by name to indicate that, "although all things are moved by God with a general motion, a special grace is needed for a person's justification" (2513). And secondly, he claims it also indicates "that the cause of our justification and of our profession of faith is to have been called by Christ" (2514).

Anyone familiar with Thomas's teaching on justification will recognize similarities with Thomas's discussion of Mary's recognition of Jesus.

Justification, according to Thomas, is the restoration of the proper relationship, or order, between the human person and God, and therefore the undoing of the disruption caused by the sin of Adam (*Summa theologiae* I–II Q113 a1corpus). This restoration is achieved by the grace of Christ, which, Thomas tells us, proceeds from the love of God (*Summa theologiae* I–II Q113 a2corpus). Like Mary, then, the justified are called to faith out of God's love. Earlier in the *Commentary*, Thomas mentions how God's chosen are called by grace, and how they know God by a "loving knowledge" (*notitia dilectionis*), a knowledge that affords them the privilege of knowing that God loves them (1412, 1417). It would appear, then, that the justified are called to faith in the same way Mary is called to hers, that is, by grace, understood here as the love of God.

Also, the case of Mary Magdalene is not the only time Thomas links justification with recognition. In an earlier chapter, Thomas says that justified believers hear the voice of Christ just as sheep recognize the voice of their shepherd: "because just as sheep recognize the voice of their shepherd due to familiar experience, so righteous believers hear the voice of Christ: 'O that today you would harken to his voice' (Ps. 95.7)" (C10 L1 1372). Elsewhere in the *Commentary*, Thomas explains this call in the same terms in which he described the process that brought Mary to recognize Jesus. In his comments on John 1.12, on the Word's power to give to any who believe in his name the power to become sons of God, Thomas explains that the Word's power consists in moving the person's free will to accept the gift of grace (C1 L6 153–54). Even though adults are called to freely assent to God's grace, God, through his grace, moves them to assent to it. Like Mary, the justified believer freely assents to God's grace under the power of God moving the will to do so. And as with Mary, Thomas describes this grace as affecting a turning out of a love for God: "'Convert us to yourself, O Lord,' by moving our will to your love, 'and we will be converted' (Lam. 5.21)" (154). Thomas names this interior moving of the will by divine grace the "interior call" to which the justified respond: "And in this sense we speak of an interior call, of which it is said, 'Those whom he called,' by inwardly moving the will to consent to grace, 'he justified,' by infusing grace (Rom. 8.3)" (154).

The grace of justification appears to illuminate recognition just as it did for Mary. Justification illuminates the intellect so that things may be recognized in the light of faith. According to Thomas, Christ established the New Law, which fulfilled the Old Law. As a fulfillment, Christianity brings something new. With the Incarnation of the Word, Thomas tells us, comes a new way for God's people and all of creation to relate to their God (C1 L7 172). The mediation of the person of Jesus Christ is to dispense God's grace and discern his will. With this new relation to God comes a new economy of revelation, in which all previous knowledge is cast in a new light. Although much of the Old Law, like the ceremonial precepts, was left behind, other aspects of it, like the moral law and certain tenants of faith, remained.[8] Christians were still obliged to follow the Ten Commandments and to attribute to God the same simplicity, eternity, omnipotence, and other divine attributes attributed to Him according to the faith of Abraham, Isaac, and Jacob. The One God of the Old Testament was to be recognized in the Trinity; the God who appeared to Moses in the person of Jesus Christ; and the people of God in the Church. Like Mary, the justified believers are expected to recognize in light of the new what was once already known in a different way. The new sight by which the old is seen anew is made possible by the illumination of faith.

Thomas talks about the effect of faith on recognition in the *Commentary*. In a discussion on spiritual blindness, Thomas explains that the humble are able to recognize their sins through the illumination of faith (1363). Faith casts a light on the world in which things are recognized in a new way. What was once seen as strength and power is seen as the sin of pride by the light of faith. It is the light of faith that allows the Centurion to recognize the divine power in Christ on the cross, the believer to recognize the Author of the Law in Jesus Christ, and the humble person to recognize the need of a saviour (*Commentary* 1425; *Summa theologiae* II–II Q22 a1corpus; III Q1 a5corpus). Faith is the gift that determines how the justified believer recognizes all of God's other gifts.

The illumination of faith also causes one to recognize the gift of faith itself. Because it implies not only the free consent of the believer, but also knowledge of what is being assented to,[9] justification implies that one recognizes grace as a gift from God. Throughout Thomas's corpus, one of the most common uses of the word recognition is in relation to the recognition of God's gifts. Often, Thomas speaks of the importance of recognizing the gifts one receives from God and recognizing that all good things have God as their origin. The greatest form of ingratitude, according to Thomas, is not to recognize a favour received (*Summa theologiae* I-II Q76 a4ad3). And the reason for sacrifices to God is the recognition of receiving goods from Him as the creator of all things (*Summa theologiae* I-II Q102 a3corpus). It would seem then that if grace is a gift from God, it should be recognized as such by the one who receives it. And if all justified believers receive the grace of justification, they should all recognize God's loving offer. In fact, Thomas says as much in his commentary on Paul's letter to the Colossians, where he interprets the Apostle's instruction to sing "with thankfulness" as "recognizing the grace of Christ and God's gifts" ("ad Col." C3 L3 169).

The recognition of grace corresponds to the mutual dimension of recognition mentioned in the scene with Mary and the risen Jesus. Thomas quotes Gregory the Great in regards to Jesus calling Mary by name: "Recognize him who has recognized you" (2514).[10] Thomas is reminding us here of Jesus's interior teaching through which he led Mary to a recognition of himself. Without Jesus's recognition of the love in Mary's heart, she would not have been able to recognize him in faith. There is a similar mutual relationship of recognition in the life of justification. The recognition of grace by the justified believer is itself an admission that God has recognized the requisite love in that person's heart.

Mutual recognition can be understood as the logical consequence of what Thomas calls "formed faith," that is, faith formed by charity. In the *Summa theologiae*, Thomas explains that the faith that justifies requires both an act of the intellect and of the will (II-II Q4 a5corpus). As an act of the intellect, faith is the assent to the true—the proper good of the intellect. But for faith to justify, it must also include a well-ordered will, that is, one directed towards the good. For without a well-ordered will there would not be the necessary rectitude of order called for by justification. The ultimate and principal good, according to Thomas, is the enjoyment of God. And to this end one is ordered by charity. And so, the faith that justifies is one formed by charity, that is, where the intellect assents to the true on account of the will's desire for God.

Because of charity we can find mutual recognition in every act of formed faith. Again in his *Summa*, Thomas tells us that charity establishes a friendship (*amicitia*) between God and the human person (II–II Q23 a1corpus). This friendship itself is established on what Thomas calls a mutual love, the love by which God shares his happiness with the faithful, and with which they love God as their happiness. And so, the mutual love caused by charity establishes a friendship between God and the human person. "Formed faith," then, is grounded in the mutual return of love between God and the person. And so, to share in this love would entail recognizing the one you love.[11] The recognition of the beloved would seem to be implied in every act of formed faith. But because this love is freely given by both parties, this recognition is not a one-way street, but mutual; for one not only recognizes one's beloved, but also that the beloved loves in return, and so returns recognition. By establishing us in a relationship of friendship with God, then, charity implies that whenever we believe we do so in recognition of the *friend* for whom we believe, a recognition we know, is returned in kind.

The close connection between faith and recognition explains why recognition and confession of faith are found linked in Thomas's writings. In his commentary on Paul's letter to the Romans, Thomas says that we bless God "when we recognize his goodness with our heart and confess it with our lips" ("ad Rom." C1 L7 144). And in his commentary on Job, Thomas explains that the remission of sins is not possible unless one "humbly recognizes and confesses his sin" (*Literal Exposition on Job* 33.23–33). If faith leads to a confession of faith, all the more will it lead to recognition of the one believed.

Therefore, the references to justification in Thomas's interpretation of Mary's recognition of the risen Jesus are not accidental, but direct the reader to the place of recognition in the Christian life, for which Mary Magdalene is a model. Just as faith illumined Mary so she could recognize Jesus in his glorified body, so too the justified believer is able to recognize all of God's gifts in light of the gift of faith. Mary's recognition also serves as a model of the recognition of God as the giver of grace, which lies at the heart of the Christian life. Mary serves as a reminder that any act of faith that is moved by grace will involve two wills—one human, one divine—poised in the position of mutual recognition of their common love, their common friendship in charity. The recognition of God's love motivates acts of piety and the confession of faith, as the justified seek to express their gratitude for God's gifts.

Thomas's interpretation of the scene with Mary and the risen Jesus also models the problem recognition can potentially pose for Christian belief. To recognize is to identify something based on a prior knowledge of it. And because the Christian faith considers itself the fulfillment of an earlier revelation, it entails the recognition of earlier held truths seen in a new context or form. The danger is that recognition, which relies on a previous knowledge, will make one closed to the new form in which it is discovered, just as Mary's recognition of Jesus might have hindered her vision of Christ's glory. Thomas's solution is to allow recognition to be transformed by the grace of faith, thereby freeing the mind from the limitations of the older knowledge and introducing into the world a uniquely Christian concept of recognition.

Author's Note

This research was originally presented in a slightly modified form at the Centre for Comparative Literature's nineteenth annual graduate conference, "From Ignorance to Knowledge: Recognition from Antiquity to the Postmodern and Beyond," at Victoria College, University of Toronto. The article in its present form benefits, I hope, from the helpful questions and comments raised by various conference attendees in response to the original.

Notes

1. Boitani, *The Bible and Its Rewritings* (1999); Ricoeur, *The Course on Recognition* (2005).
2. The *Index Thomisticus* is a searchable database of all of the works of Thomas Aquinas.
3. Translation of the Gospel text and all biblical references are taken from the English translation of Thomas's *Commentary on the Gospel of St. John*, translated and edited by James A. Weisheipl and Fabian R. Larcher, which consists of Weisheipl's translation of the text used by Aquinas up to and including Chapter 8, Lecture 4, and the Revised Standard Version for most of the remainder.
4. References to the *Commentary* will be made according to Chapter, lecture number, and paragraph number, following the scheme of the Marietti edition: S. Thomae Aquinatis, *Super Evangelium S. Ioannis Lectura* (1952).
5. In his biography of Thomas, Jean-Pierre Torrell argues against the long standing tradition that Thomas edited the John commentary (199).
6. See Thomas Aquinas, *Summa theologiae*, Prima pars, Question 1, article 9, ad2, where the obscurity of metaphors in Scripture encourages the studious.
7. References to Thomas's interpretation of Mary's recognition of the risen Jesus in the *Commentary* will be made through reference to the relevant paragraph number, according to the numbering of the 1952 Marietti edition. Other references to the *Commentary* will include chapter (C) and lecture (L) number as well.
8. On the moral precepts of the Old Law, see *Summa theologiae* I–II Q100. For the ceremonial, see *Summa theologiae* I–II Q101–103.
9. See *Summa theologiae*, II–II Q2 a5corpus.
10. Cf. *Catena* in Ioan. C20 L2, where Thomas attributes this to Gregory the Great.
11. In the *Commentary*, Thomas shows that our love can be a *sign* (signum) of God's love: "the fact that we love God is a sign that he loves us, for our being able to love God is a gift from God," and "our faith is due to God's love for us" (C14 L6 1941; C15 L5 2051).

Works Cited

Aquinas, Saint Thomas. *Catena aurea in quatuor evangelia*. Ed. P. Angelici Guarienti. 2 vols. Romae: Marietti, 1953. Print.

———. *Commentary on the Gospel of St. John*, Pt. 1. Eds. James A. Weisheipl and Fabian R. Larcher. Trans. J.A. Weisheipl. Albany, NY: Magi Books, 1980. Print.

———. *Commentary on the Gospel of St. John*, Pt. 2. Ed. James A. Weisheipl and Fabian R. Larcher. Trans. F.R. Larcher. Petersham, MA: St. Bede's Publications, 1999. Print.

———. *The Literal Exposition on Job: A Scriptural Commentary Concerning Providence.* Trans. Martin D. Yaffe and Anthony Damico. Atlanta, GA: Scholars Press, 1989.

———. *Summa theologiae.* Ottawa: Istituti Studiorum Medievalium Ottaviensis, 1943. Print.

———. *Summa Theologica.* Vol. 5. Trans. Fathers of the English Dominican Province. Westminster, MD: Christian Classics, 1981. Print.

———. "Super Epistolam ad Colossenses Lectura." *Super Epistolas S. Pauli Lectura.* Vol. II. Ed. Raphael Cai. Ed. 8 revisa. Taurini: Marietti, 1953. 125–61. Print.

———. "Super Epistolam ad Romanos Lectura." *Super Epistolas S. Pauli Lectura.* Vol. I. Ed. Raphael Cai. Ed. 8 revisa. Taurini: Marietti, 1953. 5–230. Print.

———. *Super Evangelium S. Ioannis Lectura.* Ed. P.R. Cai. 5th ed. Romae: Marietti, 1952. Print.

Boitani, Piero. *The Bible and Its Rewritings.* Oxford: Oxford University Press, 1999. Print.

Boyle, John F. "The Theological Character of the Scholastic 'Division of the Text' with Particular Reference to the Commentaries of Saint Thomas Aquinas." *With Reverence for the Word: Medieval Scriptural Exegesis in Judaism, Christianity, and Islam.* Eds. Jane Dammen McAuliffe, Barry D. Walfish, and Joseph W. Goering. 1st ed. Oxford: Oxford University Press, 2003. 276–83. Print.

Busa, Roberto. *Corpus Thomisticum Index Thomisticus.* Web edition by Eduardo Bernot and Enrique Alarcón. Pampilonae ad Universitatis Studiorum Navarrensis: Fundación Tomás de Aquino, 2006. Available from http://www.corpusthomisticum.org/it/index.age. Web.

Ricoeur, Paul. *The Course on Recognition.* Trans. David Pellauer. Cambridge, MA: Harvard University Press, 2005. Print.

Torrell, Jean-Pierre. *Saint Thomas Aquinas, Vol. 1: The Person and His Work.* Trans. Robert Royal. Washington, DC: The Catholic University of America Press, 1996. Print.

Weijers, Olga. *Terminologie des universités au XIIIe siècle.* Roma: Edizioni dell'Ateneo, 1987. Print.

NARRATIVE IDENTITY

Recognizing Oneself in Augustine and Ricoeur

JENNA SUNKENBERG

IN ONE OF HIS LAST WORKS, *The Course of Recognition*, Paul Ricoeur suggests that recognition is a process of self-evaluation and self-understanding within the production of what he terms a "narrative identity" (249). By entering into a text and reflecting upon ourselves within its imagined yet representative world, we arrive at self-understanding that we incorporate into our everyday actions and relations. As such, *The Course of Recognition* suggests that we as readers come to conceptualize our own lives as narratives, interpreting and learning from them as we would from a text. Accordingly, Ricoeur asks: "How indeed can a subject of action give his life an ethical qualification if this life cannot be brought together in the form of a narrative?...As for the vicissitudes of life, they remain in search of narrative configuration" (103).

This article will explore Ricoeur's idea of self-understanding in and through narrative identity by establishing a discourse with Saint Augustine's *Confessions*, a text explicitly confronted by Ricoeur in his work, *Time and Narrative*. While Ricoeur's work insists on Augustine's failure to conceptually correlate time and narrative within the phenomenon of self-recognition, as is Ricoeur's task, this chapter will suggest that this is exactly what Augustine's *Confessions* achieves. My discussion will begin with a brief contextualization of Ricoeur's notion of narrative identity within his greater hermeneutic theory and then move into an interpretation of Augustine's *Confessions*. My task will be to suggest that a discourse between the two thinkers, which this research begins to invite, has much to offer contemporary hermeneutics and its endeavour to conceptualize the means by which textual interpretation facilitates self-understanding.

In *Time and Narrative*, Ricoeur develops a hermeneutics founded in Augustinian and Aristotelian models, through which he conceptualizes how reciprocity between time and narrative enables fiction to reconfigure temporal experience into a narrative such that self-understanding can occur. Firstly, Ricoeur discusses Augustine's presentation of the paradox of time—that despite psychologically perceiving ourselves within a past, present, and future, time itself does not exist; it cannot be pinned down in thought or language. He summarizes Augustine's position by asking, "how can time exist if the past is no longer, if the future is not yet, and if the present is not always?" (Ricoeur, *Time and Narrative* 7). *Time and Narrative* begins with Augustine's presentation of this paradox and then, as a means of developing its own theory of time and narrative, brings Augustine's notion of time into a discourse with Aristotle's theory of mimesis as it is presented in the *Poetics*. Ricoeur's objective in focusing on the *Poetics* is to discuss how through fiction's imitative or mimetic function, a narrative's plot succeeds in re-presenting our lived experiences in time: "The tragic muthos is set up as the poetic solution to the speculative paradox of time, inasmuch as the inventing of order is pursued to the exclusion of every temporal characteristic" (*Time and Narrative* 38). Tragic mythos, Ricoeur tells us, is narrative itself: a plot's organization of events that imitate our lived experience (*Time and Narrative* 36). The discourse between the plot-driven theory of Aristotle and the psychological perspective of Augustine is that which allows Ricoeur to reach the driving thesis of his work: "Time becomes human to the extent that it is articulated through a narrative mode, and narrative attains its full meaning when it becomes a condition of temporal existence" (*Time and Narrative* 3). For Ricoeur, a reciprocal relationship develops between time and narrative. Moreover, it is only through this relation that time gains any sense of concreteness. It is the insubstantial and purely psychological character that Augustine focuses on, through the structure of narrative, demarcated into concrete divisions of past, present, and future. Similarly, narrative succeeds in clarifying and reconfiguring our experiences in the world, specifically because of the temporal framework within which a plot develops.

Arriving at his composite discourse of Aristotelian and Augustinian perspectives of time, Ricoeur concludes that Augustine captures the aporia, the innate paradox, of human time but fails to relate it to narrative's role in the production of self-understanding. He writes that "Augustine's paradoxes...owe nothing to the experience of narrating a story" (*Time and Narrative* 18). Augustine does not, according to Ricoeur, acknowledge reciprocity between time and narrative such that one gives meaning to the other. The *Confessions* performs an inquiry into the nature of time and unveils its paradoxical character, but Ricoeur argues, it offers no means of resolving that paradox within our own experiences of temporality. It is this claim that my essay will now counter. While I cannot here offer a comprehensive study of Ricoeur's hermeneutics or of Augustine's *Confessions* and theory of time, I do seek to initiate a discourse between the two thinkers in order to suggest that the *Confessions* have much to offer our contemporary views and theorizations regarding time and narrative. To proceed, I will first provide a brief summary of Ricoeur's hermeneutic theory in order to contextualize his notion of time and narrative within the act of textual interpretation and its production of self-understanding, a dynamic process I refer to as a *hermeneutics of the self*, enacted through a hermeneutics of text. I will, then, turn to the *Confessions* and suggest how Augustine's text subtly alludes to reciprocity between time and narrative that, I argue, correlates to Ricoeur's own view.

Much more than an objective interpretation theory, Ricoeur's hermeneutics always emphasize the reader's appropriating a text's truth claims into his/her perceptions of selfhood.[1] Interpretation, although initiated as an objective analysis of text, always involves subjective reflection of oneself. Accordingly, a hermeneutics of text is always a hermeneutics of the self. Ricoeur writes, "If it remains true that hermeneutics terminates in self-understanding, then the subjectivism of this proposition must be rectified by saying that to understand *oneself* is to understand oneself *in front of the text*....What is appropriated is indeed the matter of the text. But the matter of the text becomes my own only if I disappropriate myself, in order to let the matter of the text be. So I exchange the me, master of itself for the self, disciple of the text. This process could also be expressed as a *distanciation of the self from itself* within the interior of appropriation" (Ricoeur, *Hermeneutics* 192, emphasis added). In this model, a reader enters into an honest dialogue with the text that is intended to prevent the projection of one's own views and biases onto the text, whereby its meaning would be nothing more than a projection of oneself. By objectifying the text in and of itself, Ricoeur argues that one can suspend one's self-projections of meaning by becoming a "disciple of the text." The process of analysis through which we allow the text to speak in and of its self is articulated in Ricoeur's hermeneutic theory as explanation, the objective analysis of text, which then gives way to interpretive understanding. We read: "We can, as readers, remain in the suspense of the text, treating it as a worldless and authorless object; in this case, we explain the text in terms of its internal relations, its structure. On the other hand, we can lift the suspense and fulfill the text in speech, restoring it to living communication; in this case, we interpret the text" (Ricoeur, *Hermeneutics* 152).

Restoring the text to living communication is what we seek to accomplish by allowing an objective and structural explication to be fulfilled in its dialectical counterpart: understanding of the reference that structure points us toward. We read of the reference: "In the phenomenon of the sentence, language passes outside itself; reference is the mark of the self transcendence of language" (Ricoeur, *Rule of Metaphor* 74). Reference, as the discourse which marks the self transcendence of the structural matrix, is that which the story speaks of, the world it narrates. Reference may point to the mundane, the daily routine of a person's life, or it may point to a dimension of existence that is initially recognized as a feeling. Either way, the reference is a register of meaning constructed from the discourse's sense, its structural units of meaning. Taken by itself, Ricoeur considers the analysis of the text's structure to be an "undimensional approach to language" (*Interpretation Theory* 5). The text is explained, but only in terms of internal relations of structure. It remains a worldless object and therefore does not enact the discourse-like exchange with its reader, the fusion of horizons through which self-understanding can arise. We will only reach "ontological density of the reality we study" once explanation gives way to understanding (Ricoeur, *Hermeneutics* 131). Reaching the "ontological density of the reality we study" in the text we read is the purpose of reading for Ricoeur. Moreover, it is a purpose realized only through a phenomenological turn of interpretation, a turn through which explanation, as objective analysis of structure, shifts to understanding, subjective appropriation of meaning.

Once Ricoeur has developed this theory of self-understanding through a dialectic of explanation and understanding, he extends his hermeneutic of text to a study of time and narrative in order to assess how narrative enables such self-understanding to occur. In *The Course of Recognition* we read, "In this sense, quasi-plot and quasi-characters belong to the same intermediary level and have a similar function, serving as a relay station for the movement of history's questioning back toward narrative and, beyond the narrative, in the direction of actual practice" (Ricoeur 182). Here, Ricoeur extends the function of fictional narratives to the narrative or plot-driven stories we form about ourselves in order to conceptualize and understand our daily lives. "Real" events and people are configured into "quasi-plots" and "quasi-characters" as human experiences in time are configured into a plot's past, present, and future. Narratives are the means through which we conceptualize and understand our own histories, personal and cultural. Within Ricoeur's model, then, the Augustinian preoccupation with how we experience time is considered in terms of Aristotle's mimetic function of narrative. Even if we cannot explain what time is or achieve a firm mental grasping of it, we can at least recognize that our identities and notions of selfhood manifest themselves to us through the temporal frames within which narratives occur, regardless of whether those frames are historical or fictional, true or false. Through our interactions with textual and historical stories, we learn to formulate our own stories and establish our own narrative identities.

This general introduction to Ricoeur's study of the hermeneutics of the self, enacted through the interpretation of textual narratives, is in no way a comprehensive study of his hermeneutics or of his work on time and narrative. It serves only to introduce the conceptual background upon which he makes his claim that Augustine provides an inquiry into the nature of time without contextualizing that inquiry within a narrative structure. However, it is precisely within the structure and narrative of the *Confessions* that one finds a correlated dramatization of Ricoeur's reciprocity between time and narrative and its relation to self-recognition and self-understanding.

The *Confessions* is divided into two parts. The first nine books present a narrative account of Augustine's life and conversion to Christianity; while in the last four books we receive theoretical examinations of how we interpret and understand our relation to God. In these sections, Augustine discusses topics such as the memory, time, and happiness, presenting the parameters within which one comes to find God within oneself. My claim is not that these chapters are intended to be separate from the narrative account of his life, but rather, that their more theoretical-like procedures explain how narratives, such as Augustine's autobiography, serve in the production of self-understanding and, by extension, the self's journey toward God.

As stated above, Ricoeur claims that despite having captured the paradox of human time—that we exist and know ourselves within time, but cannot concretely locate time—Augustine fails to identify that "time becomes human to the extent that it is articulated through a narrative mode, and narrative attains its full meaning when it becomes a condition of temporal existence" (Ricoeur, *Time and Narrative* 3). In making this claim, I suggest that Ricoeur overlooks the *Confessions'* own narrative structure within which Augustine's description of time occurs. If his theory of time is viewed with respect to the text's meta-narrative description of textually informed identity and the philosophy of language at work in the *Confessions*, we see that Augustine does indeed develop a reciprocity between human time and narrative. In fact, he arrives at the same conclusions as Ricoeur—only through narrative can we understand our being-in-time and our belonging to the greater narrative of history.

To summarize Augustine's conclusions, we can say that time exists as a psychological manifestation and demarcation of individual experience, a necessary condition of and reaction to a living person's being-in-the-world. He writes, "It seems to me then that time is merely an extension, though of what it is an extension I do not know. I begin to wonder whether it is an extension of the mind itself" (*Confessions* 11.26). Existing as an "extension of the mind itself," time, as the past, present, and future can be afforded no concrete evidence of existing. The divisions of time are, Augustine concludes, subjectively conceived demarcations that exist only within the mind. Moreover, he extends the subjective nature of time to suggest that the past, present, and future are themselves psychological variations of the present, the only "time" that we can conceptually and visually grasp: "Some such different times do exist in the mind, but nowhere else that I can see. The present of past things is the memory; the present of present things is direct perception; and the present of future things is expectation" (*Confessions* 11.20).

Augustine then conceptualizes how these three states of psychological time—the memory, direct perception, and expectation—interact with one another to establish our ability to think and understand, a process articulated as the *distentio animi*, the distention of the mind. This *distentio animi* is the continuous distention through which the memory's past is called upon within the moment of direct perception to produce present understanding and future expectation, while, given the constant passing of time, such understanding is almost simultaneously transferred into the past and stored as memory for future interpretation. Because of the pivotal role of memory within this conception of time, the self is always involved, and therefore, all understanding is in a sense, self-understanding. For Augustine, through the interaction of present perception and past memory, we generate pictures or understandings of ourselves and come to recognize how we change throughout life. Any notion of subjective identity is one that is in constant flux and formation, but temporarily present and concrete enough to the direct perception so that self-evaluation and self-recognition can occur.

That the process of understanding oneself is inherently a process of narrative construction of self is expressed in Augustine's discussion of memory.

> In it I meet myself as well. I remember myself and what I have done, when and where I did it and the state of my mind at the time. In my memory too, are all the events that I remember, whether they are things that have happened to me or things that I have heard from others. From the same source I can picture to myself all kinds of different images based either upon my own experience or upon what I find credible because it tallies with my own experience. I can fit them into the general picture of the past; from them I can make a surmise of actions and events and hopes for the future and I can contemplate them all over again as if they were actually present. (*Confessions* 10.8)

We have here a type of parallel to what, in *The Course of Recognition*, Ricoeur refers to as narrative identity where a narrative model is required if we are to picture our lives to ourselves. For Augustine writes that in order to understand oneself, one must imagine a temporarily static picture of the past to allow for comprehension of present and future events to occur. It is the necessity of this imagined construct of a "picture" that I take as a correlation to Ricoeur's idea of narrative because it suggests the necessity of a conceptual or aesthetic mediation that actively reconfigures the disjoint of past events into a structured form or plot through which comprehension occurs.

Augustine, however, gives evidence of an even greater parallel to Ricoeur's contemporary stance because in the *Confessions* reciprocity between time and narrative is revealed only through the act of reading. In addition to the personal narratives we form as a means of imaging and recognizing ourselves, the *Confessions* suggests that we come to understand our relations to the world and to God by interpreting textual narratives (especially the Scriptures). This is, I would argue, the very model upon which Augustine's own *Confessions* is based. Accordingly, Brian Stock writes of Augustine's *Confessions*: "[It] tells a story, but it asks the narrator and through him, the reader to use this story as the basis for the self-analysis. This discourse is one part of the experience; the other consists in a set of mental exercises that follow the reading in which we do not reflect on Augustine's life but on our personal narratives. In this way, Augustine's story of his sins, conversion, and rebirth can potentially lead to the improvement of our lives" ("Reading, Ethics" 9). Augustine's notion of self-understanding through narrative, like Ricoeur's, can be considered part of a greater hermeneutic theory—a hermeneutics of the self enacted by a hermeneutics of text.

Two episodes from the *Confessions* will serve to demonstrate how textual interpretation and narrative allow us to "reconfigure" understanding of ourselves, that is, to recognize ourselves by, as Ricoeur says, distancing the self from the self—a hermeneutic process which, as Stock states, "can potentially lead to the improvement of our lives." The first moment occurs in Book III when Augustine recounts his discovery of Cicero's *Hortensius*. He writes, "The title of the book is *Hortensius* and it recommends the reader to study philosophy. It altered my outlook on life. It changed my prayers to you, O Lord and provided me with new hopes and aspirations. All my empty dreams suddenly lost their charm and my heart began to throb with a bewildering passion for the wisdom of eternal truth...So I made up my mind to examine the holy Scriptures and see what kind of books they were" (*Confessions* 3.4). Augustine tells us that reading Cicero and interpreting it with respect to his own life "altered my out look on life." Reading Cicero's words are the means through which he came to study philosophy and eventually the Scriptures, which in turn put him on the path to discovering God and himself. His initial conversion, then, occurs through reading, revealing how an interaction with text can allow us to reflect on our own lives, recognize our past and present paths, and choose to change them. If the *Hortensius* had not enacted this process within Augustine, then it would not have changed his outlook on life and Augustine would not credit it with leading him to read and interpret the Scriptures. It is in reading the Scriptures, however, that Augustine depicts his true conversion to Christianity, and in this conversion scene we receive a more explicit development of the *Confessions*' own theory of narrative identity.

Early in Book VIII, Augustine tells his readers of his hearing the story of Saint Antony. Then, as Stock has shown us, eight chapters later we discover that his mentioning Saint Antony served as a structural and thematic prefiguration of Augustine's own conversion (*Augustine the Reader* 121). The conversion scene is as follows.

> *I was asking myself these questions, weeping all the while with the most bitter sorrow in my heart, when all at once I heard the singsong voice of a child in a nearby house.... 'Take it and read, take it and read.' I stemmed my flood of tears and stood up, telling myself that this could only be a divine command to open my book of Scripture and read the first passage on which my eyes should fall. For I had heard the story of Antony, and I remembered how he had happened to go into a church while the Gospel was being read and had taken it as a counsel addressed to himself when he heard the words* Go home and sell all that belongs to you. Give it to the poor, and so the treasure you have shall be in heaven; then come back and follow me. *By this divine pronouncement he had at once been converted to you. So I hurried back to the place where Alypius was sitting for when I stood up to move away I had put down the book containing Paul's Epistles. I seized it and opened it, and in silence I read the first passage on which my eyes fell...I had no wish to read more and no need to do so. For in an instant, as I came to the end of the sentence, it was as though the light of confidence flooded in to my heart and all*

the darkness of doubt was dispelled. (St. Augustine, *Confessions* 8.12, emphasis added)

Such is Augustine's conversion. It is only by remembering the story of Antony with which Book VIII begins and appropriating its meaning through a reconfiguration of its events with respect to himself that Augustine is able to convert. By modeling his own conversion on the story of Antony, which is itself a story of conversion based on textual interpretation, and by structurally prefiguring it within Book VIII, Augustine establishes a meta-narrative discourse in which he comments on the importance of reading: by interpreting a text's meaning with respect to oneself, that meaning becomes meaningful and an individual progresses in spiritual and self-knowledge.

That this discourse between text and reader is, in a sense, a theory of *time* and narrative is expressed by connecting the *distentio animi*, the constant distention of one's own self between past and present, to the experience of reading. Accordingly, Stock assesses Augustine's conversions via reading by identifying the series of narratives as "vehicles for conversion." Books present the "clues, reminders, confirmations of inwardly understood realities. False in one context, true in another" or "false because of the nonsensory nature of the truth in question" (Stock, *Augustine the Reader* 125). Narrative, as a fictional depiction of truth, allows Augustine to engage in a discourse with himself and perceive, or to use his terminology, *remember*, truth. It allows him to conceive of images within his mind. Reflecting on himself with respect to these images, be they experiences from his own life or images presented by Scripture, then, allows him to better understand himself. Narrative, however, could not promote this discourse with the self, and the self-recognition that results, if it were not for the nature of the *distentio animi*. If our being-in-the-world were not a being-in the psychological distention of "time," being strewn between past and present within our minds, narrative would not function on a level from which notions of selfhood could be recognized to promote new understanding. Augustine's theory of language explicitly confirms this reciprocity between the *distentio animi* and reading.

In *De Magistro*, Augustine writes that "when words are spoken we either know what they signify or we don't; if we know, then it's reminding rather than learning; but if we don't know, it isn't even reminding, though perhaps we recollect that we should inquire" (127). Rather than create understanding by presenting concrete replicas of the things they represent, words can be viewed only as intermediary tools functioning within the dynamic process of remembering. Signs prompt one towards the recollection and the reorganization of past understanding to allow new discernment to occur. This is Augustine's general theory of language. When applied to reading, we can infer that by interpreting the signs, the stories of Scripture, we remember and/or imagine ourselves in conjunction with the experience depicted, and thus are able to appropriate its meaning with respect to ourselves. Accordingly, Augustine can hear the child singing, remember the story of Antony, and apply it to himself such that he can configure a narrative story for himself. In doing so, within the space of the narrative that Augustine presents us with, the past is allowed to interact with the present and facilitate future understanding. Remembering stories with respect to ourselves is thus the critical moment in recognizing ourselves, and remembering, for Augustine, is always the product of our temporality, here working in conjunction with narrative.

Is this to say that "time becomes human to the extent that it is articulated through a narrative mode, and narrative attains its full meaning when it becomes a condition of temporal existence"? Yes—this is in fact why, according to Augustine, God gave us the Scriptures. We require the Scriptures because we lack the ability to see the all-encompassing truth of the eternal present. As such, we require their narrative depictions of human and temporal experience. Through the *distentio animi*, we then experience a type of narrative reformulation of ourselves as we interact with their depictions of truth.

This view that Augustine does suggest reciprocity between time and narrative is confirmed by the fact that Augustine's meditations on time are framed entirely within his interpretation of Scripture, a point which Ricoeur mentions without fully considering its implications.[2] Again as

Stock has noted, Augustine emphasizes throughout Book XI that the aim of this book will be an exposition of God's law, of the Book of Genesis.[3] As such, only by reading and interpreting the Scripture's representation of truth will Augustine be able to suggest how individuals can progress towards God. We can then view *Confessions* I to IX as Augustine's demonstration of the fact that we understand ourselves in narrative, where his own conversions via Cicero and Saint Antony serve as meta-narrative demonstrations of this reality. Ending Book IX with his conversion, Augustine then moves onto more theoretical discussions as a means of illustrating why we require narratives, such as his, to understand ourselves. This is why his conclusions regarding reading and temporally oriented self-awareness are presented within an interpretation of the Scriptures, confirming Ricoeur's insistence that textual interpretation is the means of progressing in understanding of our being-in-the-world, which, for Augustine, because we are fallen creatures, is necessarily a being in human time.

Notes

1. Although Ricoeur's work is always grounded in a hermeneutics, his notions of interpretation explore many disciplines: a philosophy of the will, psychology, textual interpretation, poetics, and ethics. For a study of his various philosophical turns as they relate to self-understanding in and through textual interpretation see D. Jervolino's *The Cogito and Hermeneutics: The Question of the Subject in Ricoeur*.
2. Ricoeur acknowledges Augustine's framing of Book XI within an exegesis of Genesis, but chooses to "isolate" the meditation on time, thereby isolating Augustine's conclusions from their relation to interpretation itself. For Ricoeur's acknowledgement see *Time and Narrative*, 5.
3. See Stock, *Augustine the Reader*, Chapter 8: "Memory, Self-Reform, and Time."

Works Cited

Augustine. *Against the Academicians and The Teacher (De magistro)*. Trans. Peter King. Indianapolis, IN: Hackett, 1995. Print.

———. *Confessions*. Trans. R.S. Pine-Coffin. Harmondsworth, UK: Penguin, 1961. Print.

Colish, Marcia L. *The Mirror of Language: A Study in the Medieval Theory of Knowledge.* Lincoln: University of Nebraska Press, 1968. Print.

Jervolino, Domenico. *The Cogito and Hermeneutics: The Question of the Subject in Ricoeur.* Trans. Gordon Poole. Dordrecht, NL: Kluwer Academic Publishers, 1990. Print.

Marshall, Donald G. "Rhetoric, Hermeneutics, and the Interpretation of Scripture: Augustine to Robert Basevorn." *Rhetoric and Hermeneutics in Our Time.* Eds. Walter Jost and Michael J. Hyde. New Haven, CT: Yale University Press, 1997. 275–89. Print.

Ricoeur. Paul. *The Course of Recognition.* Trans. David Pellauer. Cambridge, MA: Harvard University Press, 2005. Print.

———. *Hermeneutics and the Human Sciences.* Ed., Trans. John B. Thompson. Cambridge: Cambridge University Press, 1981. Print.

———. *Interpretation Theory: Discourse and the Surplus of Meaning.* Fort Worth, TX: Christian University Press, 1976. Print.

———. *The Rule of Metaphor: Multi-Disciplinary Studies in the Creation of Meaning in Language.* Trans. Robert Czerny with K. McLaughlin and J. Costello. Toronto: University of Toronto Press, 1977. Print.

———. *Time and Narrative.* Vol. 1. Trans. Kathleen McLaughlin and David Pellauer. Chicago: University of Chicago Press, 1985. Print.

Stock, Brian. *Augustine the Reader: Meditation, Self-Knowledge, and the Ethics of Interpretation.* Cambridge, MA: Harvard University Press, 1996. Print.

———. "Reading, Ethics, and the Literary Imagination." *New Literary History* 34.1 (2003): 1–17. Print.

Tracy, David. "Charity, Obscurity, Clarity: Augustine's Search for Rhetoric and Hermeneutics." *Rhetoric and Hermeneutics in Our Time.* Eds. Walter Jost and Michael J. Hyde. New Haven, CT: Yale University Press, 1997. 254–74. Print.

8

THE INTERRUPTION OF TRAUMATIC DOUBLING IN THE INTERPOLATED TALE OF DOROTEA

JEFFREY NEIL WEINER

THE INTERPOLATED STORY OF DOROTEA occupies a special place in *Don Quijote* both because of its structural placement in the middle of the novel and because it offers one of many possible resolutions to the repetitive gestures that characterize the Aristotelian "middle" of the plot. After her initial forceful seduction and betrayal, Dorotea flees her parents' home only to find herself demonically pursued by similar attempts of sexual violation in the manner that Freud vividly describes in his essays on "the uncanny" and the "compulsion to repeat." As Freud discusses, traumatic experience spawns a series of similar, mirroring narratives whereby the subject attempts to master the painful, often forgotten memory and thereby bring about a satisfying closure. These "daemonic" repetitions correspond to the structural "middle" of the genres of comedy and romance, as outlined by Northrop Frye, which portrays a descent into an infernal underworld before returning the hero to a rehabilitated world. The desecration of social and religious laws creates the underworld: don Fernando betrays the confidence of his vassals, Dorotea's parents, and furthermore breaks a sacred vow of marriage, which catapults Dorotea into an anarchic space. While blinding desire causes the collapse of social justice, Cervantes restores society through the production of religious *maravilla*—the audience's awe, compassion, and desire for Dorotea as she tells her story. Within the improvised religious sanctuary created by the presence of the curate and a compassionate audience, Dorotea seduces don Fernando into a ritual of purgation in which he struggles with and finally renounces destructive desire; experiences contrition; and completes the act of restitution that returns all the lovers to their rightful spouses.

The reader's desire—and in the case of Dorotea, all the men who take pleasure first in her vulnerable distress and later in her beautiful body and words—lies behind the many detours in the romance narrative, the repetitions and complications of plot that lead to the resolution. The implacable desire of the audience, however, is to end the detours of the middle and experience a happy resolution (Frye 155). Dorotea's story, dominated as it is by the "compulsion to repeat," threatens to spiral downward and devolve into an improper end. As Peter Brooks explains in "Freud's Masterplot," "Repetition is a *return* in the text, a doubling back. We cannot say whether this return is a return *to* or a return *of*: for instance, a return to origins or a return of the repressed" (Brooks 334, emphasis original). For Dorotea there can be no restitution of her original identity since don Fernando definitively changes her body: the puncturing of her hymen manifestly takes her out of the conventional romance narrative and threatens to thrust her into the kind of realistic burlesque typical of Boccaccio's deflowered nuns and maidens. In Dorotea's tale, the repressed is the suffocating isolation and the tyranny of expectation of her parents, which she describes to her audience as Eden. However, the repressed knowledge pursues Dorotea and forces her to map out her trajectory through the underworld even though in reality there is no possibility of a return to a pre-lapsarian state, the kind of resolution provided in the genre of romance. Cervantes offers instead a comedy in which destructive desire is responsible for the dissolution of society and restrained desire literally reconfigures society. He does this by inscribing the traumatic story—characterized by the "compulsion to repeat"—within a comedy where the repetitive middle corresponds to the demonic underworld. Cervantes goes further by making religious *maravilla* the vehicle of ascent, using the enclosure of the sacramental confession as the space where the restoration of society rightfully occurs.

I have described several ways of experiencing transformation over time: the Freudian theory of traumatic repetition; the paradigm for comedy and romance outlined in Frye's oeuvre, and especially in *The Secular Scripture*; and the Catholic ritual of purgation. All of these theories are attempts to provide models for how experience is turned into a narrative; they provide their own rules for interrupting repetition and bringing about a resolution. Although these models are quite different—and are generated during different if overlapping historical periods—they all plot experience as co-ordinates upon the same two axes, space and time. The fulfillment of time in narrative—the plot—occurs in these overlapping spaces: in Freud's nomenclature, the repressed unconscious, the compulsion to repeat, and the death drive; in Frye's terminology, the Edenic birth place, the nocturnal world, the restored society; in Roman Catholic theology, the various spaces of the phases of purgation—contrition, confession, restitution. Desire moves the hero through these spaces and the important co-ordinates of all three discourses crystallize experiences of transformation and movement: sixteenth-century Spain articulated as *maravilla* what Freud would call the "uncanny," which is not unlike the miraculous moment of grace leading to contrition and starting the process of purgation that results in the reincorporation of the sinner into the body of Christ.

I

At the end of the twenty-eighth chapter of Part I of *Don Quijote*, a recently introduced character, Dorotea, recounts her story to an audience of seemingly sympathetic men. She tries to make sense of why, in spite of her attempts to act with integrity, she has been subject to repeated visitations of sexual violation. She conjectures, "Pero como suele decirse que un mal llama a otro, y que el fin de una desgracia suele ser principio de otra mayor, así me sucedió a mí" (I.xxviii.355; "But as they say, one misfortune attracts another, and the end of one disgrace tends to be the beginning of the next").[1] The reference to a colloquial saying brings together the main part of her narrative about how she was aggressively pursued, deceived, and then discarded by don Fernando, with the rest of the story—the explanation of how the servant, in whom she confides and who accompanies her in her escape from her parents, attempts to rape her.[2] The same happens when the cowboy, whom she goes to work for after throwing the servant off of a cliff, sees through her disguise as a boy, and tries to rape her.[3] But by bringing up the aphorism, Dorotea also signals her understanding of how trauma works. Her manner of describing the events has an air of inevitability: one misfortune or, a more literal translation of the Spanish, one "bad," attracts another. There is no break between one disgrace and the next—the end of one event begets another. Dorotea captures the sense of the repetition of cycles of sexual violence, the way in which the victim is cast over and over into the same role.

Dorotea is not a pushover: she runs away from her parents and after don Fernando to give him a piece of her mind and persuades him to honour those marital vows he made privately; she pushes the servant off a cliff; and, as she puts its, finding no precipice from which to hurl the cowboy, she does the next best thing, which is to flee from him. While Dorotea clearly shows her audience that she has not been vanquished by the aggressions of her male suitors, she also recognizes her abject situation. She seems to intuit that she is being pressed to play a role in a story that has already been written for her.

In his essay on the "uncanny," or "unheimlich," published in 1919, a year before *Beyond the Pleasure Principle*, Freud remarks upon a dreamlike experience in his own life, prefiguring the "compulsion to repeat," the central pathology of the 1920 text.

> As I was walking, one hot summer afternoon, through the deserted streets of a provincial town in Italy which was unknown to me, I found myself in a quarter of whose character I could not long remain in doubt. Nothing but painted women were to be seen at the windows of the small houses, and I

> hastened to leave the narrow street at the next turning. But after having wandered about for a time without enquiring my way, I suddenly found myself back in the same street, where my presence was now beginning to excite attention. I hurried away once more, only to arrive by another detour at the same place yet a third time. (Freud, "Uncanny" 237)

The innocuously "uncanny" quality of the experience—this mysterious, perplexing, and ultimately unsettling sensation—develops into the agony of the "compulsion to repeat." This phenomenon explains not only the haunting repetition of nightmares, but also the recurrent dramatization in real life of painful memories, "cases where the subject appears to have a *passive experience,* over which he has no influence, but in which he meets with a repetition of the same fatality" (Freud, *Reader* 604). Freud describes the "woman who married three successive husbands each of whom fell ill soon afterwards" as an example of this kind of repetition (*Reader* 604–05). Thus, Freud's example of walking down the street of prostitutes three times, furnished a year earlier as an example of the uncanny, becomes easily resolvable under the category of the daemon of the compulsion to repeat. The seemingly "passive experience" betrays a compulsion of the mind.

Dorotea acknowledges that there is a script—a demonically repetitive story created and reified by a hostile other's desire. The only thing that can stop it, she explains, will be either divine intervention in this life or death. Only "the sky," as she euphemizes God, can stop the authorial hand of aggressive desire and rewrite a new narrative. She concludes her story: "no hallé derrumbadero ni barranco de donde despeñar y despenar al amo, como le hallé para el criado, y así, tuve por menor inconveniente dejalle y asconderme de nuevo entre estas asperezas que probar con él mis fuerzas o mis disculpas" (I.xxviii.355; "I did not find a *precipice* nor a *cliff* from which to *punish* or *fling* the cowboy, as I had found for the servant"). She describes how she did the second best thing, which was to run away into the wilderness, and continues:

Digo, pues, que me torné a emboscar y a buscar donde sin empedimento alguno pudiese con suspiros y lágrimas rogar al cielo se duela de mi desventura y me dé industria y favor para salir della, o para dejar la vida entre estas soledades, sin que quede memoria desta triste, que tan sin culpa suya habrá dado materia para que de ella se hable y murmure en la suya y en las ajenas tierras. (I.xxviii.355; I say, then, that I went back to hiding myself in the forest and looking for where one could, without impediment, pray to the sky with sighs and tears of my misadventures and receive the knowledge and the help to escape from them. Or, if not, to end my life in this desolation, without leaving behind a memory of this sad woman, who without meaning to, has given cause for gossip at home and in foreign lands.)

In her linguistic choices, Dorotea captures the sense of chaos implicit in her dramatic situation through her play with words, namely through repetition and doubling. She makes extravagant use of synonyms and homonyms: in the original Spanish, her repetition of cliff and precipice in "I did not find a precipice nor a cliff" is redundant: "No hallé derrumbadero ni barranco" (I.xxviii.355). Following, she alludes to this confusion through her use of homonyms: "fling the cowboy and punish him" is "despeñar and despenar"; "Hiding myself in the forest" and "looking for" is "emboscar y...buscar" (I.xxviii.355). This conspicuous linguistic coupling of homonyms and synonyms is mirrored in the conceptual coupling with which the passage ends: she will pray with "tears" and "sighs," two signs of suffering, to receive both "knowledge" and "favour," two divine gifts. Or, as an alternative to the outcome of "favour" and "knowledge," she asks to finish her life in the obscurity of the wilderness.

We get the sense, then, of Dorotea's grasp—both consciously and unconsciously—of the tremendous force behind the doubling and repetition of experience. The image of Dorotea hiding in the dark of the forest echoes the beginning of the story, as she tells it, in which she describes herself completely shrouded from the gaze of a male suitor and sealed up in her parent's hacienda.[4] When the barber, the priest, and Cardenio spy on Dorotea, she is hiding away in the wilderness, washing her feet by a river; she attempts to run away and they force her to stay, echoing don Fernando's invasion of her bed chamber, and in her flight, the more recent sexual assaults by the servant and the cowboy. There are even intertextual repetitions: Dorotea's description of her exquisite imprisonment in her parents' estate powerfully alludes to Adam and Eve's divinely sanctioned incarceration in Eden. Cervantes seems to deliberately reproduce spaces of "enclosure," which are precarious sanctuaries, and then express their violation. The text establishes a dialectic between protected spaces and their transformation into infernal spaces. However, he also demonstrates the reverse in the translation of scenes of potential violence into the opposite, a sanctuary. Therefore, we see the curate, the barber, and the priest spy upon Dorotea in a sexually-charged setting, which turns into a place of peaceful meeting and reconciliation; the threesome meeting her at the river recalls the conventional situation in medieval Spanish lyric of the lover meeting his mistress at the river (Boyle 137), and heightening the already high pitch of sexual tension. The encounter at the inn, traditionally a space of transgression and violence, becomes the space for a sublime reconciliation and social restitution.

Dorotea concludes the story of her misfortunes, leaving the audience on the edge of knowing, caught in that moment of suspense between the conclusion of one cycle of trauma and, as Dorotea has foreshadowed, the beginning of another. To repeat her explanation of how trauma repeats itself: "one misfortune attracts another, and the end of one disgrace tends to be the beginning of the next" (I.xxviii.355). The question, at this juncture, is what will repeat itself, what will the good priest, the kind-hearted barber, and the chivalrous Cardenio—all of whom have promised to protect and help Dorotea—allow to repeat?

The answer is: absolutely everything. Right after she finishes her story, the priest enlists Dorotea in a scheme to lure don Quijote back to his home and to force the deluded Caballero de la Triste Figura to assume his previous identity as an hidalgo from a town in La Mancha, which even the author would prefer to forget. They want to end his wandering in fantasies and return him to his impoverished reality. The priest enlists

Dorotea because she has shown herself to be such a wonderful storyteller. Dorotea's story translates the substance of her own narrative from one genre to another, from romance to chivalry. It is, in its own right, an extremely comic episode in the story; at the same time, it is, if we consider it carefully, something that should make us uneasy.

The episode is a complete parody of what has preceded it. As in Dorotea's "true" story, there are strange linguistic footprints that obliquely suggest the traumatic doubling of Dorotea's true story of sexual violence. We see this in many details, ranging from the name that the curate chooses for Dorotea, "Princessa MicoMicona" with its repetition of "Mico" to Dorotea's calling Spain, the Spains: "las españas" (I.xxx.370). We even see this in the fact that the characters we know under one identity are now using flimsy disguises, which fall off, to double their identities and tell a story that mimics the "authentic" story of Dorotea's life. Dorotea throws herself at don Quijote's feet seeking the same kind of help from the crazy knight errant that she just received from Cardenio, a man who in his own words appears exactly like don Quijote: "Soy el desdichado Cardenio... roto, desnudo, falto de juicio, pues no lo tengo sino cuando al cielo se le antoja dármele por algún breve espacio" (I.xxix.357; "I am the unfortunate Cardenio...as you see me, broken, naked, without human comfort, devoid of reason, because I only have it when the heavens decide to give it to me for a moment"). Cardenio offers his help to Dorotea as part of that same soliloquy as a "gentleman and a Christian" (I.xxix.357) just as don Quijote now offers to help her only if it does not compromise his first allegiance to king, country, and lady, and will accomplish this with the help of God and his strength, "con la ayuda de Dios y la de mi brazo" (I.xxix.362). This parodic doubling immediately raises the question: what use is the help of Cardenio and was it even real? And speaking of identifying what is real or not, when Cardenio offers his help to Dorotea, he offers it based on the premise that she has told the truth: "siendo verdad, como creo que lo es, lo que aquí habéis contado" (I.xxix.357; "being true, as I think it is, the story you have told"). But at the end of the play-acting, the priest praises Dorotea for her ability to fabricate a story that was brief and closely resembled a chivalric tale. Dorotea's facility for fabricating should at the very least make her audience uneasy, particularly after she prefaces it to her audience as "my true story," *mi verdadera historia* (I.xxx.370). But it does not.

The episode goes further by parodying one of the most important structural elements of the genre of comedy to which Dorotea's "authentic" story belongs: the way in which people are recognized and identified. Calling on the convention in romance and comedy of recognizing a hero through a special birthmark, Dorotea recalls that her father, the great magician, predicted that her saviour would have a mole with some bristly hairs on it located on his left shoulder. Don Quijote, taking this at face value, goes to undress, but Sancho stops him and reminds don Quijote that he has a birthmark like that halfway down his spine. Dorotea replies that that is good enough since it is all of the same flesh. Thus, the parody absolutely empties this convention of the genre of any meaning because, according to generic convention, the object of recognition need be specific.

Similarly, the parodic play-acting questions another convention of the genre: the discovery of one's true identity. At a crucial juncture, Dorotea almost causes the whole spoof to collapse when she forgets the name that the curate assigned her. In another hilarious episode, the curate supplies the name, saying, "No es maravilla, señora mia, que la vuestra grandeza se turbe y empache contando sus desventuras; que ellas suelen ser tales, que muchas veces quitan la memoria a los que maltratan, de tal manera, que aun de sus mesmos nombres no se les acuerda, como han hecho con vuestra gran señoría, que se ha olvidado que se llama la princesa Micomicón" (I.xxx.369–70; "It's no wonder, my lady, that your majesty should become disturbed and embarrassed by telling the story of your travails; because they seem to be the kind of hardships that many times take away all memory from those they mistreat, that they even forget their own names, as has happened to you"). In romance, it is conventional for a peasant of impeccable virtue to discover that she is actually a princess. But, in this parody of romance, Dorotea is assigned the role of princess and cannot even remember her name. Harsh trials and tribulations bring about the recovery of one's true identity in romance. In this comedic parody, however, the curate acknowledges the truth that embarrassing and distressing realities eat away at the memory and cause the collapse of identity.

What I wrote about the company of men, who promise to protect her but actually subject her to repetition, is both true and untrue. It is true in that parts of her story are duplicated, distorted, translated into the genre of chivalric romance. It is also true that the very dramatic structures with which her own story is plotted are at best poked fun at and at worst, problematize how we read Dorotea and her story, possibly emptying it of any meaning or moral interest. The ability to fabricate a convincing story extemporaneously, the *discreción* for which she is roundly applauded, makes suspect her veracity earlier. And perhaps more disturbing is the resemblance of the futile don Quijote to Cardenio, the man who has vowed to help her. If that does not cause us to despair, then the parody of the providence by which Dorotea runs into Cardenio in the wilderness with the farcical encounter with don Quijote, should. The coup de grace would seem to be in Dorotea's ridicule of "legitimate marriage" in promising herself to don Quijote as part of her father, the magician's prophesy.

Finally, Dorotea creates a giant as part of the fantasy to entrap don Quijote. Dorotea personifies her trauma with don Fernando and all of the subsequent sexual assaults in the figure of giant, Pandafilando of the Creepy Face, who is so named, she says, "llamado Pandafilando de la Fosca Vista, porque es cosa averiguada que, aunque tiene los ojos en su lugar y derechos siempre mira al revés, como si fuese bizco, y esto lo hace él de maligno y por poner miedo y espanto a los que mira" (I.xxx.370; "as a matter of corroborated fact, because even though he has eyes in their rightful place and straight on his face, they look backwards, as if he were cross-eyed. And he does this because he is malicious and he wants to instill fear and terror in all those who look at him"). Pandafilando duplicates and magnifies don Fernando's bad traits and he clarifies and translates into metaphor the traumatic substance of Dorotea's encounters with don Fernando: he has eyes that should look forward because they are positioned in "their rightful place." What particularly irks Dorotea, and she emphasizes this, is that they function contrary to nature in spite of their appearance of being "straight on his face." In other words, what dismays her about being tricked by don Fernando is that, by all appearances, he seems to be all the right things (noble and a marrying man), but is in fact a man of no integrity in spite of his nobility. Furthermore, emulating the repeated episodes of attempted violation following her initial encounter with don Fernando, her experiences always draw her backward. And they do this precisely because the subject (don Fernando or the giant) will not properly look at her. Dorotea explains that the giant has demanded her hand in marriage in spite of the disparity of class; she a princess and he something clearly lower, thereby inverting her situation with don Fernando. His eyes look every which way except at her. He cannot, in fact, recognize the humanity of whomever he faces, but only fill them with fear and terror. Thus, the giant functions as the conspicuous metaphor for everything we have been talking about with regards to trauma: by its very nature, it draws one backward, paralyzes, and terrifies precisely because the initial traumatic situation is one in which she is not humanized fully. Sancho Panza exclaims on the stupefying confusion resulting from this situation: "Todo puede ser...pero no hay de qué maravillarse, que un diablo parece a otro" (I.xxxi.379; "Everything is possible... there is no reason to marvel, that one devil looks just like another"). The phrase "Everything is possible" (echoed again sixty-some pages later by the priest) suggests an openness not only to doubling, but also to the possibility for change and transformation.

This doubling, mirroring, and parodying of the same experiences in the tale of Dorotea corresponds with Freud's exposition of textual moments of repetition. For Freud, this particular reiteration of trauma is the "most moving poetic picture of a fate such as this" (Freud, *Reader* 605). In Torquato Tasso's *Gerusalemme Liberata*, the hero, Tancred, "unwittingly kills his beloved Clorinda in a duel while she is disguised in the army of an enemy knight" (Freud, *Reader* 605). After his recognition of killing the one he loves and following her burial, "he makes his way into a strange magic forest which strikes the Crusaders' army with terror. He slashes with his sword at a tall tree; but blood streams from the cut and the voice of Clorinda, whose soul is imprisoned in the tree, is heard complaining that he has wounded his beloved once again" (Freud, *Reader* 605). Here, repetition depends upon disguise: the beloved comes in the guise of the enemy in one scene and then as something completely outside the realm of human intimacies—the tree. The narrative thematizes the dispersal of identity into different, unrecognizable manifestations, similar to Dorotea's story of Pandafilando the Giant. The beloved other takes on multiple forms at different points in time. This unrecognizability—and the suggestion of the difficulty in identifying the subjectivity of the other—also becomes linked in this story to confusion of affect. Both fateful wounds occur during heightened emotional states. In the duel, the primitive urge of fight or flight fuels the hatred behind the seemingly blind crime. In the second scene, Freud describes the army's terror in the "magic forest." This magic forest is the place of fantasy and dream, experienced at the emotional level by "terror." The metaphorical second generation of Clorinda—her iteration as a tree, bound in silence by the untellable "nonstories" it has inherited—remains equally susceptible to the "fate" of violent aggression as the previous generation.

From Freud's examples, we can begin to map out the spatial and temporal landscape of the "compulsion to repeat." In both examples, the behaviour occurs under a "spell." In his essay "The Uncanny," Freud describes a "deserted," foreign town in the dead of summer; we imagine him worn down by the heat, at liberty because the Italians are taking their siesta; the torpor and desolation of the scene characterizes it as a dreamscape. In the "poetic example," Freud explicitly describes a "magical," liminal space in the "forest," and the heightened emotion of terror puts it beyond the realm of normal experience. Both examples articulate the "compulsion to repeat" in a spatial framework, involving movement from a "normal" space to an exceptional space.

This "spatial" movement also describes the experience of the various parts of the mental topography. Whether we label them as the "unconscious," the "conscious," the "ego," the "repressed unconscious," we are clearly dealing with different imaginary locations in the psyche: from the dreamy vulnerability and the unguarded manifestations of fantasy in Freud's *détours* to the various guises of Clorinda's subjectivity, as enemy knight and victim tree. Furthermore, Freud's division into the self that keeps taking him down the same street and the one that is astonished and embarrassed describes fragmentation; his circular walks spatially articulate that fragmentation.

By its nature, the subject experiences the "compulsion to repeat" as a temporal phenomenon. In retrospect, Freud becomes unsettled by the "uncanny" quality of his returns to the *quartier infâme*, only after he has returned three times. Likewise, while Tancred may have felt remorse and guilt from his first "fateful" crime against his lover, the second iteration brings about the experience of terror in the nightmarish "magic" forest.

Northrop Frye plots the timeline of comedy and romance in similar literal and figurative spaces, characterized by parallel emotional experiences. Frye appropriates the "myth" of Christianity, that is, the larger cosmological and theological narrative of Christ's incarnation, his descent into the underworld (the Harrowing of Hell), his ascension to the world (the resurrection) and revelation, and finally his return to heaven, as being the paradigm for romance and comedy. This Christian paradigm suggests the major categories of experience in romance and comedy: descent into an underworld whether through socioeconomic decline (Frye 119) or a psychological and spiritual plunge (Frye 66–67) into a dream-like space in which the narrative movement either elevates the hero through the realization of desire or plunges him into an anguished, nightmarish state (Frye 67). The hero descends into a nocturnal world and returns to an idyllic world (Frye 69); this parallels humanity's fall from Eden into reality and the return to Eden (Frye 111–12). Travel from one space to another is coupled with a change of identity (Frye 157), and these transformations of self-presentation can take place in a metonymic fashion through the abundant disguises and costume changes to which we are accustomed in romance and comedy (Frye 88, 122). In the end, the besieged hero must succeed in rescuing his or her original identity (Frye 169).

Dorotea narrates a story that moves her through these spaces, in the beginning only in the doubling spaces of the "compulsion to repeat," later through the full trajectory of Frye's cosmos. Initially, she describes a claustrophobic sanctuary, a space startling similar to Eden. Her parents allow her to rule the household, controlling the finances, the estate, and the servants. However, she pays for this by her image of perfection, an unblemished mirror for them: "Era el espejo en que se miraban...todos sus deseos" (I.xxviii.347; "I was the mirror in which they looked at themselves...all of their desires"). In the Eden of Genesis, the Creator bestows a conditional liberty upon the original couple, the terms of which are obedience to Him and reflecting the Creator without distortion. Similarly, Dorotea buys her "freedom" by being the perfect image of her creators. A breach thereof hurls her into the nocturnal world of *descensus* Frye maps out, which corresponds to the space of repetition named by Freud. The underworld, however, provides the opportunity for transformation. The enclosure of her parents' gaze leads ineluctably to the prison of male scrutiny and finally to the freedom of the inn where she reveals herself literally and metaphorically to the circle of her audience's eyes and ears. Part of the audience's *admiración* necessarily emerges out of the overlap of these enclosures, through a kind of repetition reminiscent of Tancred's re-encounters with Clorinda, producing awe, fear, and suspense. Apropos of Frye's spatial scheme for comedy and romance, the descent and ascent will occur in spaces that mirror each other—as in a dark mirror; I add that the contiguity through resemblance provides the "middle" term of the syllogism, allowing for a transformation. Thus, the Eden from which Dorotea descends is related to the underworld and the restored world to which she returns through space of the enclosure.

II

The complexity of the definition of *admirar*, the verb form of *admiración* stems from its paradox. According to the *Tesoro de la Lengua castellana o española*, the most influential dictionary of Cervantes's time, *admiración* "is to be moved and awed before something extraordinary, whose cause is ignored. In addition to other characteristics attributed to man is to admire. This causes inquiry, reflecting upon whatever comes to mind, until he discovers the truth. From here we can infer that the man who does not 'admire' anything, or pretends to know the cause of all things, or is so worldly that nothing moves him, these are the simple, the stupid, and the impaired" (Covarrubias 44).[5] The author sternly reproaches anybody who would reason to come up with an explanation. This is the reaction of a fool. Rather, there is a built-in dilatory reaction to knowing in *admiración*. It involves savouring the experience of the extraordinary and allowing that experience of the marvellous to impact the rational process, to inspire inquiry, reflection, and discovery of the truth, while still ignoring the "obvious" or "reasonable" causes. In this sense, Tancred remains under the compulsion to repeat because he does not allow an appropriate *admiración* to interrupt the duplication of violence. This is precisely what we see in the above encounter, this causal reaction between seeing something beautiful; being moved to astonishment and rapture; and then being moved to inquiry, a desire to know more. According to the *Tesoro*, *maravilla* (what I translate simply as "marvellous") is something that causes *admiración*. And *maravillarse* is synonymous with *admirarse*, meaning "es admirarse viendo los efectos e ignorando las causas" (Covarrubias 1242; "to see the effects and ignore the causes").

For Aristotle in the *Poetics*, wonder is the human response to three components of plot: (1) an unexpected reversal in the course of events, (2) a character's recognition, and (3) events that occur contrary to reason (Minsaas 147). The experience of wonder is meant to enhance the experience of fear and pity. Aristotle would not have regarded the kinds of marvellous improbabilities that arouse wonder in the romances and epics of the Renaissance as a superior kind. We saw above how in the tradition of romance and comedy, an unexpected reversal in the course of events often involves highly unlikely coincidences, and a character's recognition is often of equally spectacular truths. According to Kirsti Minsaas, wonder became particularly important to epic theory in the Renaissance, "regarded as the major element in the affective appeal of a work, working its effect severed from other emotions" (161).

In his discussion of *admiratio*, E.C. Riley points out another facet of the concept, asserting that "seventeenth century writers aimed to startle and impress their readers not only because this was pleasant, but in order to engage their attention and put them in a receptive frame of mind in which a moral lesson could be driven home, a universal truth conveyed... The methods used to stimulate one, however, sometimes suggested not so much a concentration on the reader as a positive assault, and they were indeed not unconnected with the militant techniques of the Jesuits" (91). I believe what Riley is alluding to in Jesuit practice is the use of *enargeia*. Marjorie Boyle describes it as "the rhetorical term for the representation of reality that evoked a physical—primarily visual—scene in all its line, texture, and color. It was a stylistic effect that appealed to the senses and so described the scene that the listener became a spectator" (6). In Loyola's *Spiritual Exercises*, immensely popular during Cervantes's life, the reader is called to imagine sections from the gospels from every possible perspective—literally all over the imaginary tableau—the woman touching Christ's robe, the onlooker watching the woman touch the robe, etc.—and then again, using all the senses: what does the robe feel like? What does the market place smell like? What noises do you hear? The idea is to call to life a text by working all the senses. Boyle continues, "This vivid pictorial description penetrated to the very emotions" (6).

In the final scene, we see masked strangers arrive at the inn, forcing Dorotea to cover her face and Cardenio to go into hiding behind a door. The atmosphere is one of high suspense. In response to the extreme hiddenness of identity, the obfuscation behind masks, disguises, closed doors, the young man employed to accompany the band of strangers confides in the priest. He wonders who these disguised people might be and what they are hiding. The priest responds with a comment worth more than all the earlier cues to the audience that they should feel *maravilla* and *admiración*: "Todo podría ser" (I.xxxvi.440; "Everything could be."). The openness of this suggests the posture of *admiración* as a response to the world that is undogmatic, to circumvent the process of ascribing cause and allow the improbable.

The resolution is nothing exceptional and proceeds according to the conventions of romance: disguises fall; the true identity of the characters is revealed; there is a great deal of conspicuous staring; and Cervantes meticulously describes the gazes of one lover pursuing the beloved—Dorotea and don Fernando, don Fernando and Luscinda, Luscinda and Cardenio, Cardenio and Luscinda, and, finally, don Fernando and Dorotea. Dorotea's traumatic repetition is finally interrupted in this enclosure. Dorotea has been telling and retelling the story; she has magnified the memory of don Fernando into the figure of the giant Pandafilando. But the resolution actually happens through an invisible structure obscured by the fireworks of the stock romance techniques. Dorotea tells her story once again, in front of a rapt audience. She persuades don Fernando to honour the vow that he made, in other words to acknowledge the sacramental nature of marriage after the intensity and "unreason" of his passion has caused him to disavow the reality of God's order. This occurs within the framework of the sacrament of a confession presided over by the priest and performed *for* don Fernando by Dorotea. It is a self-conscious, religious affirmation of the narrative structure of this sacrament and of the sacramental nature of storytelling performed for an audience. Dorotea's retelling of the story serves not only to entertain and give pleasure. The divine grace, which has given her the complex, exquisite understanding of her situation, also allows her to tell a story of herself—in effect, a public confession—which informs, horrifies, induces contrition, and finally brings about reconciliation between the discordant loves of all the players.

In past episodes, Cervantes sets the curate up as a master of ceremonies, the director of action. For example, in the first encounter with Dorotea, the curate is present; he calls the others to see; and his presence prevents Cardenio and the barber from being overwhelmed by their desire. His presence is also, most likely, what allows the scene to move from voyeurism, lust, and curiosity to wonder and awe: *maravilla* and *admiración*. Rather than having a situation in which the senses incite lust (as they have done in the notorious cases of don Fernando, the servant, and the cowboy) they produce a sensation of wonder. Likewise, the curate orchestrates the Princess Micomicona ruse, and thereby parodies the mechanisms that romance uses in its attempts to bring closure. In this final scene, the curate helps to bring about a spiritual conclusion by allowing the endless possibilities of the *maravilloso* to occur within the sacrament of confession: again, as he marvels aloud, "Todo podría ser." There is no limit on what is to be discussed, nor even a cap put on the intensity of emotion that the participants, the audience, and we are to feel.

Specifically, the curate presides over the particular kind of confession popularized by the Jesuits after the council of Trent: the "general confession" (Maher 184). The Society of Jesus's *Formula of the Institute*, approved by Pope Julius III in 1550, described the goal of the Society as "the spiritual consolation of Christ's faithful through hearing confessions" (Maher 184). In contrast with the annual confession, which was prescribed by the Fourth Lateran Council (1215), in the general confession "the priest hearing the confession placed a greater emphasis on the intention and general trends of a person's sinful behaviour rather than on specific sins... the penitent reviewed sinful patterns in his or her life and sought counselling on how to eradicate habits that manifested themselves in sinful behaviour" (Maher 185). Before the confession, the priest exhorted the penitent to closely examine his or her conscience, to visit the Jungian dark shadow of the soul, in order to fully comprehend the enormity of one's inner malice. Loyola writes in his *Spiritual Exercises*, "to make [a general confession] brings...profit and merit, because of the...sorrow experienced at present for all the sins and evil deeds of one's entire life. During these Spiritual Exercises one reaches a deeper interior understanding of the reality and malice of one's sins than when one is not so concentrated on interior concerns. In this way, coming to know and grieve for the sins more deeply during this time, one will profit and merit more than was the case on earlier occasions" (Maher 192). Only through this emotional experience of one's sins is it possible for the penitent to move past them and receive consolation from God. "For Ignatius...no spiritual advancement could occur without removing sinful patterns" (Maher 200). Those sinful patterns could only be removed once a narrative had been made, a pattern given to the list of wrong actions. They need to be emotionally, viscerally, palpably re-experienced.

In *Don Quijote*, then, the stock situations of comedy and romance induce *admiración*, but there seems to be a superior purpose for the wonder that accompanies those situations presided over by the priest. In the final scene, the confessional structure offers Cervantes a powerful site to show the marvellous at work. Perhaps with more force than ever in Counter-Reformation Spain, the sacraments were the locus, par excellence, for the manifestation of God's grace. As the Protestant movements furthered their emphasis on a personal, direct experience of God through reading His Holy Scripture, Catholic Spain stressed the necessity of ecclesial mediation between God and the laity. The force of papal authority and the majesty of the Spanish crown give credence to the fact—not the idea—that properly administered, the marvellous may occur through the sacraments: "The Catholic Church, at the Council of Trent, affirmed that the seven sacraments existed as special actions in which participating persons could avail themselves of God's saving grace. The Jesuits agreed fully with official Church teaching that only by means of the sacrament of confession was unity restored between God and the sinner seeking forgiveness" (Maher 188).

In Dorotea's beautiful speech at the end of chapter 36, she reconciles don Fernando to his duty as a husband and a Christian. She exhorts him to give meaning to the sacrament of marriage and to renounce his sins. In a sense, then, Dorotea functions as his confessor, presided over by the priest. Or perhaps more accurately, she simply creates the narrative, the reasons, the enumeration of his wrongs, with feeling and reason, to facilitate his contrition. But there is already the outer frame of the priest who, in the end, compels don Fernando to honour his debt to God. The priest presides over the displays of emotion, Luscinda and Dorotea's copious tears of grief and desperation, and the audience's cries of *admiración*. I refer you to the extravagant sixteenth-century crying rituals in Spain on Good Friday. The production of copious tears would have been considered in and of itself a source of consolation and a sign of participating in the miracle of Christ's passion.[6]

The confessional enclosure at the inn unites three temporal processes—contrition, confession, and restitution. In addition, this particular manifestation of the space of enclosure figures as the last in aeries of such enclosures corresponding to the lost Edenic world, the underworld, and the restored world. In accordance with the goals of Ignatian-inspired confession, don Fernando's emotional response to the displays of Luscinda and Dorotea brings about the completion of purgation. This temporally situated resolution transforms the world; we witness the metamorphosis of the underworld into the resurrected and redeemed world before our eyes. The confessional enclosure allows the interruption of the compulsion to repeat by giving don Fernando the opportunity to see the patterns of repetition through the depiction of the underworld that his misguided desire has created.

The convergence here of a stock romance climax of recognition, conversion, reconciliation and resolution with the sacrament of confession in this scene outlines what they have in common. It maps the newly revived and recreated sacrament—the general confession—onto an older paradigm, comedy and romance. In doing so, Cervantes solves a psychoanalytic impasse inherent in both the nature of trauma and of comedy and romance. The structure of trauma—like the structure of romance and comedy—seeks to give meaning to the repetitive middle part of the narrative by constantly searching for lost origins, for a beginning that will give meaning to the endless wandering of the middle, the insufferable repetitions, the painful and violent doublings of the initial, perhaps lost memory. For the entire first half of Dorotea's interpolated story, her language reveals that she has started to make sense of this tendency of traumatic experience. She is forced to wander through endless repetitions, searching for her initial identity as obedient and cared-for daughter by virtue of being both a victim of sexual violence *and* a character in a comedy.

However, she can never truly return to her identity as virgin daughter, which is why she runs away in the first place. In her former role, she was entombed by her parents' desires: she can serve them and be their "mirror" only by adhering to their immaculate standards by meticulously conforming her will to their own. Cervantes plays with the popular notion of *admiración*—an obsessive literary topos of the sixteenth and early seventeenth centuries—and expands the possibilities for it from merely enhancing the pleasure of the storytelling for the audience to actually effecting a spiritual renewal. He does this by bringing theology to bear on literary theory. The revivified importance of confession, with its newly forged relationship to storytelling, make it an important narrative structure to allow the resolution of trauma and to bring closure to the tale of Dorotea. The confessional enclosure interrupts temporal repetition and spatial doubling—at last resolving these in ascent from the underworld to a rehabilitated society of married lovers.

Notes

1. This and all translations of *Don Quijote* (*DQ*) that follow are my own.
2. Continuing from the previuos quote, Dorotea explains, "porque mi buen criado, hasta entonces fiel y seguro, así como me vio en esta soledad, incitado de su mesma bellaquería antes que de mi hermosura, quiso aprovecharse de la ocasión que, a su parecer, estos yermos le ofrecían, y, con poca vergüenza y menos temor de Dios ni respeto mío, me requirió amores" (I.xxviii.354–55; "because my good servant, who had been faithful until then, seeing me alone and moved more by his own wickedness than by my beauty, wanted to take advantage of the occasion which he believed this wasteland afforded. Shameless, with neither fear of God nor respect for me, he demanded my favours").
3. See *DQ*, I.xxviii.355: "mi amo vino en conocimiento de que yo no era varón, y nació en él el mesmo mal pensamiento que en mi criado." ("My master came to understand that I was not a boy and the same wicked feelings were born in him as in my servant.")

4. "Es, pues, el caso que, pasando mi vida en tantas ocupaciones y en un encerramiento tal, que al de un monasterio pudiera compararse, sin ser vista, a mi parecer, de otra persona alguna que de los criados de casa...y yo tan cubierta y recatada" (I.xxviii.347; "So it was that, having spent my life encloistered as completely as if I had been in a monastery, without having been seen by anybody but the servants of the house...so enshrouded and modest in my demeanour was I").

5. The original reads: "es pasmarse y espantarse de algún efeto que ve extraordinario, cuya causa inora. Entre otras propiedades es ser admirativo; y de aquí resulta el inquirir, escudriñar y discurrir cerca de lo que se le ofrece, hasta quietarse con el conocimiento de la verdad. De aquí se infiere que el hombre que no se admira de nada, o tiene conocimiento de las causas de todos los efetos...o es tan terrestre que en ninguna cosa repara; tales son los simples, estúpidos y mentecaptos."

6. In fifteenth- and sixteenth-century Spain, "emotional experiences were measures of the health of the soul, and religious weeping was evidence of the disposition of the heart toward God. Tears were especially important as signs of contrition.... Collective weeping was both a dramatic admission by townspeople that they had transgressed God's law and an appeal to God for mercy and forgiveness" (Christian 33).

Works Cited

Boyle, Marjorie O'Rourke. *Loyola's Acts: The Rhetoric of the Self*. Berkeley: University of California Press, 1997. Print.

Brooks, Peter. "Freud's Masterplot." *The Novel: An Anthology of Criticism and Theory 1900–2000*. Ed. Dorothy J. Hale. Malden, MA: Blackwell, 2006. Print.

Cervantes Saavedra, Miguel de. *Don Quijote de la Mancha*. Ed. John Jay Allen. Vol. 1. Madrid: Cátedra, 1994. Print.

Christian, William A. Jr. "Provoked Religious Weeping in Early Modern Spain." *Religion and Emotion: Approaches and Interpretations*. Ed. John Corrigan. Oxford: Oxford University Press, 2004. 33–50. Print.

Covarrubias Horozco, Sebastian de. *Tesora de la lengua castellana o española*. Ed. Ignacio Arellano y Rafael Zafra. Madrid: Centro para la Edición de los Clásicos Españoles, 2006. Print.

Freud, Sigmund. *The Freud Reader*. Ed. Peter Gay. New York: Norton, 1989. Print.

———. "The Uncanny." *The Standard Edition of the Complete Psychological Works of Sigmund Freud*. Eds. James Strachey and Anna Freud. Vol. 17. London: Hogarth Press, 1953. 217–56. Print.

Frye, Northrop. *La Escritura Profana: Un estudio sobre la estructura del romance*. Trans. Edison Simons. Barcelona: Monte Avila Editores, 1980. Print.

Fuchs, Barbara. *Romance*. New York: Routledge, 2004. Print.

Maher, Michael. "Confession and Consolation: The Society of Jesus and its Promotion of the General Confession." *Penitence in the Age of Reformations*. Ed. Katharine Jackson Lualdi and Anne T. Thayer. Aldershot, UK: Ashgate, 2000. 184–200. Print.

Minsaas, Kirsti. "Poetic Marvels: Aristotelian Wonder in Renaissance Poetics and Poetry." *Making Sense of Aristotle: Essays in Poetics*. Ed. Øivind Andersen and Jon Haarberg. London: Gerald Duckworth and Company, 2001. 145–71. Print.

Riley, E.C. *Cervantes's Theory of the Novel*. Oxford: Clarendon Press, 1962. Print.

9

SPENSER'S BAD ROMANCE

"First, Astonishments; Then, Consolations" in The Faerie Queene

JOSEPH RING

AT THE BEGINNING OF HIS CLASSIC STUDY of the sublime, Samuel Monk looks "in vain" for traces of interest in Longinus in sixteenth-century England that might have registered the appearance of his treatise *Peri Hypsos*, or *On the Sublime*, on the continent (18). Francesco Robortello published the *editio princeps* in Basel as early as 1554, and a printed Latin translation, by Domenico Pizzimenti, was published in Naples in 1566 (Weinberg, "Translations" 145–51). Yet while Spenser "knew the 'lofty style,'" Monk observes, "there is no hint that he or his circle had any interest in the conception of the sublime as Longinus discusses it" (18–19). Longinus's treatise failed to capture much attention even on the continent, where Aristotle's *Poetics* dominated the critical landscape, but it was not without influence. Intriguingly, Robortello was the first to publish not only *Peri Hypsos*, but also commentaries on the increasingly ascendant *Poetics*, in 1548. However theoretically discrete, *Peri Hypsos* and the *Poetics* are nevertheless further bound by a shared valorization of the central passion in Renaissance literary theory—namely, wonder or astonishment. For example, Francesco Patrizi, a student of Robortello's and the literary theorist in the period most under the spell of Longinus's treatise, attempts to demolish Aristotelian poetics insofar as it demands imitation and verisimilitude in literary works, in a never-published manuscript, *La deca ammirabile* (1587) (Weinberg, *History* 765–86). But he does so somewhat paradoxically by elevating wonder, an already essential element in Aristotle, to a supreme position. Alternatively, Boileau's *Traité du Sublime ou du Merveilleux dans le Discours Traduit du Grec de Longin* (1674), the translation of Longinus's *Peri Hypsos* most credited for the rising popularity of the sublime in the eighteenth century, acknowledges in its title an inherent connection between the earlier category of the marvellous, which comprises wonder and astonishment, and the sublime.[1] Although a Longinian tradition in this period "is as yet unborn" in England (Monk 19), the key terms that it shares with Aristotelian poetics of the marvellous open the possibility of affinities between the two, especially in a peripheral and belated English Renaissance literary culture unsystematic at best in applying continental theory.

If the inclusive "or" in Boileau's title articulates the sublime with the earlier tradition of the marvellous, troubling the conventional narrative of the sublime as an eighteenth-century invention *tout court*, early critics of the sublime were also wont to detect it in classical and Renaissance writers. Indeed, despite Monk's dismissal—and even perhaps one reason for it—Spenser was frequently deemed an exemplary poet of sublimity. Employing a critical vocabulary drawn from Longinus, readers praised him for lifting them to elevated states of enthusiasm and transport.[2] Writes John Hughes, eighteenth-century critic and Spenser's first editor, "Spenser abounds with such Thoughts as are truly sublime" (26). Citing Longinus's famous reading of a sublime passage in Euripides that describes Phaeton's chariot ride through the heavens, in which "the Soul of the Poet seems to mount the Chariot with him, and to share all his Dangers" (24), Hughes follows this precedent, already embedded in Longinus's treatise, for applying the sublime retroactively in his praise of Spenser. Thus Hughes judges Spenser's account of Duessa's chariot ride to the underworld in *The Faerie Queene* as commensurately sublime: "The Reader will find himself in a like manner transported throughout this whole Episode; which shews that it has in it the Force and Spirit of the most sublime Poetry" (24). Joseph Warton, another eighteenth-century critic, writes in the same vein, quoting selected stanzas that describe allegorical figures like Payne, Strife, Gealosie, Feare, Sorrow, and Shame: "Here all is in life and motion; here we behold the true Poet or Maker; this is creation; it is here, might we cry out to Spenser, it is here that you display to us, that you make us feel, the sure effects of genuine poetry, 'when carried away by enthusiasm and passion, you think you see what you describe, and you place it before the eyes of your hearers' (Longinus, *On the Sublime*, sec. 15)" (113). Edmund Burke also finds Spenser at moments to be sublime in his *Enquiry* on the sublime and beautiful, and some of the passages considered most sublime in Milton, for example, from the Sin and Death episode in *Paradise Lost*, trace directly back to Spenser.

Exulting in a transfer of "Force and Spirit" from poet to text to reader, these early evaluations of Spenser's epic romance as sublime were not mere anachronism. For *The Faerie Queene* not only achieves the central effect of the sublime in Longinus, that of "transport," according to early readers such as Hughes and Warton, but the poem in many respects also centres on the same elevated passion most associated with *ekstasis* in Longinus, namely astonishment (*ekplêxis*). Astonishment is the passion of the sublime *par excellence* both in Longinus and in its later prophets. Burke, for example, describes it as "the effect of the sublime in its highest degree" (53). Of course, insofar as it is also associated with the marvellous, astonishment in *The Faerie Queene* finds more immediately affiliation with chivalric romance, if not Aristotelian poetics. But by recasting the passion of astonishment both in embodied and in quasi-religious terms, Spenser's poem develops an early modern poetics of the sublime not by way of Longinus, but through the contested form of romance.[3]

I

Drawing a partly ironic comparison between Spenser's *The Faerie Queene* and the Italian epic romance tradition from which it springs, C.S. Lewis observes that Spenser is "hopelessly inferior" to his continental models when it comes to satisfying a taste for such things as "speed and gaiety" (305).[4] Yet from a different angle, the refinement and "briskness" of the Italians can be seen as mere gloss. Thus Lewis hastens to add, "If, on the other hand, you are a romantic, if your taste is more for Wonder than for wonders, if you demand of poetry high seriousness and an admission to worlds of sensation which prose cannot enter, then you will find it just as easy to turn the tables" (306). For although "Spenser and the Italians are equally full of marvels" and would sound alike were they presented "in a prose abstract," the resemblances between the two are as superficial and deceptive as the very marvels in Italian romance: "The marvels of Boiardo and Ariosto are a literary form of one of the oldest games in the world—the 'tall story,' the brag, the lie: they belong to the same world as the adventures of Baron Munchausen. The marvels of Spenser, quite apart from his explicit allegory, are always gravely imaginative" (Lewis 307).[5] The fault line Lewis draws here might be cast as a split between poetics and experience: whereas Italian romances traffic in an Aristotelian poetics of the marvellous that calls for plausible impossibilities and the "scandalous" use of paralogism or faulty reasoning, Spenser's poem elicits a deep psychology of wonder.[6] In Lewis's account, Spenser begins *The Faerie Queene* "like a man in a trance" (310), his real concern is not the "merely entertaining" (306), the stuff of fantastic romance adventure, but "the primitive or instinctive mind, with all its terrors and ecstasies" (312). Leaving aside the ultimate merits of his somewhat tongue-in-cheek comparison, I want to argue in this essay that Lewis puts his finger on a profound, if much overlooked, truth about *The Faerie Queene* when he places passional wonder at the core of the poem's aesthetic energies.

My own view is that moments of extreme wonder or astonishment in Spenser's poem do indeed mark a break from the marvellous. However, in contrast to Lewis, I suggest that these sublime episodes register a programmatic ambivalence toward, rather than an absolute difference from, the epic romance marvellous. Attention to this ambivalence will enable us to see astonishment in Spenser not only as an over-determined link between the categories of the marvellous and the sublime, but also as an aesthetic and hermeneutic middle space between the "darke conceit" of the poem's allegorical mode and its apocalyptic unveiling in the "great light" of revelation (Spenser 737).[7] Given the resurgence of interest in the categories of wonder and the marvellous over the past couple of decades, it is surprising how little remarked wonder in *The Faerie Queene* is in recent criticism.[8] However, if we shift categories a bit and recall the poem's reception among early critics of the sublime, we can see that Lewis's insight into wonder and even more extreme passions like terror and ecstasy in the poem was not new. Of course, not only readers of the poem but characters within *The Faerie Queene* meet with some form of wonder or astonishment—extreme states that range from a staggering overloading of sensation to an anaesthetized blankness—in nearly every canto of the poem.

Astonishment is also central to *The Faerie Queene* in a quite literal sense. For example, the Redcrosse Knight's astonishment from the wind of Orgoglio's errant club, which "all his sences stoond, that still he lay full low" (1.7.12), marks the precise middle of book 1 (Cheney 268–69).[9] And both alternate endings of book 3, in the 1590 and in the 1596 editions, enact scenes of astonishment. As the 1596 edition added books 4 through 6, what was the final moment of astonishment became the midway point of the poem. The 1590 edition ends with the statuefied bodies of Amoret and Scudamour ecstatically fused, "like two senceles stocks" (3.12.46). But this astonishment is replaced with another in the later edition: a shocked Britomart, "whose noble heart [is] stonisht sore" (3.12.44) when she returns from Busirane's vanished castle with Amoret, only to find Scudamour and her squire Glauce likewise vanished. By turning to several scenes of epic combat, I shall argue that this middle but extreme space of astonishment in *The Faerie Queene* often marks moments of "sublime blockage" (Hertz 54) that destabilize conventional boundaries between the marvellous and the verisimilar, antipodal imperatives within chivalric romance. Spenser's epic romance thus anticipates and antecedes the sublime as much as it recalls the discourse of the marvellous from its Italian predecessors.

In the preface to his English translation of a 1674 tract on Aristotle's *Poetics*, Thomas Rymer does not see the distinction Lewis draws between Spenser and the Italians, but rather "blame[s] the *Italians* for debauching *Spencer's* judgment" (168), having seduced him with their marvels. Spenser had "a *Genius for Heroick Poesie*" that rivalled Virgil's, "yet he rather suffer'd himself to be misled by *Ariosto*; with whom blindly rambling on *marvellous* Adventures, he makes no Conscience of *Probability*. All is fanciful and chimerical, without any uniformity, without any foundation in truth; his poem is perfect *Faery-land*. They who can love *Ariosto* will be ravish'd with *Spencer*, whilst men of juster thoughts lament that such great Wits have miscarried in their Travels for want of direction to set them in the right way" (167–68, emphasis original). The juster-thinking Rymer thus rues Spenser's wayward turn, punningly likening the poet's abandonment of epic for romance to Redcrosse's unfaithful forsaking of Una for Duessa ("without any uniformity, without any foundation in truth"). But to the contrary, Spenser in fact distances himself from the moral taint of the marvellous in naming the first marvel to appear in the poem Errour, whose "huge long taile" overspreading her den, yet "in knots and many boughtes upwound" (1.1.15), figures another kind of tale, the wandering, episodic structure of romance itself. Indeed, Redcrosse the knight errant having become "wrapt in *Errours* endlesse traine" (1.1.18), his amazement in response to the monster—which likewise finds geographic correspondence in the mazy "labyrinth" (1.1.11) of the Wandring Wood, the *selva oscura* of romance narrative—registers primarily disgust, as he looks on the brood devouring her to bursting self-destruction at the end of the encounter: "That detestable sight him much amazde" (1.1.26).

This is not to say, however, that Spenser rejects the marvellous entirely. For counterpart to the dark amazement at the revolting sight of Errour is the redemptive wonder that Una casts upon the "rude, misshapen, monstrous rablement" (1.6.8) that flock around her when she is found by the satyrs in canto 6 of book 1, even as she withholds herself from them: "The doubtfull Damzell dare not yet commit / Her single person to their barbarous truth, / But still twixt feare and hope amazd does sit" (1.6.11). The satyrs, in turn, "amazed" and "astonied" (1.6.9), are stirred to sympathy and adoration: "They in compassion of her tender youth, / And wonder of her beautie soveraine, / Are wonne with pitty and unwonted ruth" (1.6.11). Indeed, however idolatrous in their worship of Una, the satyrs at least recognize the supremacy of what has been termed the "Christian marvellous," perhaps the purest and most powerful formulation of which is Fidelia, in the House of Holiness, whose "heavenly documents," or teachings, "weaker wit of man could never reach" and "wonder was to heare" (1.10.19).[10] She possesses miraculous powers to kill and resurrect with words, to command the hasty sun to "stay" or turn back its course, to dismay great hosts of men, to part floods in two, and to throw mountains into the raging sea: "Almightie God her gave such powre, and puissance great" (1.10.20). Book 1 of the poem would thus seem to proceed teleologically from the allegorical darkness of Errour's cave to the revelatory light of Fidelia's disclosure, toward a Christianization of the marvellous. On "things which seeme most wonderful in our Scriptures" (449), Philippe de Mornay writes, "The Scriptures (say they) doe tell us things unpossible and uncredible, more lyke the fond fables of Poets, than the reportes of sound Histories....But when things that are unpossible to Creatures, are reported of GOD, whose power is infinite: although men doubt whether they were doone or noe; yet can they not deny but that hee was able to doe them" (456). Somewhat like the doubtful Una between fear and hope, or like the sun stopped in its course, astonishment in *The Faerie Queene* sits ambivalently between the marvellous and the sublime.

The very first occurrence of astonishment in the poem strikingly registers neither the conventional romance marvellous nor the Christian supernatural, but the violent shock of war: Redcrosse's encounter with the Saracen knight Sansfoy in mounted combat. As Victoria Kahn points out, Longinus recognized dramatization of literary combat, not just nature, as a source of sublimity (194). But if Aristotle's *Poetics* associates astonishment with epic and tragic *anagnorisis* or recognition, this opening moment of astonishment parodies both in its literalness.[11] Punning on the petrifactive quality of astonishment, the blockage results from sheer physical force, intensified by passional energies and military assemblages of horses and riders.

> *The knight of the Redcrosse when him he spide,*
> *Spurring so hote with rage dispiteous,*
> *Gan fairely couch his speare, and towards ride:*
> *Soon meete they both, both fell and furious,*
> *That daunted with their forces hideous,*
> *Their steeds do stagger, and amazed stand,*
> *And eke themselves too rudely rigorous,*
> *Astonied with the stroke of their owne hand,*
> *Do back rebut, and each to other yeeldeth land.*
>
> *As when two rams stird with ambitious pride,*
> *Fight for the rule of the rich fleeced flocke,*
> *Their horned fronts so fierce on either side*
> *Do meete, that with the terrour of the shocke*
> *Astonied both, stand sencelesse as a blocke,*
> *Forgetfull of the hanging victory:*
> *So stood these twaine, unmoved as a rocke,*
> *Both staring fierce, and holding idely*
> *The broken reliques of their former cruelty.* (1.2.15–16)

One distinction that critics have made between romance and epic is that whereas the former genre converts what at first appears to be the alien knight or other into a feudal ally, the latter turns the "same" into an "other" for the purposes of imperial conquest (Quilligan 44; Jameson 141). Yet here, temporarily at least, in this suspended middle space of astonishment, we have neither, or something in-between. Although Redcrosse graphically cleaves Sansfoy's head after they recover in the following stanzas, in this arresting and traumatic jostling, formally recapitulated by several caesural pauses in stanzas 15 and 16, the two become indistinguishable, both literally blocked, turned to stone by the shock of their collision.

Somewhat ironically included under the category of "Courage" (though oddly, not under "Astonishment") in Robert Albott's compilation *Englands Parnassus* (440–41), this moment is at once sublime and ridiculous: in the violent clash, both knights recoil, not only losing ground, but also momentarily forgetting their martial objectives. Astonishment simultaneously marks their failure to recognize each other as doubles and their profound identity. Of course, the allegorical significance within the poem as psychomachia is unmistakable, the faithless Redcrosse meeting Sansfoy having just abandoned Una. That is, his physical victory over Sansfoy is also his own moral defeat. In the wake of their collision, Redcrosse and Sansfoy stand "twaine" or as two, but in contradictory senses: as twins (united in the single "rocke" of astonishment), yet sundered and estranged from themselves (*OED* "twain," a. 2 and 3). This specular structure obtains on several further registers, in the mirroring between amazed steeds and astonished riders—which in a sense anticipates the simile of the rams—and between the two stanzas, tenor and vehicle of the epic simile. Astonishment is here a species of error, but if amazement in the Errour episode suggests the episodic wandering of romance, astonishment brings that wandering to an abrupt and traumatic halt.

This opening feat of arms, the first of what Lewis derisively calls Spenser's "reiterated single combats" (306), is unmistakably the very stuff of chivalric romance, wherein knights attempt to balance their public duties of winning glory through martial valour with their private obligations of courtly love. Consider, for example, Arthur's battle with Pellinore in book 1, chapter 23 of Thomas Malory's *Morte Darthur*, which might well have informed Spenser's simile: "thenne they wente to the batayl ageyne/ and so hurtled togyders lyke two rammes that eyther felle to the erthe." Moreover, scenes of battle astonishment are also standard in romance, wherein knights regularly get stunned by some heavy blow. Indeed, a joust between Orlando and the Saracen knight Gradasso in canto 41, stanzas 62–63 from John Harington's translation of *Orlando Furioso* (1591) could easily be placed next to Redcrosse and Sansfoy's encounter.

> *The weaker horse on which Orlando rode,*
> *Was brused so with this so fearfull shocke,*
> *As now he could no longer beare his lode,*
> *But sinking downe, lay senseless with the knocke.* (41.63)

Only Orlando's beleaguered horse, which he abandons "lying senseless like a stocke" (63), is astonished, but these are comparable moments. There are, however, distinctions to observe. For example, in the ensuing mêlée Gradasso discovers that he is unable to wound Orlando: "For God had made his skinne impenetrable" (68), or "charmed" (86). Additionally, Orlando's sword Balisard is fashioned by the sorceress Falerina, and Gradasso thinks himself invulnerable because he possesses Orlando's sword Durindana. In famous remarks on epic poetry, Thomas Hobbes mentions in disapproval those who "would have impenetrable armours, enchanted castles, invulnerable bodies, iron men, flying horses, and a thousand other such things, which are easily feigned by them that dare" (614). Of course, more than a few of these items furnish Spenser's romance, but at least in the collision between Redcrosse and Sansfoy, which is devoid of such enchantments, Spenser refuses the marvellous, or rather re-defines it in the experiential or passional terms of astonishment, as traumatic shock.

"And what els is vyolence, but a justling of two bodies together?" (239), Philippe de Mornay asks in the *Trueness of the Christian Religion* (1587). Mornay's question is pertinent here, for astonishment in this scene is largely to do with overwhelming physical force. Rider, horse, spurs, and couched spear combine to generate a powerful weapon, and the collision between the two vectors of energy steps up the violence all the more. And this maximum degree of violence in turn calls for proportional representation, delivered in grand terms, such as "hideous," "amazed," "rigorous," "astonied," "terrour," and "shocke." If the delayed pun on "rebut" in stanza 15 sets up the turn toward the rams in the next stanza, the uncontained martial force nonetheless resurfaces in the "terrour of the shocke" produced by the rams' butting horns. Possibly related to the Middle

Dutch *shokken*, meaning "to collide," the word "shock" was first adopted in English as a military term, and here specifically invokes an encounter between mounted warriors or jousters charging one another (*OED* "shock" sb. 3.1).

Yet the astonishment results not only from sheer physical force, but also from the warriors' equally heightened passions. Fittingly, the words "astun," "astony," "astonish," and "astound," of common origin, in the period carry both physical and psychological senses of the blow or strike (*OED* "astone," "astun," v.). The senseless, immobile, and anaesthetized state—a kind of stoical *apatheia*—that the shock induces in these two hotspurs ("unmoved as a rocke" suggests affective as well as physical paralysis) is interestingly the endpoint of an extreme movement of passions. Much as the horse and rider, irascible passions "stird" in these stanzas, like "dispiteous rage," fury, and "ambitious pride," assemble into a devastating weapon in service of concupiscent desire for the lady. But astonishment in this scene paradoxically seems at once an excessive overloading of sensations and a zero degree of emotion. The fierce staring of the knights, the fixed look that denotes astonishment, is intense and blank at the same time, "holding idely" aptly modifying not only their hands but also their frozen eyes, which (be)hold but fail fully to apprehend their objects. In his sonnet "To Sir Philip Sidney's Soul," included in the prefatory matter of Sidney's *An Apologie for Poetrie* (1595), Henry Constable belatedly laments, "I did not feel the grief I did sustain" on Sidney's death, which followed his wounding by musket shot at the battle of Zutphen in 1586: "The greater stroke astonisheth the more; / Astonishment takes from us sense of pain" (463).[12]

The collision not only knocks the combatants senseless, bringing them to a literal standstill, but also threatens prematurely to check the poem itself. In this respect, the epic simile of the rams, occasioned by the staggering blow of the joust, functions as a kind of poetic shock absorber or stimulus shield in order to displace this traumatic excess of astonishment. The simile that replays the collision thus attempts to make sense of the astonished knights' senselessness in order to avoid absolute stoppage.

Albeit violent, the image of fighting rams, vying for rule over "the rich fleeced flocke," naturalizes the battle between the two knights. The simile shifts registers, relocating human violence within the green world of pastoral romance. While the appearance of the word "shocke" jars this figurative retreat to the natural, it simply emphasizes *a fortiori* the need for the simile as a shielding or numbing agent. Indeed, when the two knights resume their fight, the function of armouring and the shield is emphasized, not only by breaches in armour, out of which flow "streames of purple bloud," as each seeks to "perce" through the other's "iron sides," but also by Sansfoy's belief that Redcrosse's shield is charmed, keeping his "body from the bitter fit" (1.2.7). Of course, Redcrosse's armour—yet another source of sublime identification—is charmed, insofar as it is, as Spenser explains in his prefatory "Letter to Raleigh," "the armour of a Christian man specified by Saint Paul" in his epistle to the Ephesians. The "broken reliques" that the two knights are left holding at the end of stanza 16 suggest the overall aestheticization of the martial encounter by the simile, even as the relics counter the anaesthetic forgetting. But the relics also figure a form of marvellous power that confers compensatory wholeness and potency. The phrase "broken reliques" is ironically and paradoxically redundant. For, on the one hand, relics already evoke fragmentary, broken body parts or remnants. And on the other hand, they also suggest protection for the body and contact with the divine. Once again, however, there is a hint of the ridiculous, not only in the image of dazed knights grasping their broken swords, but also in the dubious authenticity of relics generally in the period.

Although it resists the conventional enchantments of romance, the battle nevertheless produces a version of the marvellous through its "wondrous" force and passions. That is, the knights are astonished, but for readers also, the force of their collision is, if not astonishing, at least worthy of admiration. Moreover, the blow might have knocked the two knights senseless, but Spenser withstands the energies, appropriating and distributing them in order to galvanize his poetic labour. This shifting or even numbing effect that the simile achieves resembles what

Neil Hertz has called the "sublime turn" in Longinus's *On the Sublime*. As Hertz points out, Longinus is fascinated by literary passages involving extreme violence, risk, or near-annihilation whose passions transfer into or are taken over by poetic activity, such as a heroic simile in the *Iliad* that likens Hector attacking the Greeks to a storm that blasts a ship at sea, terrifying and nearly killing its sailors, or an ode by Sappho in which her passions for a lover render her speechless and threaten her with bodily and psychological dissolution. In these examples, "the turning away from near-annihilation, from being 'under death' to being out from under death…is, characteristically, the sublime turn…and it is rightly seen here as bound up with a transfer of power (or the simulation of such a transfer) from the threatening forces to the poetic activity itself" (Hertz 6). In this reversal, the poet endures the threat of overwhelming force or dissolution along with his or her heroes, but then heroically appropriates and masters it formally. Following the literal moment of "sublime blockage," Spenser's epic simile of the rams enacts this "movement of disintegration and figurative reconstitution" that Hertz tracks in Longinus's treatise (14).

A related scene of mounted combat, between Blandamour and Paridell at 4.2.15–16, which reworks the first martial meeting of Redcrosse and Sansfoy, develops this alternately disabling and enabling, threatening and armouring dialectic of astonishment in *The Faerie Queene*. Curiously, it is also included in Albott's *Englands Parnassus*, in this case under the heading "Astonishment" (462). These two scenes are strikingly linked not only because they contain the only two instances of the word "shocke" in the poem, but also because the words appear precisely three books apart (to the canto, stanza, and nearly the line).[13] In the latter encounter in book 4, "The Book of Friendship," the combatants are former friends rather than religious enemies. More immediately, Blandamour and Paridell are parodic doubles of Cambell and Triamond, whom they meet later in the same canto, and who conversely begin as enemies but emerge as friends. But in this doubling, like Redcrosse and Sansfoy, Blandamour and Paridell are both temporarily stunned by their collision. Once again, excessive passions and the horse and armoured rider assemblage channel powerful, "untamed" force into the spear. Yet the epic simile that follows shifts not into the green but surprisingly into the modern world, a present-day scene of naval warfare.

> *Their firie Steedes with so untamed forse*
> *Did beare them both to fell avenges end,*
> *That both their speares with pitilesse remorse*
> *Through shield and mayle, and haberieon did wend,*
> *And in their flesh a grisly passage rend,*
> *That with the furie of their owne affret,*
> *Each other horse and man to ground did send;*
> *Where lying still a while, both did forget*
> *The perilous present stownd, in which their lives were set.*
>
> *As when two warlike Brigandines at sea,*
> *With murderous weapons arm'd to cruell fight,*
> *Doe meete together on the watry lea,*
> *They stemme ech other with so fell despight,*
> *That with the shocke of their owne heedlesse might,*
> *Their wooden ribs are shaken nigh a sonder;*
> *They which from shore behold the dreadfull sight*
> *Of flashing fire, and heare the ordenance thonder,*
> *Do greatly stand amaz'd at such unwonted wonder.* (4.2.15–16)

This scene of astonishment, like the earlier, is also marked by doubling and by appropriation and dispossession. Both fight for the woman as trophy (in this case False Florimell), but temporarily forget the object of the battle in the wake of the collision. If previously the "dispiteous" rage of the rider flows into spurs and then horse, connecting affect to shock combat, here the weapon itself is charged with affect—"pitilesse remorse." Indeed, the spears are so overcharged with affect that they cancel altogether. For while the primary sense of "remorse" in this instance is "biting or cutting force," another available sense, "pity," is paradoxically conjured and dismissed by the adjective "pitilesse" (*OED* "remorse," sb. 3 and 6). As before, this moment of astonishment registers both the physical force of the exchange, the armour- and flesh-piercing trauma of the spear, and the passional dimension of the blow. The word "stownd" in stanza 15 primarily carries the sense of "a time of trial or pain," but it also suggests the knights' benumbed stupefaction and amazement (*OED* "stound," sb. 1.2a and b and 2).[14]

The turn to the epic simile here could signal either an escapist, anaesthetic forgetting, and repression of historical content—somewhat like the marvellous itself within traditional romance—or its shocking re-surfacing. Rather than shift to the green world in order to absorb the shock, however, the epic simile in this case intensifies the degree of violence by abruptly transporting the reader to a vaguely contemporary sea battle in the present tense. The naval battle not only magnifies the violence, but also breaches the anachronistic illusion of the chivalric romance, much as the word "shocke" disrupts the pastoral turn in the rams simile. Wonder alone registers the new or unfamiliar, but that the stemming brigantines at sea, accompanied by the thunder and fire of artillery, amaze the onshore beholders as an "*unwonted* wonder" intensifies this jolt of the present to the anachronistic fiction of romance.[15] Like the two knights, readers "forget / The perilous present stownd" of the narrative set within the poem, but are momentarily thrust back into their own present. If following their astonishment the knights "At length...both upstart... in amaze, / As men awaked rashly out of dreme" (4.2.17), what was the knights' dream, the epic simile, constitutes the readers' rash and amazed awakening to the present.

Readers are shocked into the present temporarily, as the solid ground of the battlefield turns "watry," and hence feel heightened rather than diminished threat, however imaginary. But they are quickly placed again at a distance from the action, safely onshore with the other spectators. However, the amazement and wonder of these observers *ab extra* put the violence of these encounters to question. On the one hand, the intensified firepower is once again a counterpart to the marvellous, generating in its beholders the admiration that has long been viewed as the governing passion of epic (Aristotle 24.1460a). Douglas Biow, for example, has explored connections in *Orlando Furioso* and in Renaissance culture more broadly between marvels and firearms (113–18). The distancing effect in the simile, which affords amazed viewers both access to and shelter from the fire and thunder of the naval shock, would seem to recall and condense two scenes in a famous passage from book 2 of Lucretius's *De rerum natura*, the first, in which a spectator watches a ship in peril from the protection of the shore, and the second, where the beholder witnesses a battlefield from a safe coign of vantage: "It is sweet, when on the great sea the winds trouble its waters, to behold from land another's deep distress; not that it is a pleasure and delight that any should be afflicted, but because it is sweet to see from what evils you are yourself exempt. It is sweet also to look upon the mighty struggles of war arrayed along the plains without sharing yourself in danger" (qtd. in Wasserman 293). Evidently with the Lucretius passage in mind, Hobbes remarks: "Nevertheless there is in it both joy and grief. For as there is novelty and remembrance of our own security present, which is delight; so is there also pity, which is grief. But the delight is so far predominant, that men usually are content in such a case to be spectators of the misery of their friends" (*Elements of Law* qtd. in Thorpe 1117). Although Hobbes rejects the exorbitancies of romance, he praises the effects of novelty insofar as admiration and curiosity at the new lead to scientific investigation (Thorpe 1117). More generally relevant to the social strife signified by this clash between former friends, the Lucretius passage identifies the security of the observer *ab extra* with the transcendent view enjoyed by the wise. Discussing the diversity of religious opinion, wherein scholars "be divided among themselves, having confused language like to the builders of Babel," one John Boys cites the Lucretius passage to affirm truth "guided by Gods spirit," translating the lines as they continue in *De rerum natura*: "'but it is a greater pleasure for the minde of man to be firmely setled in the certaintie of truth, and from thence to descry the manifold perturbations, errours, waverings and wanderings up and downe of other [sic] in the world.' Blessed is *Peter*, and blessed are all such, as *endevour to keepe the unitie of the spirit in the bond of peace* [Ephesians 4:3]*, confessing one Lord, one Faith, one Baptisme*" (43, emphasis original). The sublime turn of the brigantines simile offers a Longinian twist to the Lucretian spectacle, allowing readers at once to share in and to escape the danger.

On the other hand, aside from being an epic end in itself, the "unwonted wonder" of the spectators at the power of the ships does not really lead to anything, such as ethical action. They do not, for example, experience the catastrophe as tragedy, and pity its victims, who are, after all, pitiless themselves. Likewise, when the Squire of Dames shows up on the scene to intervene, he "first laide on those Ladies [the spectators, who include False Florimell, Duessa and Ate, "the mother of debate, / And all dissention" (4.1.19)] thousand blames, / That did not seeke t'appease their deadly hate, / But gazed on their harmes, not pittying their estate" (4.2.20). For that matter, neither does the temporary astonishment of the knights, who on coming to consciousness merely resume their battle, produce anything virtuous. Moreover, the forgetting of the stound is itself framed within another amnesia at the beginning of the conflict, the knights being "Forgetfull each to have bene ever others frend" (4.2.14). There are other signs to suggest a negative evaluation of the violence. However grand, the "forse" of the steeds and the "might" of the brigantines are respectively "untamed" and "heedless." By the same token, the "murderous weapons" of the brigantines imply a critique of firearms in warfare. Romance writers in general, for whom the gun posed particularly stark problems to their anachronistic fictions, tended to identify the use of the gun as opposed to the chivalric code.[16] The gun was frequently deemed a demonic invention and thus considered morally suspect in romance,[17] famously figured by Orlando's throwing Cimosco's gun into the North Sea in the Olimpia story, cursing it as an "*abominoso ordigno*," or abominable engine (*Orlando Furioso* 9.91 qtd. in Murrin 127).

II

In the violent astonishment of these scenes of epic combat Spenser inscribes a critique of the romance marvellous, but this shifting of the marvellous away from the supernatural into the realm of experiences that verge on the traumatic does not resolve the lingering question of legitimacy. For example, the martial collisions produce their own form of epic admiration, but Spenser also suggests that astonishment is a form of error. The tension between these valences of astonishment in the poem can be viewed within an unlikely background, the so-called Descensus Controversy, a long-running debate among English Protestants over an article in the Apostles' Creed that affirmed Christ's descent into Hell.[18] The conformist side understood Christ's descent as local, that is, as a literal visit by Christ's soul, while the Puritan side interpreted the descent figuratively, as Christ's suffering hell pains in his soul on the cross. More specifically, a series of exchanges between Bishop of Winchester Thomas Bilson and radical Puritan Henry Jacob on the question of Christ's suffering "hellish sorrowes," wherein astonishment became a significant bone of contention, offer a non-secular context for the Spenserian sublime.

In his *Treatise of the Sufferings and Victory of Christ* (1598), Jacob claims that at three places in Christ's life great horror of punishment "did so stonish and amaze and overwhelme his humane weakenes...For a man in such amazednes, doeth easilie on a suddaine become *forgetfull* of himselfe" (52–53).[19] According to Jacob, Christ could not "but be *affrighted, astonished, forgetfull, & all confounded* in his wholl humanity, both in all the powers of *his soule*, and senses of his bodye" (53–54, emphasis original). That Christ nevertheless did not sin despite his mind being "*astonished* at the furious violence of this unspeakeable horrour" (70), Jacob illustrates with a metaphorical experiment of two glasses, one filled with muddy water that settles at the bottom and the other with crystal clear water: "shake both these glasses, in the one the mudde ariseth straightway, and defileth all the water there: in the other, although you shake it never so much, yet the cleere water, though troubled likewise, remayneth still all cleere as christal: Even so if anie of us bee shaken and disquieted with anie trouble, our Muddy affections arising doe presentlie defile us all over: but Christ...being likewise shaken, hee remained still cleere from anie the least spott of sinne at all" (56). Thus shaken, Christ's "nature desiring and wishing suddenlie ease and rest, he mighte suddenlie utter somewhat, which els reason in him would have controuled: which quicklie it did agayne, we see in saying: *Yet not my will, but thine bee done*, as it were, suddenlie coming to him selfe agayne" (71). Christ's lapses do not have as a consequence his lost confidence in God, for those "who by some violence are striken into astonishment, or naturallie fall on sleepe" nevertheless retain their faith (72), since presumably they come to themselves or wake again. Being forgetful is not a sin, but nature's infirmity: "If a man in distresse fall a sleepe, and then lift not up his heart to God, he sinneth not, nor he that being amazed with some violent blowe on the head, calleth not upon God: because nature is oppressed, and can not doe that which hee would and should doe. Also in this man so astonished, or in him a sleepe, we can not saye, there is any lesse grace" (56–57). For Jacob, "Not only all Christs *paines* were meritorious, but even all his very *infirmities* also: his wearines, his hunger, his sleepe, and so his astonishment & amazednes... was exceeding meritorious in him and highly accepted with God" (*Defence* 128–29, emphasis original).

Jacob and Bilson argued not only the merits of astonishment, but also the degree and cause of Christ's astonishment. Citing Bilson that "both in the causes and effects [of amazedness and astonishment] there be divers degrees," Jacob avers that "in Christ both the one and the other was in the extreamest and most violent *degree* that might be. And therefore no marvaile though his Astonishment were far greater, then is to be seene in any man ells that ever was or shalbee [sic]" (*Defence* 128). Taking Jacob to task for inflating his argument with "a fardell of phrases, to express that *all the senses of his bodie, and al the powers of his soule were amazed, astonished, distempered, disturbed, distracted, forgetfull, overwhelmed, and all confounded*," Bilson provides in *Full Redemption* a definition of astonishment that, I would argue, anticipated later formulations by Bacon, Descartes, and Burke.

> As in feares and sorrowes there bee divers degrées; so are there likewise in astonishments. To be astonished is to joine feare with admiration, which draweth the minde so wholie to think of some special thing above our reach, that during the time we turne not our selves to anie other cogitation. Even as the eie, if it be bent intentivelie to behold anie thing, for that present it discerneth nothing else: So fareth it with the soule, if she wholie addict her selfe to thinke on anie matter, she is amused; if it bee more then she conceaveth, or more fearefull then she well indureth, she is amazed, or astonished; but not of necessitie so, that she looseth either sense or memorie; onlie for that time she converteth neither to anie other object. (293, emphasis original)

Bilson acknowledges that Christ experienced astonishment, but neither to the degree, nor for the cause that Jacob asserts: "this religious astonishment...might for a season suspend all other thoughtes in our Saviour, yet is there no neede it shoulde deprive him of understanding, sense or memorie" (293). Nevertheless, Bilson had in *Full Redemption* conceded: "It is true that a mightie feare may so affect a man for the time, that it shall hinder the sences from recovering themselves, and stop the faculties from informing one the other. But this must bee some suddaine object astonishing the heart; and so terrible that it suffereth us not presentlie to gather our wits together, and to consider of it" (120).[20]

Bilson's and Jacob's treatment of astonishment illuminates *The Faerie Queene* not because it resolves the contradiction between the shattering violence and the admiration that astonishment commands in epic combat, but because their argument recalls the contradiction, both defining and collapsing astonishment's polarities—infernal and divine, meritorious and unmeritorious. Jacob's hypothetical man who receives a violent blow on the head seems a particularly apt figure for Spenser's knights, who, to bring another fardel of phrases, are knocked out, forgetful, beside themselves, and shaken, as in the "wooden ribs" of the brigantines "shaken nigh a sonder." Redcrosse's repeated astonishments and re-collections point at once to his purification and defilement, and to his self-alienation and self-remembering, though it is often too muddy a task to distinguish between the two. The hellish association that the ordnance evokes in the brigantines simile is likewise oddly pertinent to the dispute over hell pains, and their ambiguous merit.

In a way, Bilson's own various definitions of astonishment best illustrate the difficulty of drawing distinctions among the "divers degrees" of astonishment. Under the heading "What astonishment is" in his *Survey of Christs sufferings*, Bilson returns to his running dispute with Jacob over the degree of Christ's astonishment in Mark 14.33, pointing out that the word *ekthambeisthai* "signifieth either admiration alone, or els a mixion thereof with some feare upon any suddaine or strange sight" (440). Citing the astonishments at the healing of the cripple by Peter and John in Acts 3.10ff and at Christ's transfiguration, Bilson notes that neither moment strikes people "with such great feare, that should take their senses from them," and that in the latter occasion the people explicitly run to Christ, *ekthambeisthai* thus importing "a sudden admiration sometimes without feare, and sometimes permixed with feare for the sight of some strange or unknowen thing" (441). In these instances, the word does not signify "any hellish paine, or confusion; but either admiration, or such sudden feare joined with some wondering, as a strange or unknowne sight breedeth; though we feare no hurt towards our selves" (441). Although Bilson insists on sharp distinctions here, his definitions paint astonishment as a passion that mixes with others. This last definition bears some resemblance to the albeit more intense situation of the amazed but safe spectators in Spenser's simile who gaze on the sea battle with "unwonted wonder." By contrast, however, the simile also includes the hellish pains of those caught up in the collision. Bilson rehashes this discussion later, under the expanded heading "What astonishment with feare is," again centring his argument on the word *ekthambeisthai*, which "signifieth either admiration alone, as I have formerly shewed, or feare mixed with some wondering. So that the word neither in the Scriptures, nor in any Grammar, signifieth your hellish astonishment for intolerable pains and torments, but suddenly to stand defixed, or somewhat afraid at an unwoonted sight" (468). Christ may have experienced "no such astonishment as [Jacob] dream[s] of" (468), but the controversy over this question helps to elucidate the astonishments *The Faerie Queene* dreams of in the wake of the marvellous, whose causes and effects are likewise diverse, and both meritorious and unmeritorious.

III

The exact midpoint of book 1, in canto 7, marks a decisive turning point in the poem with an astonishment whose merits are open to question: Redcrosse's first defeat by the giant Orgoglio. The defeat is paradoxically his first victory, since it ushers a Christian hero into the poem. Canto 7 opens with the knight, somewhat like those who experience Jacob's "meere naturall" shaking, "desiring and wishing suddenly ease and rest" (*Treatise* 71), though not from hellish pain, but out of sexual pleasure. "Disarmed all of yron-coted Plate" (1.7.2), Redcrosse drinks from the nymph-inhabited fountain by which he and Duessa recline, whereupon the narrator reports "his manly forces gan to faile" (1.7.6). This onset of infirmity immediately occasions the appearance of Orgoglio, who defeats Redcrosse both because he has drunk from the lethargic waters of the stream and because he surprises him, "Pourd out in loosnesse on the grassy grownd" (1.7.7), without his armour of faith. These two causes seem related, however; for it is almost as if, underneath his armour, Redcrosse is nothing but liquid. His armour serves as an external skeleton, and without it, Redcrosse pours out onto the ground like the waters of the fountain nymph. The water may feminize Redcrosse, causing his manly forces to fail, but his disarming also exposes his interior itself as fluid and feminine. Ironically at the nadir ("at the last") of this dissolution, Redcrosse is "astownd[ed]" by the sound of Orgoglio's loud bellowing: "That all the earth for terrour seemd to shake, / And trees did tremble" (1.7.7). For as this hardening intimates, Orgoglio—whose Italian name suggests pride—turns out to be something of a giant erection, a projection of Redcrosse's inflated sexual pride. Orgolio's genealogy—son of mother Earth and Aeolus—figures him as a personified earthquake, but "this monstrous masse of earthly slime, / Puft up with emptie wind, and fild with sinfull crime" (1.7.9) also evokes an erection, thought in the period to be caused by an influx of air into the penis.[21] It is thus somewhat ambiguous whether Redcrosse's hardening at Orgoglio's entrance follows a post-coital moment or is rather a kind of coitus interruptus.

Redcrosse's further astonishment and humiliation, when the wind from Orgoglio's errant blow overthrows him, "And all his sences stoond, that still he lay full low" (1.7.12), produces another phallic image in the ensuing simile.

> As when that divelish yron Engin wrought
> In deepest Hell, and framd by Furies skill,
> And ramd with bullet round, ordaind to kill,
> Conceiveth fire, the heavens it doth fill
> With thundering noyse, and all the ayre doth choke,
> That none can breath, nor see, nor heare at will,
> Through smouldry cloud of duskish stincking smoke,
> That th'onely breath him daunts, who hath escapt the stroke. (1.7.13)

As in the brigantines simile, this simile jolts the reader out of romance into a present-tense scene of modern warfare. The former transports the reader to Lucretian safety, while here even those who escape the stroke are daunted by the mere smoke or smell of the cannon. The virile, iron cannon presents at once an image of Redcrosse's erection and a transmuted counterpart, a militant opposite to the liquefied venal figure spilled out in the grass.[22] Moreover, the cannon also seems at once phallus and male womb ("ramd with bullet round," "Conceiveth fire"), thus free from the taint of woman. The iron ball rammed into the barrel of the cannon replaces Redcrosse's fluid interior. And manufactured in hell, the cannon is "framd" rather than born of woman.

Along these lines, the cannon might be seen not so much as a figure for orgasm as the latter's displacement in violent combat. Klaus Theweleit's comparison of the cadet's blackout in the fascist military drill after excessive physical exertion to "the moment of tension-and-release in orgasm" (166) is worth recalling here. Rather than produce bodily equilibrium, like the orgasm, the blackout, according to Theweleit, disrupts it. In blackout, the soldier does experience a momentary release: "his armor, as 'masculine' repressor, merges with the repressed—his incarcerated 'feminine' interior" (166). And this fashions a new subjectivity: "In the coma, a new structure, a new body grows onto him. When he awakes from this process of transformation, he has become physically and psychically another, a new man" (169). The result, a new "man of steel," is nevertheless a deformed and "delibidinized" ego: "The blackout...is in fact a form of punishment for his attempt to obtain forbidden pleasure: but more than this, it is a function of a body incapable of the experience of pleasure in any form" (195). However masculine, the knight as reinforced cannon cuts a somewhat ridiculous, anachronistic figure. As Theweleit points out, for example, knights responded to the rise of feudal absolutism and merchant capital across Europe by attempting to "technize" their bodies, which only reinforced their anachrony.

> Faced with the advance of the cannon and the gun, the knights began to subject their bodies to intense physical training: suits of armor too were extended and reinforced, to produce a totality [sic] mechanization of the body....The cannon barrel that appears as a thick iron mantle around the body of the knight is a parody of progress....He "mistakenly" responds to the new (cannons, guns, the greater mobility of unarmored troops) by reinforcing the old (his suit of armor), as if he hoped to make the new serve the purposes of the old. What he produces in the process is a monstrosity that expends every ounce of its energy in maintaining the appearance of invulnerability. (202)

The epic simile's temporal shift into the modern thus reinforces the power of the giant Orgoglio's blow, but it also raises to consciousness the anachronism of romance and the knight's obsolescence on the modern battlefield. As a figure for armoured subjectivity, moreover, the cannon may replace Redcrosse's liquid viscera with an iron bullet, but it also disturbingly suggests a hollowed out interior, rammed from the outside with metallized content.[23]

Redcrosse's humiliation, his being laid "full low," fits into a Protestant paradigm of salvation, in which the sinner must experience total abjection before receiving divine grace. Orgoglio reduces Redcrosse to mere carcass—"he tooke the slombred senceless corse, /...ere he could out of his swowne awake" (1.7.15)—throwing him into his dungeon at Duessa's intercession, rather than simply killing him. But Redcrosse's blackout, as with the fascist's, is the beginning of a process of transformation the end result of which is putatively a new man and a stronger subject. The agent of grace is, of course, Arthur, a Christian hero of the spirit, rather than a classical hero of the body, one essentially fallen and dependent upon spiritual salvation. This process of astonishment and armouring, as I have been tracing it, bears significant resemblance to the experience of the sublime. As Steven Knapp writes, "For Kant, the sublime experience always involves a temporary failure or humiliation of the subject" (74). Yet, this fall serves a larger transcendence: "the humiliation is short-lived, since failure on the level of sense is interpreted as a sign of the mind's supersensible vocation. The agent responsible for this providential translation of defeat into victory is the reason, which takes the moment of discontinuity as an opportunity to assert its superior claims" (74).

It will be useful here, however, for my discussion of the kind of armoured subjectivity depicted in the cannon simile to draw more from Knapp's qualification of the experience of sublime transcendence. Writing on the relation between the sublime and the agency of personified allegorical figures, Knapp states: "Kant, along with Burke and the English satirists, was aware of the intriguing proximity of *hypsos* to bathos, of subjective 'freedom' to a mad or comical inflation of the self. The sublime, as Kant explains it, is therefore programmatically ambivalent: it demands a simultaneous identification with and dissociation from images of ideal power. Unless the subject in some degree identifies with the ideal, the experience reduces to mere pretense. But total identification collapses the distinction between ideal and empirical agency and leads to a condition of 'rational raving' that Kant designated 'fanaticism'" (3). In Orgoglio, we have quite literally a personification of this kind of proximity of *hypsos* to bathos, "a mad or comical inflation of the self" that Knapp describes. Arthur deflates this self when he defeats Orgoglio with the aid of his shield, reducing the "Castle"-like giant to nothing, "like an emptie bladder" (1.8.23–24). Fanatical over-identification with the iron cannon and the ideal security of spiritual or body armour—as in the case of the fascist armoured body—ironically collapses into bathos.

IV

Astonishment from the violent blow in *The Faerie Queene* has a destabilizing effect not only on the formation of the self, but also on problems of knowledge and hermeneutics. In a 1625 Easter sermon on John 5.28–29, verses in which Christ speaks of a coming resurrection, John Donne deems wonder as a kind of middle state. Donne first glosses the opening lines of the passage from John, "Marvell not at this," as an injunction against "extraordinary wonder," but then proceeds to qualify it.

> But it is, *Ne miremini hoc,* Wonder not at this; *but yet, there are things, which we may wonder at.* Nil admirari, *is but the Philosophers wisdome; He thinks it a weaknesse, to wonder at any thing, That any thing should be strange to him: But Christian Philosophy that is rooted in humility, tels us, in the mouth of* Clement of Alexandria, Principium veritatis est res admirari, *The first step to faith, is to wonder, to stand, and consider with a holy admiration, the waies and proceedings of God with man: for, Admiration, wonder, stands as in the midst, between knowledge and faith, and hath an eye towards both. If I know a thing, or beleeve a thing, I do no longer wonder: but when I finde that I have reason to stop upon the consideration of a thing, so, as that I see enough to induce admiration, to make me wonder, I come by that step, and God leads me by that hand, to a knowledge, if it be of a naturall or civill thing, or to a faith, if it be of a supernaturall, and spirituall thing.* (265, emphasis original)

Although Donne opposes the Stoic refusal to admire against Christian humility, the quotation from Clement of Alexandria reworks within a

Christian frame the Aristotelian and Platonic commonplace that wonder is the gateway to philosophy. Wonder stands "in the midst" not only between knowledge and faith, but it also stands more humbly between false and "true" knowledge. Donne's recuperation of wonder, which might suggest an attitude of weakness toward the object, within a Christian tradition of humility recalls Erich Auerbach's depiction of the merging of *humilitas* and *sublimitas*, or low and elevated styles, within that same tradition. Whereas classical rhetoric strictly separated these antithetical styles, Auerbach argues, the Christian tradition, following the humble example of Christ, collapsed the rigid hierarchy of styles, situating the sublime in the plain or lowly. Indeed, Tasso says in his *Discourses on the Art of Poetry* that the sublime style is proper for epic, insofar as it works toward wonder. But he also warns against the vices or defects of the style, for example, magnificence becoming swollen (134). This inflated style or tumidity "is like vainglory, which exults in virtues that it does not possess and employs those that it does at the wrong moment" (141). Although Donne locates wonder between ignorance and knowledge, this middle ground is a space not only of potential enlightenment, but also of estrangement, alienation, and even implicit danger. As Bilson points out, in fixing the mind wholly on "some special thing above our reach," admiration and amusement can turn into amazement and astonishment, if the object of thought is more than the soul can conceive, "or more fearefull then she well indureth."

Astonishment in *The Faerie Queene* thus occupies a kind of ambivalent third space between the darkness of allegory and the unbearable light of revelation. To shift to the second episode of the diptych that book 1, canto 7 forms, Arthur's shield, for example, itself figures the dichotomy of revelation and allegory, but also produces astonishment as a third term. Unveiled, the exceeding brightness of the shield dispels all falsehood, yet also vanquishes any mortal exposed to it: "And when him list the raskall routes appall, / Men into stones therewith he could transmew, / And stones to dust, and dust to nought at all" (1.7.35). The literal astonishment, and even pulverizing, of the "rascall routes" is at once the blinding opposite and terrifying effect of revelation. Before the shield of faith and revelation, ironically, fallen men and women require the protection of another shield, the veil that "closely cover[s]" it (1.7.33). Yet if Arthur's adamantine shield is impenetrably framed "that point of speare it never percen could" (1.7.33), the allegorical veil that covers it can be equally so. As we learn at the start of the poem, the trees of the Wandering Wood "did spred so broad, that heavens light did hide, / Not perceable with power of any star" (1.1.7). But the shield of allegory provides only false security, and threatens those shrouded in its darkness with astonishment from the opposite direction of revelation. Spenser admits in the start of his "Letter to Raleigh" to knowing "how doubtfully all Allegories may be construed," and thus "discover[s]" in the letter his "general intention and meaning" for Raleigh's "better light in reading." But if his choice of Arthur provides the "most fitte" example by which "to fashion a gentleman," that this ancient figure is "also furthest from the daunger of envy, and suspition of present time" nevertheless renders the allegory even more open to being misconstrued or even impenetrable by any light.

Writing about sublime blockage, Hertz notes that its most rigorous formulation comes from Kant's notion of the mathematical sublime, whose sense arises out of "sheer cognitive exhaustion, the mind blocked not by the threat of an overwhelming force [as in the dynamical sublime], but by the fear of losing count or of being reduced to nothing but counting—this and this and this—with no hope of bringing a long series or a vast scattering under some sort of conceptual unity" (40). This "momentary checking of the vital powers," in which the rational faculties are overwhelmed, is followed by "a compensatory positive movement," a kind of quasi-transcendent expansion of the bounds of reason into the territory of irrational feelings (40). Hertz offers Wordsworth's phrasing of the moment of blockage, the latter repeatedly representing himself as "thwarted, baffled and rescued in his own despite," that is "checked in some activity… then released into another order of experience or of discourse" (44). He goes on to cite Samuel Monk, who traces this pattern of sublime experience (confrontation with absolute greatness, failure, and then bafflement and wonder) from Addison to Kant. "Eighteenth-century writers," states Hertz, "do not use the word 'blockage'; they use verbs like 'baffle' and 'check' or nouns like 'astonishment' or 'difficulty'" (46). Hertz nevertheless gestures here toward even earlier traditions, pointing out "that the metaphor of blockage draws much of its power from the literature of religious conversion, that is, from a literature that describes major experiential transformation, the mind not merely challenged and thereby invigorated but thoroughly 'turned round'" (47).[24] Moreover, "difficulty," along with absolute blockage, also draws its origins from religion, and here Hertz quotes Angus Fletcher's account of "difficult ornament," blockage that takes place at the level of interpretation (47).

Arthur's second battle with Maleger, captain of a monstrous rabble of troops, outside Alma's Castle of Temperance in book 2, condenses astonishment as both the physical overwhelming of the senses and the failure of reason. Arthur thinks the fight ended after felling Maleger with his mace, but his withered and emaciated foe possesses a kind of Sadean body, capable of sustaining infinite abuse. Hence the extreme violence Arthur unleashes on Maleger gives way to absolute bewilderment: "Ne wist he, what to think of that same sight, / Ne what to say, ne what to doe at all" (2.11.39). After considering a series of supernatural options to explain Maleger—"magicall / Illusion" or "wandring ghost" or "aerie spirit" or "hellish feend" (2.11.39)—Arthur looks for rational support.

His wonder farre exceeded reasons reach,
That he began to doubt his dazeled sight,
And oft of error did himself appeach:
Flesh without bloud, a person without spright,
Wounds without hurt, a bodie without might,
That could do harme, yet could not harmed bee,
That could not die, yet seem'd a mortal wight,
That was most strong in most infirmitee;
Like did he never heare, like did he never see. (2.11.40)

Maleger thus turns from being sublime physical foe to cognitive, even textual, paradox.[25] Arthur's sublime blockage—"A while he stood in this astonishment" (2.11.41)—ultimately reinvigorates him, but also causes him to change tactics.

 Throwing away sword and shield, Arthur resorts first to "naked" grappling (2.11.41) and then gives up direct engagement altogether when that too proves futile: "Nigh his wits end then woxe th'amazed knight" (2.11.44). What begins as an insuperable physical foe turns into a figurative challenge, or "difficult ornament." Fletcher explains: "'Difficulty' implies here a calculated obscurity which elicits an interpretive response in the reader. The very obscurity is a source of pleasure, especially to the extent that the actual process of deciphering the exegetical content of a passage would be painfully arduous and uncertain. Obscurity stirs curiosity; the reader wants to tear the veil aside. 'The more they seem obscure through their use of figurative expressions,' says Augustine, 'the more they give pleasure when they have been made clear'" (*Allegory* 234–35). The solution comes in a strange flash of recognition, a surfacing memory of Maleger's genealogy: "He then remembred well, that had bene sayd, / How th' Earth his mother was, and first him bore" (2.11.45). Arthur then conceives to throw Maleger into a "standing lake" (2.11.46), placid as his finally subdued affections: "without remorse, / Ne stird, till hope of life did him forsake" (2.11.46). Particularly bizarre is the possibility that Arthur has in fact heard about Maleger's mother from the narrator, who makes this genealogical connection for the first time in stanza 42 and then again in stanza 44, immediately before the moment of recollection. While perhaps a reassertion of reason over wonder, the interjection of Arthur's sudden memory seems rather a marvellous, even paralogistic, literary device. If a few stanzas earlier, Arthur "need[s] the helpe of weaker hand; / So feeble is mans state, and life unsound, / That in assurance it may never stand" (2.11.30), here the memory of Maleger's origin seems to materialize out of the ether, adventitious like the earlier intervention, when "had not grace thee blest, thou shouldest not survive" (2.11.30). Hertz writes that the sublime drama of collapse and compensation can be thought of as "the story of Ethics coming to the rescue in a situation of cognitive distress" (50).

But this drama can be thought of in religious terms, as well. In a seventeenth-century sermon on Jesus's Transfiguration, Bishop of Exeter Ralph Brownrig writes of the apostles who witness the event: "*Primò territi, nunc gaudio affecti*; First, we saw them cast into a kind of Astonishment, *In somno ecstatico*; now see it ends in Joy and Comfort. It is the order of Gods making himself known; first, to strike us with fear, to bring us comfort; first, Astonishments; then, Consolations" (98).[26] Brownrig's "first, astonishments, then, consolations" formula clearly draws on a letter in which Augustine justifies the compelling of religious belief.[27] Bilson quotes the letter approvingly in discussing "the calling of Paul; first as a Jew...then strooken with blindnes, & amased with terror from heaven; and therefor compelled to Christianitie by corporal violence...Behold (saith that learned father) *in Paul, Christ first compelling, afterward teaching; first striking, then comforting*" (*True Difference* 17, emphasis original). Taking up the general astonishment at Peter's healing of the lame beggar in Acts 3.1–15, on which we have already heard Bilson's commentary, the Swiss reformer Rudolph Gwalther recounts from Luke that "being striken with marveylous admiration," the people "were provoked to runne to the Apostles, and to bethinke them of so straunge and unwoonted a matter" (157). This is proper, Gwalther continues:

> *For we ought diligently to consider the workes of God, and to marveyle at the excellencye of them, for the which ende some Philosophers, not altogether unwittily, have sayde, that God made manne. Because that observation and marveyling, stayeth not in a certaine blinde and amazed dulnesse of the minde, but is a certayne preparation of the mynde, whereby we are drawne to the true knowledge of God....such is the corruption of our minde, that unlesse we be drawne by some forcible motion, we can never be brought from earthly things to the consideration of heavenly. Wherefore God joyneth to his*

worde many times certain signes, and most singuler works, that they may awake our minds out of that dull sleepe, and bring them to the consideration of his worde and will. And for this cause Christ oftentimes, eyther before his teaching, or in his teaching, used myracles, to make men the more ready to recyve his doctrine. (157)

This "forcible" marvelling, a "wholesome feare and amazednesse" (87) Gwalther distinguishes from the blind and dull sort precisely because it snaps the mind to attention, is all the more necessary in "these...daungerous dayes" wherein "we [are] lying bolt upright and snorting" (158): "the sluggishnesse of this age" renders many deaf and blind to "the thinges whereby God puncheth us and waketh us up to acknowledge our salvation" (157).

It is worth noting one further entry in this Augustinian shock doctrine. Citing both Augustine and Gwalther, Gervase Babington argues against sparing the rod, in certain cases: "For divers men being of divers manners and dispositions, one and the same way of preaching agreeth not to them all. Some it sufficeth to have doctrine plainely delivered to them, others must have earnest admonition also, & many must have exhortation, yea, sharpe rebukes and chidinges, or else they profite not....The Magistrate may compel, whom the Preacher can not perswade to serve God" (550–51). Babington's magisterial way of delivering doctrine anticipates somewhat Spenser's own method of "historical fiction" to the "general end" of fashioning a gentleman "in virtuous and gentle discipline," as he explains it his letter to Raleigh: "To some I know this Methode will seeme displeasaunt, which had rather have good discipline delivered plainly in way of precepts, or sermoned at large, as they use, then thus clowdily enwrapped in Allegoricall devises. But such, me seeme, should be satisfide with the use of these dayes, seeing all things accounted by their showes, and nothing esteemed of, that is not delightfull and pleasing to commune sence." To the extent that Spenser's "doctrine by ensample" rather than "by rule" proposes to instruct by delighting, it would seem the opposite of Augustinian compulsion. But both methods are alternatives to plainly delivered doctrine, and both are occasioned by the dangerous days of the present. Moreover, the veil of allegory demands a hermeneutics not unlike that of the miracle, as Gwalther argues of the men who are "astonied and wonder at the great miracle" of the Pentecost in Acts 2.1–13, an anti-Babel moment in which the multitude from different nations understand one another in their own tongue: "Yet they stande not styll in this bashement, but goyng further, they seeke the ende and use of this matter: saying: *What meaneth this?*" (88).

However, Hertz cites a competing interpretation of this sublime drama, a suspicion that the distress is "slightly fictitious, staged precisely in order to require the somewhat melodramatic arrival of Ethics" (50). Indeed, the suspicious resolution puts to question whether Arthur's remorseless drowning of Maleger in the standing lake figures mastery over the passions or anaesthetizing repression.[28] And this returns us to Lewis's own blockage that began this discussion: his belittling of the marvels of Boiardo and Ariosto as deceitful tricks. It is not, as Lewis claims, "only the surfaces of the English and Italian poems that are alike," beneath which they are "essentially different" (308). There are both deep resemblances and differences, and it is his alternating avowals and disavowals of the marvellous that make Spenser an early, but overlooked, antecedent of the sublime. Likewise, astonishment in Spenser oscillates between Descartes's valuation of the passion as "never anything but bad" and Burke's regard for it as the "effect of the sublime in its highest degree," marking sublime blockage in the poem not simply as an anachronistic precursor of the eighteenth-century sublime, but as its, to borrow from Lewis, "primitive" other.

Notes

1. Boileau writes in his Preface to this translation: "Il faut donc entendre par sublime, dans Longin, l'extraordinaire, le surpenant, et comme je l'ai traduit, le merveilleux, dans le discours" (qtd. in Thorpe 1125).
2. As Richard Macksey points out, *Peri Hypsos* is not just a treatise on "'the high style' in the tradition common to many ancient critics of a rhetoric of stylistic gradation

(e.g., High, Middle, and Low)," but is concerned instead with "distinctions of conception and expression, with the sources and effects achieving a state of elevation that he calls 'transport' (*ekstasis*, in the quite literal sense of being 'carried outside' oneself)" (471–72). If Longinus variously locates sublimity in the author, in the text, and sometimes in its impact on the audience, its consequences are nonetheless "irresistible and lend themselves to a rhetoric of astonishment (*ekplexis*) and domination" (Macksey 472).

3. For a related argument, see Cascardi, who argues for the Spanish Baroque as an antecedent of the sublime not indebted to Longinus. Debates over romance in the sixteenth century largely were centred on the genre's relationship to Aristotle, who made no mention of it in the *Poetics*. For an account of these debates, see Weinberg, *A History of Literary Criticism in the Italian Renaissance*, 954–1105.

4. Spenser's fairy knights, for example, are "slow moving and heavy-spoken" dullards compared to their Italian counterparts, and next to Ariosto's inimitable Bradamant, "Britomart is little better than a big-boned country girl" (Lewis 306). Delivering the coup de grace, Lewis concludes: "Nor will Spenser's small zoo of monsters, his reiterated single combats, his monotonous forest (relieved by no change of season), stand comparison for a moment with the inexhaustible inventions of the Italians" (306).

5. See chapter 24 (1460a) of Aristotle's *Poetics*: "It is Homer especially who has taught the other poets how to tell lies as they should be told. This is done through the use of paralogism [or false inference]" (74).

6. On the scandal of the Aristotelian marvellous, see Cave, 1–2, 40–43, and passim.

7. See the letter to Raleigh, "annexed" to the 1590 edition of the poem. All further citations of the poem are to the Longman edition.

8. Notable recent work that addresses wonder in *The Faerie Queene* includes Guenther and Fletcher (not to be confused with the author of *Allegory: The Theory of a Symbolic Mode*, which I cite elsewhere in this article). Although Guenther interestingly situates wonder in Spenser within a Neoplatonic discourse of magic and performativity, I would argue that insofar as wonder in *The Faerie Queene* is linked to magic, it also evokes less serious traditions of magic in the period— such as street juggling, illusion, and legerdemain—that undercut belief in the "instrumental" power of magic which Guenther argues is at work in the poem. The wonder of this more popular tradition of magic finds a counterpart in the probable impossibilities and deceptive paralogisms of the Aristotelian marvellous. Focusing on the *Mutability Cantos*, Fletcher argues that Spenser incorporates "wonder into a methodical proceeding of thought that results in a marvelous affirmation"

("Marvelous Progression" 6). My argument runs in the opposite direction, where astonishment is not methodically recuperated in knowledge, but registers experiences that exceed reason's grasp and even threaten bodily integrity.

9. In the 1596 edition "stoond" becomes "stound."
10. See Hathaway, 133–51 and Tasso, 103–04.
11. On epic and tragic anagnorisis and the marvellous in Aristotle, see Cave, 41–46.
12. In his *Touchstone of complexions* (trans. 1581), the Dutch physician Levinus Lemnius describes the body's terror "in daungerous adventures and perilles hazarded by Sea and lande (which to the eyes and mynd represent a very Image of death)": "when as all the parts of the body be forsaken of theyr vitall juyce, there is none of them that throughlye and well executeth his righte function and office: the feete stagger and stumble, the eyes dazzel, the lustynesse of the mind drowpeth and is dulled, the cheeks seeme flaggie and hanging downe, the tongue stammering and the teeth gnashing and whetting. [Quoting Virgil's *Aeneid* 4.280:] His hayres for feare stand staring up, / his tongue is tyed fast" (93–94). To Lemnius's further claim that no creature is immune from dread and terror of death "because it bringeth destruction and utter dissolution to all," except "such whose myndes bee stupefied and their Senses blunted and unperfecte," a marginal gloss adds, "Astonishment of mind taketh away the feeling of pain" (94).
13. The word "shocke" occurs at 1.2.16, line 4 and at 4.2.16, line 5.
14. See also *OED* "stound," v. 1, where the word carries an obsolete dialectal sense: "*Stound*, to stop, to stand still, esp. in order to listen."
15. The verb "stemme" here should be glossed as "ram," but another sense, "to stop, check; to dam up," suggests astonishment.
16. See Murrin, 123–37; Hale; and Biow, 113–18.
17. Hale traces the genealogy of this association, and both Murrin and Biow draw from Hale's work for this point. See also Langer.
18. For an account of this debate, see Quantin, 114–30.
19. For the three moments of Christ's horror, Jacob notes John 12.27ff, when Jesus says that his soul is troubled and asks if he should say to the Father, "save me from this hour"; Matthew 26.32ff, in agony in the garden of Gethsemane, when Jesus is grieved "even to death"; and his hanging on the cross.
20. Also quoted by Jacob in *Defence*, 123.
21. Helkia Crooke offers a standard account in his *Mikrokosmographia* (1615): "the true cause of erection...is partly Natural, to wit, an abundance of winde and spirits filling the hollow Nerves" (245).

22. J.R. Hale asserts that "English Renaissance drama shows that the gun took over from the sword as a virility symbol at about the same time that it became a symbol of war itself" (409).

23. Theweleit writes, for example: "Since the 'ego' of these men cannot form from the inside out, through libidinal cathexis of the body's periphery and identification, they must acquire an enveloping 'ego' from the outside" (164).

24. Hertz remarks that the pseudo-transcendence of sublime blockage, in which utter self-loss paradoxically confirms the unitary status of the self, "is only legible in a specular structure," wherein the self identifies with the blocking agent (54–55).

25. In *The Arte of English Poesie*, George Puttenham calls the figure of *Paradoxon* "the Wondrer," which effects a reflective moment of pause: "Many times our Poet is carried by some occasion to report of a thing that is marvelous, and then he will seeme not to speak it simply but with some signe of admiration" (225–26). Following *Paradoxon*, Puttenham next considers the figure of "*Aporia*, or the Doubtfull," which is "Not much unlike the *wondrer*" (226).

26. Brownrig earlier states that the apostles' sleep may be estimated disparately, "As a Natural infirmity," "As a carnal indisposition," or "As a Spiritual amazement, and consternation" (86). According to the third account, "The terrour of this glorious Vision, it hath amazed them; so overcome their spirits, that they are sunk into astonishment" (89).

27. Augustine, 641 (Letter 185.6.22).

28. I would recall but revise Lewis's discussion of the difference between Boiardo's "magically difficult to kill" Orrilo in *Orlando Innamorato* and Spenser's Maleger. In Boiardo, Lewis notes, "the conflict with Orrilo leads up to the moment at which the knight has the ingenious idea of cutting off both his arms in quick succession, picking them up, and throwing them into a river. It is such a problem, and such a solution, as we should expect from Mickey Mouse. We are a thousand miles away from this when we read of Maleger 'of such subtile substance and unsound / That like a ghost he seem'd whose grave-clothes were unbound.' The one story is fun, the other nightmare" (308). If at this description we are a thousand miles away, Arthur's own solution several stanzas later closes the distance significantly, with a little hint of Mickey Mouse. Eighteenth-century critic Joseph Spence's remarks speak to the mixture of the sublime and the ridiculous in Spenser: "I am apt to believe that he [Spenser] considered the Orlando Furioso, in particular, as a poem wholly serious, tho' the author of it certainly wrote it partly in jest. There are several lines and passages in it that must have been intended for burlesque; and they surely consider that poem in the truest light, who consider it as a work of a

mixed nature: as something between the professed gravity of Tasso, and the broad laugh of Berni and his followers. Perhaps Spenser's taking some things to be said seriously, which Ariosto meant for ridicule, may have led him now and then to say things that are ridiculous, where he meant to be very serious" (36).

Works Cited

Albott, Robert. *Englands Parnassus: or the choysest flowers of our moderne poets, with their poeticall comparisons.* London, 1600. Early English Books Online. Web. 28 Sept. 2008.

Ariosto, Ludovico. *Orlando furioso in English heroical verse, by John Haringto[n].* London, 1591. Early English Books Online. Web. 28 Sept. 2008.

Aristotle. *Poetics.* Trans. James Hutton. New York: Norton, 1982. Print.

Auerbach, Erich. *Literary Language and Its Public in Late Latin Antiquity and in the Middle Ages.* Trans. Ralph Manheim. New York: Pantheon, 1965. Print.

Augustine. *A Treatise Concerning the Correction of the Donatists.* Trans. J.R. King. A Select Library of the Nicene and Post-Nicene Fathers of the Christian Church. Ed. Philip Schaff. Vol. 4. Buffalo, 1887. Print.

Babington, Gervase. *A profitable exposition of the Lords prayer.* London, 1588. Early English Books Online. Web. 28 Sept. 2008.

Bilson, Thomas. *The effect of certaine sermons touching the full redemption of mankind by the death and bloud of Christ Iesus.* London, 1599. Early English Books Online. Web. 28 Sept. 2008.

———. *The suruey of Christs sufferings for mans redemption and of his descent to Hades or Hel for our deliuerance.* London, 1604. Early English Books Online. Web. 28 Sept. 2008.

———. *The True Difference betweene Christian Subjection and Unchristian Rebellion.* Oxford, 1585. Early English Books Online. Web. 28 Sept. 2008.

Biow, Douglas. *Mirabile Dictu: Representations of the Marvelous in Medieval and Renaissance Epic.* Ann Arbor: University of Michigan Press, 1996. Print.

Boys, John. *The third part from S. John Baptists nativitie to the last holy-day in the whole year.* London, 1615. Early English Books Online. Web. 28 Sept. 2008.

Brownrig, Ralph. *Twenty five sermons.* London, 1664. Early English Books Online. Web. 28 Sept. 2008.

Burke, Edmund. *A Philosophical Enquiry into the Origin of our Ideas of the Sublime and Beautiful.* Ed. Adam Phillips. New York: Oxford University Press, 1990. Print.

Cascardi, Anthony. "The Genealogy of the Sublime in the Aesthetics of the Spanish Baroque." *Reason and Its Others: Italy, Spain, and the New World.* Ed. David

R. Castillo and Massimo Lollini. Nashville, TN: Vanderbilt University Press, 2006. 221–39. Print.

Cave, Terence. *Recognitions: A Study in Poetics*. 1988. Oxford: Clarendon Press, 2002. Print.

Cheney, Donald. "Envy in the Middest of the 1596 Faerie Queene." *Edmund Spenser: Modern Critical Views*. Ed. Harold Bloom. New York: Chelsea House, 1986. 267–83. Print.

Constable, Henry. "To Sir Philip Sidney's Soul." *New Oxford Book of Sixteenth-Century Verse*. Ed. Emrys Jones. New York: Oxford University Press, 1991. 463. Print.

Crooke, Helkiah. *Mikrokosmographia: A Description of the Body of Man*. London, 1615. Early English Books Online. Web. 28 Sept. 2008.

Descartes, René. *The Passions of the Soul*. Trans. Stephen H. Voss. Indianapolis, IN: Hackett, 1989. Print.

Donne, John. *The Sermons of John Donne*. Ed. E. Simpson and G. Potter. Vol. 6. Berkeley: University of California Press, 1953–1962. Print.

Fletcher, Angus. *Allegory: The Theory of a Symbolic Mode*. Ithaca, NY: Cornell University Press, 1964. Print.

Fletcher, Angus. "Marvelous Progression: The Paradoxical Defense of Women in Spenser's 'Mutabilitie Cantos.'" *Modern Philology* 100 (2002): 5–23. Print.

Guenther, Genevieve. "Spenser's Magic, or Instrumental Aesthetics in the 1590 Faerie Queene." *English Literary Renaissance* 36.2 (2006): 194–226. Print.

Gwalther, Rudolph. *An hundred, threescore and fifteen homelyes or sermons, upon the Actes of the Postles, written by Saint Luke*. London, 1572. Early English Books Online. Web. 28 Sept. 2008.

Hale, J.R. "Gunpowder and the Renaissance: an Essay in the History of Ideas." *Renaissance War Studies*. London: Hambledon Press, 1983. 389–419. Print.

Hathaway, Baxter. *Marvels and Commonplaces: Renaissance Literary Criticism*. New York: Random House, 1968. Print.

Hertz, Neil. *The End of the Line: Essays on Psychoanalysis and the Sublime*. New York: Columbia University Press, 1985. Print.

Hobbes, Thomas. *The Answer of Mr. Hobbes to Sir Will. D'Avenant's Preface before Gondibert*. 1650. *English Renaissance Literary Criticism*. Ed. Brian Vickers. New York: Oxford University Press, 1999. 608–25. Print.

Hughes, John. *Remarks on the "Fairy Queen."* 1715. *Spenser's Critics: Changing Currents in Literary Taste*. Ed. William Mueller. New York: Syracuse University Press, 1959. 18–27. Print.

Jacob, Henry. *A defence of a treatise touching the sufferings and victorie of Christ in the worke of our redemption.* Middelburg, 1600. *Early English Books Online.* Web. 28 Sept. 2008.

———. *A treatise of the sufferings and victory of Christ, in the work of our redemption.* 1597. Middelburg, 1598. *Early English Books Online.* Web. 28 Sept. 2008.

Jameson, Frederic. *The Political Unconscious: Narrative as a Socially Symbolic Act.* Ithaca, NY: Cornell University Press, 1981. Print.

Kahn, Victoria. "Allegory and the Sublime in Paradise Lost." *John Milton.* Ed. Annabel Patterson. New York: Longman, 1992. 185–201. Print.

Knapp, Steven. *Personification and the Sublime: Milton to Coleridge.* Cambridge, MA: Harvard University Press, 1985. Print.

Langer, Ulrich. "Gunpowder as Transgressive Invention in Ronsard." *Literary Theory/Renaissance Texts.* Eds. Patricia Parker and David Quint. Baltimore, MD: Johns Hopkins University Press, 1986. 96–114. Print.

Lemnius, Levinus. *The touchstone of complexions...Englished by Thomas Newton.* London, 1581. *Early English Books Online.* Web. 28 Sept. 2008.

Lewis, C.S. *The Allegory of Love: A Study in Medieval Tradition.* 1936. London: Oxford University Press, 1953. Print.

Macksey, Richard. "Longinus." *The Johns Hopkins Guide to Literary Theory and Criticism.* Baltimore, MD: Johns Hopkins University Press, 1994. Print.

Malory, Thomas. *Le morte darthur.* London, 1485. *Early English Books Online.* Web. 28 Sept. 2008.

Monk, Samuel. *The Sublime: A Study of Critical Theories in XVIII-Century England.* New York: MLA, 1935. Print.

Mornay, Phillipe de. *A woorke concerning the trewnesse of the Christian religion, written in French: against atheists, Epicures, Paynims, Jewes, Mahumetists, and other infidels...Begunne to be translated into English by Sir Philip Sidney Knight, and at his request finished by Arthur Golding.* 1587. *Early English Books Online.* Web. 28 Sept. 2008.

Murrin, Michael. *History and Warfare in Renaissance Epic.* Chicago: University of Chicago Press, 1994. Print.

Puttenham, George. *The Arte of English Poesie.* 1589. Eds. Gladys Willcock and Alice Walker. Cambridge: Cambridge University Press, 1936. Print.

Quantin, Jean-Louis. *The Church of England and Christian Antiquity: The Construction of a Confessional Identity in the 17th Century.* New York: Oxford University Press, 2009. Print.

Quilligan, Maureen. "On the Renaissance Epic: Spenser and Slavery." *Edmund Spenser: Essays on Culture and Allegory*. Eds. Jennifer Klein Morrison and Matthew Greenfield. Burlington, VT: Ashgate, 2000. 43–64. Print.

Rymer, Thomas. Preface to the Translation of Rapin's Reflections on Aristotle's Treatise of Poesie. 1674. Critical Essays of the Seventeenth Century. Vol. 2. Ed. J.E. Spingarn. Oxford: Clarendon Press, 1908. 163–81. Print.

Spence, Joseph. The Defects of Our Modern Poets, in Their Allegories: Instanced from Spenser's "Fairy Queen." 1747. Spenser's Critics: Changing Currents in Literary Taste. Ed. William Mueller. New York: Syracuse University Press, 1959. 32–36. Print.

Spenser, Edmund. The Faerie Queene. Ed. A.C. Hamilton. New York: Longman, 1997. Print.

Tasso, Torquato. Discourses on the Art of Poetry. Trans. Lawrence F. Rhu. The Genesis of Tasso's Narrative Theory: English Translations of the Early Poetics and a Comparative Study of Their Significance. Detroit: Wayne State University Press, 1993.

Theweleit, Klaus. *Male Fantasies*. Trans. Erica Carter and Chris Turner. Vol. 2. Minneapolis: University of Minnesota Press, 1989. Print.

Thorpe, Clarence DeWitt. "Addison and Some of His Predecessors on 'Novelty.'" *PMLA* 52.4 (1937): 1114–29. Print.

Warton, Joseph. An Essay on the Genius and Writings of Pope. 1756. Edmund Spenser: A Critical Anthology. Ed. Paul J. Alpers. Harmondsworth, UK: Penguin Books, 1969. 112–13. Print.

Wasserman, Earl R. "The Pleasures of Tragedy" ELH 14.4 (1947): 283–307. Print.

Weinberg, Bernard. A History of Literary Criticism in the Italian Renaissance. Vol. 2. Chicago: University of Chicago Press, 1961. Print.

———. "Translations and Commentaries of Longinus, On the Sublime, to 1600: A Bibliography." Modern Philology 47.3 (1950): 145–51. Print.

10

THE HOME, THE PALACE, THE CELL

Places of Recognition in Le rouge et le noir *and* Great Expectations

ROSA MUCIGNAT

WHEN JULIEN SOREL, the hero of Stendhal's *Le rouge et le noir*, first arrives at the famous Hôtel de la Mole in Paris, he is taken to what he sees as "the ugliest of rooms," where he finds "un petit homme maigre" (Stendhal 337; "a small thin man" [Slater 250]); his uneducated glance cannot recognize the sober elegance of the Marquis. Earlier, in Verrières, he had mistaken Mme de Rênal's tender interest in him for a display of aristocratic arrogance. Similarly, in Dickens's *Great Expectations*, Pip is blinded by the upper-class grandeur of Satis House, and when Biddy expresses her misgivings about his plan to become a gentleman, he mistakes her genuine concern for malevolent jealousy. Both Julien and Pip underestimate "home" and think too highly of the rewards promised by the "palace." As a consequence, their ability to assess the value of a place is defective and they incur a sort of tragic *hamartia*. But as Aristotle teaches, after confusion comes recognition: in both novels there is a third space, the "cell," which is nearly devoid of attributes and offers no possibility of movement, but is the place where heroes are left to unravel the strands of their own story.

Recognition is a narrative force that moves characters toward a reinterpretation of their place in the world and of their relations to events, people, and objects. In a sense, it realigns the narrative along the correct cardinal points that were lost in the confused flourishing of the middle section, when the hero is caught in a series of adventures, travels, and metamorphoses, losing his sense of direction. But narrative plots often correspond to trajectories in space in a real and not only in a figural sense. Progressions in the story are frequently marked by changes of setting, and the atmosphere and layout of the different locales influence the characters and their actions. Thus, if we consider that the plot is structured also according to a spatial pattern, it becomes interesting to observe what happens to space when the narrative is involved in "a change from ignorance to knowledge," as Aristotle defines *anagnorisis* (65).

Recognition is an old trope, from the toolbox of tragedy and myth, yet it is still at work in Stendhal and Dickens. Narratologists, such as Yuri Lotman, and advocates of the continuity between romance and the novel, such as Northrop Frye and, more recently, Margaret Ann Doody, have shown how modern novels incorporate parts of the ancient machinery, adapting them to express new ideas about society and the self and new images of reality. In his study on Dickens and the permanence of romance, Ian Duncan has argued that a narrative plot is constructed upon "a grammar of formal conventions, that is, a shared cultural order distinct from material and historical contingency" (2). But even if recognition, together with other features of older texts, is still in operation, the modern novel refashions it on the basis of new concerns. In particular, localization and space descriptions become central, as they convey a sense of the material conditions of life, of the daily negotiations of relationships, and even of the character's inner dynamics of choice and action. In this way, recognition itself "takes on flesh" and becomes closer to everyday experience, losing the appearance of a prodigy announced by oracles, which miraculously discharges all tensions and solves all riddles. Novelistic recognition is not an instantaneous shift but a process initiated by previous events.

Stendhal and Dickens, like Greek myths and biblical stories, use recognition to represent the reconnection of what has been unduly separated, removed, suppressed; but unlike their ancient counterparts, they use it to connect larger slices of reality, and not only the two severed ends of a single thread. As I will attempt to show, Julien and Pip not only rediscover forgotten emotional or blood ties as in the traditional family romance, they also operate a mediation between two levels of the wider social and geographical reality—on the one hand, the provincial world of the home, and on the other, the metropolitan high-life of the palace. Moreover, the moment of recognition implies a reconsideration of the narrative status of the two worlds the heroes have visited: the palace, adorned with the romantic fantasies of richness and gentility, is nothing but a false track; it was instead the unremarkable space of the home that contained the germ of self-satisfaction and constructive energy, now irremediably dispersed. The Aristotelian plot structure, the traditional family romance, and the realist's attention to the concrete everyday world are all brought together in mid-nineteenth-century novels, whose structure we can read as a more complex and at times contradictory form of the old recognition pattern.

Following Aristotle's definition of anagnorisis as "a change from ignorance to knowledge," Terence Cave adds that "it is also a shift into the implausible: the secret unfolded lies beyond the realm of common experience; the truth discovered is 'marvellous'" (1–2). But, in actuality, the opposite is true in the case of Pip and Julien Sorel: their recognition brings them from a lofty imagined world to the heaviness and irrevocability of the real world, from the romance of Satis House to Newgate, and from the *salon* de la Mole to the guillotine. In both novels, recognition has the function of a reality check, allowing the characters to distinguish between "real" and "unreal" places, between places of rightful belonging and places of alienation. Interestingly, Cave defines the plots of recognition as characterized by "a compulsive returning to the 'same' place, a place already known, as if one were discovering it for the first time" (489). Recognition is therefore also a reassessment of spatial values, which makes one aware of being in the wrong place, and leads to an attempt to return home. And this is the kind of recognition experienced by Julien at the end of his social ascent, when, confined in a prison cell, he thinks back to Verrières and Mme de Rênal's artless charms. The same illumination hits Pip when, after Magwitch's death, he re-emerges from a long illness with the intention of returning to the forge and marrying his childhood friend Biddy.

Recognition is thus also a matter of space and location, and here we aim to consider the different sets of places in which characters move, analyzing the relations established between them. Both *Le rouge et le noir* and *Great Expectations* are structured around three different types of space: the home, which is both a simple country idyll and a place of mundane everyday life; the palace, where the games of ambition and sexual desire are played out, threatening the hero's identity and integrity; and the cell, which represents the condition of isolation and deep self-reflection in which the ultimate process of recognition takes place. In particular, I argue that both novels contain, on the one hand, a superficial plot of transition from a space of oppressive sameness (the home) to a space of exciting novelty (the palace) and, on the other hand, include a subterranean plot that assigns to the first the value of reality and to the second the value of deception. The shift from one plot to the other is performed through the trope of recognition, which takes place in the neutral space of the cell.

The Home
The starting point for Julien Sorel and Pip is a provincial backwater and a life bound to manual labour. The two novels belong to that class of education novels that traces the itinerary of a young hero from the country to the city, and from innocence to experience. Both deal with questions of paternity, legitimacy, and in general with all the range of identity problems arising from social and spatial displacement. Both can be defined as plots of ambition: the ambition to know more, to have more, and to be more. First, the characters struggle to acquire education and manners. Then they strive for money, power, and women, so that, inevitably, ambition becomes associated with bad temptations and delinquency, with a

sinful disdain for the native condition, and with a criminal attempt to trespass social borders. Julien Sorel's title of "monster" and Pip's early association with convicts and prisons signal their intrinsic flaw, their mark of difference, and their being invariably alien and out of place.

In fact, their common status of orphaned or bereft children is no longer an opportunity to be recognized as the king's son, as it was in the Greek New Comedy. Their evident otherness does not indicate a sign of election but demonstrates a taint that makes them restless; and their itinerary in the world is not in the shape of a comic ascent, but ensues from a tragic rise and fall. The moments of recognition thus assume a crucial function that represent the point where the illusory family romance and the real "shameful genealogy" plots intersect, shedding light on the course of the heroes' actions and their destiny.

At the beginning of *Le rouge et le noir*, Stendhal situates the imaginary small town of Verrières in the region of the Jura mountains, a landscape of picturesque beauty, with jagged peaks, tumbling mountain streams, and splendid valleys. But while guiding an imaginary Parisian visitor through the town, the narrator soon remarks on the villagers' utilitarian, rather than aesthetic, views: "*Rapporter du revenu* est la raison qui décide de tout dans cette petite ville qui vous semblait si jolie" (Stendhal 52, emphasis original; "*Bringing in money* is the consideration which settles everything in this little town you found so pretty" [Slater 8–9]). In fact, Verrières is a fake country idyll: the natural setting has been altered and twisted to suit the new sawmills and the iron manufactures; and M. de Rênal, the local *ultra* mayor, applies a strict royalist policy even to the trimming of the trees along the municipal promenade, reducing them to ridiculous works of topiary, instead of leaving them to grow freely, as the liberals wish, and show "ces formes magnifiques qu'on leur voit en Angleterre" (Stendhal 51; "the magnificent shapes they display in England" [Slater 8]).

Patriarchal despotism and greed dominate in old Sorel's sawmill, too. With his slender and almost feminine frame, Julien is not cut out to be a manual worker and is more often found sitting on a rafter of the mill-shed reading a book rather than looking after his father's mechanical saws.

Julien is clearly of a different breed from his father and older brothers, to the point where he suspects Sorel of not being his real father. From an early age, his efforts are concentrated on finding the way to escape from his home. This intention is reported in Julien's distinctive tone, one of merciless harshness and exactness: "Pour Julien, faire fortune, c'était d'abord sortir de Verrières; il abhorrait sa patrie. Tout ce qu'il y voyait glaçait son imagination" (Stendhal 71; "For Julien, making his own fortune meant first and foremost getting out of Verrières; he loathed his native town. Everything he saw there froze his imagination" [Slater 26]). As a matter of fact, his imagination is inflamed enough, feeding on the bundle of books bequeathed by the old surgeon, and endlessly fantasizing about Parisian women and military exploits.

In *Le rouge et le noir*, the figure of home is discontinuous and fragmented, since it only appears in the recesses of wider and less congenial spaces: on top of a rafter in old Sorel's sawmill, in a solitary mountain cave, and in Verrières or Vergy when M. de Rênal is away. In Vergy, the family's summer residence, Julien makes a total conquest of both Mme de Rênal and her children, with whom he forms a cheerful little family (which does not include M. de Rênal). There he enjoys freedom in beautiful natural surroundings and an initation in love with Mme de Rênal. His resentful temper, however, and the fear of suffering and ridicule prevent him from enjoying life there. His days in Vergy are brought to an abrupt end by his own self-imposed sense of duty, which impels him to abandon this temporary idyll and proceed further on the road to Paris. When he is tempted by the idea of settling down in the Rênal household, living an easy life with his books and his secret mistress, Julien reminds himself of the higher destiny awaiting him: "Le voyageur qui vient de gravir une montagne rapide s'assied au sommet, et trouve un plaisir parfait à se reposer. Serait-il heureux si on le forçait à se reposer toujours?" (Stendhal 362; "A traveller who has just climbed a steep mountain sits down at the summit and finds perfect pleasure in resting. Would he be happy if forced to rest for ever?" [Slater 162–63]). High-mountain hikes and visits to mountain cottages and grottos are a constant presence in *Le rouge et le noir*. They are fragments of that secure, inviolable space Julien is secretly longing for, but which he nonetheless continues to abandon for the sake of ambition and dreams of future glory. The appeal of the palace is too strong, and life in these makeshift homes too precarious to offer an alternative to the powerful swelling tide of events, which carry Julien farther and farther away into the Parisian imbroglio.

What Victor Brombert called the "aerial prison" (91) is a major feature of Stendhalian imagery and it returns unfailingly later in the novel. Julien, like other Stendhalian heroes such as Fabrice Del Dongo and Lucien Leuwen, yearns for the heights, and during one of his solitary high-mountain hikes he discovers a small cave where he takes refuge for the night: "Ici, dit-il avec des yeux brillants de joie, les hommes ne sauraient me faire de mal" (Stendhal 130; "Here, he said to himself with delight shining in his eyes, no man can do me any harm" [Slater 76]). In this place of solitary reflection, he lets his imagination run freely to Parisian courtesies and daring feats, unaware that he is resting in his own future sepulchre. In fact, the burial place where his body will be taken at the end of the novel is precisely a wild grotto "vers le point le plus élevé d'une des hautes montagnes du Jura" (Stendhal 660; "at the summit of one of the highest mountains in the Jura" [Slater 529]). Surrounded by a brutal masculine world of fathers and husbands, Julien carves out small refuges for himself and his loving women, where he lives brief happy moments of childlike play and familial intimacy. As Leo Bersani has it, "love in Stendhal seeks out cloistered retreats" (121)—shadowy gardens, locked bedrooms, attics, prison cells. But the narrative does not follow Julien on these awkward routes. The scattered bits of home remain only fragments, episodes of the larger sequence that moves irresistibly toward the palace, the *salon*, and the wider world.

Pip's native landscape possesses a different sort of fascination—not the rough verticality of the mountains but the enigmatic lure of the marshes, with their unbroken flatness and misty gloom, punctuated by solitary lights: the forge, the church, the fingerpost. Just as Julien feels at home high on a mountain top, Pip's identity is indissolubly linked to the marshes. "Pip's cogito," as Peter Brooks calls it (116), takes place in the bleak and barren churchyard, in the presence of his parents' tombstones, and outlines the phenomenology of Pip's homeland: the horizontal line of the marshes, where the scattered cattle feed, severe witnesses of all his crimes; the low line of the river; and the distant origin of the wind, the sea. On these data Pip founds his knowledge of himself and the world, and this landscape resurfaces in hallucinatory flashes of vision whenever he is confronted with the problem of his identity. For example, when he recognizes the destructive yet irresistible nature of his love for Estella (Dickens 250) and later when he recognizes in Magwitch the old convict of his childhood. Moreover, the marshes become a metaphor of his condition when he compares the flatness and darkness of the place with the monotony and obscurity of his working days at the forge in contrast to the light vessels skipping across the waves, which stand for Estella and Miss Havisham (Dickens 107).

Pip too has been an unwanted and unloved child, raised "by hand" by his pugnacious sister and bullied by everyone but Joe, his slow-witted guardian angel. He has no qualms about confessing his dislike for his sister, but it is only with an acute self-accusatory tone that he admits to his "black ingratitude" for Joe, and to his disgraceful condition of feeling "ashamed of home" (Dickens 106). But unlike Julien, who feels he was born different from his kin, Pip realizes that he "should never like Joe's trade" and wants a gentleman's life only after coming into contact with another world, that of Satis House. Pip's disloyalty to his position in society and his own domestic hearth is a dreadful crime in Dickens's Victorian world, even if the home he betrays is characterized by injustice and discomfort. Just like Julien's, Pip's home is precarious and essentially inhabitable, dominated by the shrewish Mrs. Joe and greedy uncle Pumblechook. "If I could have settled down," he tells Biddy, "I know it would have been much better for me" (Dickens 128). But even the much anticipated apprenticeship at Joe's furnace has become a dreary burden now, and Biddy, although "comfortable enough," cannot compare with the cold and dazzling Estella.

Pip's desire for a gentleman's life and to appear worthy and to be worthy of Estella contradicts the moral imperative of respecting home and the hard-working life of Joe and Biddy. Robin Gilmour has shown that the fracture in Pip's identity is related to a specific historical juncture, the early Victorian era, when English lower middle class was caught "in its most anxious phase of self-definition, struggling out of trade and domestic service and clerical work into the sunshine of respectability" (Gilmour 106). And this anxiety is one of the knots in Pip's personality that recognition will unravel. The topography of the novel bears the trace of conflict between morally justified and culpable intentions: next to the forge are the prison hulks, and Pip's lodgings in London are but a short walk to Newgate prison. Pip's apparently groundless feeling of guilt, stimulated by the recurring apparition of prison-related figures, like Julien's constant self-reproach, are symptoms of both characters' failure to recognize that their ambitions are leading them on the wrong track.

To some extent, Julien Sorel and Pip reproduce the function of the typical folktale hero who ignores the interdiction and crosses the border, leaving the familiar world of home behind. But their transgression is not represented as simply wrong, or a whim. The urge that both characters feel to rise above their humble background, their idealism, and their desire for beauty and culture are positive impulses in themselves. Yet, they lead to a series of difficult choices, misunderstandings, and ambiguities that characterize the complex phase of their life at the palace.

The Palace
The next level in both heroes' experience is the space of the palace, the residence of a higher class, where the two working-class heroes discover that they are "coarse and common" and both undertake a strict training in order to erase these qualities. The palace is a place of intrigue and hypocrisy, a labyrinth populated by attractive female presences and alluring prospects of grandeur. Here the hero, blinded by his hubris, turns aside from the straight course and enters a masquerade in a disguise that does not suit him and that he cannot hold for long. The plain black suit of the

secretary conceals Julien's delirious plans of ascent to power and sexual domination; Pip's well-tailored suits and the stylish décor of his London apartment are not enough to erase the obscure sense of kinship with the sinful and the criminals. The new palace identity works like a cover thrown over the character's complex and contradictory self, a "bundle of shivers," as Pip calls himself, or a "mystery," a "monster," as Abbé Pirard defines Julien. In the same way, the glittering space of the palace is superimposed on a deeper layer of experience, the space of the home, which continues to work underground, is ready to explode in a disastrous volcanic recognition.

Following the discovery of his affair with Mme de Rênal, Julien is removed to the seminary in Besançon, and from there he makes his final leap to Paris and the Hôtel de la Mole. Here he has to learn how to dress, move, and talk according to the rules of the place and goes through a series of transformations: he is given new shirts by the marquis's tailor, takes dancing lessons, practices horse-riding, and struggles, like a cuckoo, to establish himself in the foreign nest. The transformation is complete when the marquis invents for him a new identity as the illegitimate son of a nobleman, which the society of the *salon* is keen to endorse because it rectifies the scandalous incongruity of his low birth with his innate nobility.

Living among balls, ultra-reactionary plots, and radical conspiracies, Julien jettisons his revolutionary ideals and forgets all about Mme de Rênal. The narrator marks the completion of his metamorphosis with the remark that "Julien était un dandy maintenant, et comprenait l'art de vivre à Paris (Stendhal 386; "Julien was a dandy now, and understood the art of living in Paris" [Slater 293]). The *salon* is the realm of Mathilde de la Mole, and there the haughty countess-to-be shines above all others. But she has no supremacy over Julien in the less public spaces of the house, especially the Marquis's library and the garden, where his strategy of seduction unexpectedly succeeds. When he is finally engaged to Mathilde, and the Marquis has made him a lieutenant of the Hussars, he reflects: "Après tout…mon roman est fini, et à moi seul tout le mérite"

(Stendhal 639; "When you come to think about it...my story is ended, and all the credit goes to me alone" [Slater 462]). Julien reads his own story as an eighteenth-century tale of audacity rewarded, à la Marivaux, and prepares himself for the expected happy ending. What is to end instead is the "roman" of the palace, the corrupted make-believe that alters and covers reality. Julien's new identity is destroyed by a letter from Mme de Rênal, which reveals their illicit love story to the Marquis and thus ends his plans to marry Mathilde. Past events, which he had removed as inconsequential to his new life at the palace, resurface as the forsaken home takes revenge on Julien, crushing the illusory "novel" of his social ascent. At the same time, the return of the past triggers a beneficial process of self-recognition and helps the hero to reconnect to his initial noble aspirations.

But let us now go back to *Great Expectations*. Here the palace is Satis House in a ruin, where the old Miss Havisham lives entombed in a state of near mummification, having removed herself and her house from the natural flow of time. But Pip's dazzled eyes see only elegance and aristocratic splendour in Satis House and are blind to the place's insanity and decay. Like the Rênals' house, Satis House is "up town" (Dickens 51), and before he can access it, the commoner Pip must purify himself in a bath (officiated by his rough-handed sister) and cover himself with a penitential sackcloth, in the form of a rigid Sunday suit. In fact, all his visits to Satis House have the character of a spiritual and corporal mortification. Mistaking Miss Havisham for a "fairy godmother" (Dickens 157), he consents the temptation of a world of sterility and death and allows a deadly *belle dame sans merci*, the beautiful Estella, to enchant him.

Unlike *Le rouge et le noir*, the first-person narrative of *Great Expectations* is illuminated by a retrospective view, so it is Pip himself who draws attention to his blindness and failure to recognize the poisonous nature of Satis House: "What could I become with these surroundings? How could my character fail to be influenced by them? Is it to be wondered at if my thoughts were dazed, as my eyes were, when I came out into the natural light from the misty yellow rooms?" (Dickens 96). Satis House awakens Pip's ambition, and when he is presented with his great expectations, he naturally credits them to Miss Havisham for removing the memory of Magwitch, the convict he saw on the marshes and for whom he felt pity. This belief finds confirmation in the fact that the London circles in which Pip moves are full of Miss Havisham's relations and collaborators. It appears for Pip that London is nothing but an extension of Satis House, the place that obsesses him and to which he regularly returns. As John Hagan has remarked, "The alternation between two different locales is basic to the whole. Pip tries to make his home in London, but he is forced a number of times to return to the site of his former life, and each return brings him a new insight into the truth of his position" (63). On each return Pip gains an increased intimacy with the mystery of Satis House, culminating with an overnight stay at the house, during which he spies a ghost-like Miss Havisham prowling around the rooms. Still, there is no true knowledge acquired from Satis House. The marshland, with its churchyard and its hulk, is where the truth about his identity lies.

Meanwhile, his life in London is a disappointment: in tune with the anti-urban bias of Victorian England and compatible with Dickens's description of an ugly, dirty, and corrupt city. Pip's rooms at Barnard's Inn are expensively decorated, but Joe declares he "wouldn't keep a pig in it [himself]" (Dickens 221). Compared to the simple comforts of the country home, the urban palace is nothing but a glittering surface laid over a rotten frame in London like at Satis House. Pip's free money buys him a comfortable drawing room at the temple, and there he sits oblivious to the east winds that engulf London, blowing straight from the marsh country and carrying with them the shadow of the old convict.

For John Carey, the storm belongs to the category of Dickens's symbolic devices, which involves "the use of objects as portents, heralds of momentous happenings" (123). Thus, Dickens preserves part of the prodigious character of recognition, here still announced by an upheaval in nature (the east wind) and by a white-haired man in rags, weary of sea travel, not unlike an Odysseus arriving incognito on Ithaca. Magwitch also re-enacts the age-old gesture of showing his tokens of recognition—two one-pound notes, admittedly not as emblematic as the traditional birthmarks or scars, but more in keeping with the prosaic concerns of the nineteenth century. In *Le rouge et le noir* the process of recognition is triggered by a letter delivered to the Marquis, in which Mme de Rênal exposes Julien's past conduct and reveals their affair. His plans to marry into aristocracy undone, Julien travels to Verrières almost in a state of trance, buys a pair of pistols and shoots Mme de Rênal in the back as she is attending Mass. He then lets himself be carried away by police and is locked up in the Besançon fortress. This whole sequence is told in a brisk matter-of-fact tone, with little insight into Julien's thoughts and intentions. After he has fired his gun twice, the narrator tells us, Julien "resta immobile, il ne voyait plus" (Stendhal 592; "stood motionless with unseeing eyes" [Slater 469]). This momentary paralysis and blindness represents the lowest point of Julien's *hamartia*, while also marking his removal from the artificial palace life and the moment when his awakening begins.

Julien and Pip are banished from the palace precisely when they seem to have reached the peak of their expectations. Prepared by signals and premonitions throughout the narrative, the moment of recognition arrives when illusory great expectations crash against the hard, unyielding certainties of life and the space of the palace is infiltrated by the rejected and forgotten spirit of home, which forces characters to throw off the cover of their constructed identities and to recognize their guilt. In *Le rouge et le noir* and *Great Expectations*, the experience of the palace ends disastrously with the reappearance of events and people from the past, such as Mme de Rênal and Magwitch, whose importance had been overlooked by the protagonist. But in both cases recognition is not immediate and does not take place directly in the instant of confrontation. Pip struggles for a few chapters to accept that his great expectations came indeed from Magwitch and his hopes about Satis House were "all a mere dream" (Dickens 323). It takes Julien some fifteen days of self-analysis and meditation in the solitude of his cell before the narrator announces that "l'ambition était morte en son coeur" (Stendhal 616; "ambition had died in his heart" [Slater 490]). So, even after they have been shown the tokens of recognition, Julien and Pip still have to renounce ambition and the world of the palace and reconcile themselves with the re-emergence of their past lives, their homes, and their real selves. The space where this extended process of recognition happens I have called the cell.

The Cell

The final stage of the two novels sees the protagonists reduced to a state of immobility and isolation. Julien, as we have seen, sits in his cell in Besançon. Pip lies on his sickbed after a failed attempt to smuggle the convict out of the country and following Magwitch's death in prison. After these action-filled sequences, the plot suddenly decelerates and space contracts, as if the motive force of ambition was exhausted, leaving Julien and Pip to rest in a space of confinement. The cell works as a decompression chamber where characters can readjust to reality, after the abrupt shift caused by the resurfacing of home. But it is also the place where movement stops, and with it, the narrative.

Prisons and cells are a major theme in *Le rouge et le noir* and *Great Expectations*. This mirrors the growth of public interest in penitential institutions in the nineteenth century. The first half of the century saw the consolidation of a vast process of reform of the judicial system in Europe and in the United States. In Michel Foucault's words, "it saw a new theory of law and crime, a new moral or political justification of the right to punish; old laws were abolished, old customs died out" (*Discipline and Punish* 7). Public execution, torture, chain-gang transports, and hulks gradually disappeared and were replaced by what was regarded by contemporaries as the most rational and equitable of penalties: the prison.

Both Stendhal and Dickens are fascinated by the image of the cell. Dickens's concern with the judicial system, penal institutions, the police, and crime in general has been widely discussed, both in terms of his own personal interest and of his literary reworking of the theme. Philip Collins, for instance, details his visits to prisons and madhouses, his subscription to legal journals and court gazettes. Edmund Wilson investigates Dickens's sympathy for the figures of criminals, convicts, and thieves who populate his novels, and his antagonism toward repressive institutions. Pip's sense of kinship with the convicts and, even more, his personal involvement with Magwitch show that Dickens's world is not one of segregation and pre-determination, but it is one of mutual influence and interrelatedness, in which recognition retraces the missing links between individuals across the social classes.

Nevertheless, neither Dickens nor Stendhal are in the least prepared to affirm the injustice of punishment per se and to see their convict heroes go free. D.A. Miller, in what he defines "a Foucaldian reading of the Novel," has exposed the self-contradiction inherent in the repudiation of policing power professed by Dickens and other nineteenth-century novelists, bringing to light a "radical entanglement between the nature of the novel and the practice of the police" (2), both of whom ultimately consist in active regulation and the preservation of an order, albeit in the fluid and less intrusive manner of modern surveillance techniques.

For Stendhal, the prison, and in particular the cell on top of a tower, is a place charged with spiritual and emotional resonances. It is the hermit's cell where Julien studies his books and rethinks his own story. And it is also the allegorical *carcel d'amor* of the late-medieval tradition where Julien is visited by his lover. The novel, which had begun with a dispute over the workhouse in Verrières, finds its circular conclusion in a prison cell on top of a gothic keep. The enclosed space is remote from every human contact, but opens onto a superb view of the Jura. Julien has found his eagle's nest again, and is overwhelmed by the same euphoric sense of freedom he had experienced in the mountain cave: "D'ailleurs, la vie m'est agreeable; ce séjour est tranquille; je n'y ai point d'ennuyeux, ajouta-t-il en riant, et il se mit à faire la note des livres qu'il voulait faire venir de Paris" (Stendhal 651; "Besides, I'm finding life enjoyable; this place is quiet; I don't have any tedious visitors, he added laughing, and he began to make a note of the books he wanted to have sent from Paris" [Slater 475]). The cell is a place of seclusion and privacy, free from external pressures, where time dilates and the compass of the story is finally allowed to adjust itself to the right direction. It is only in his cell that Julien regains, or actually finds for the first time, the freedom to orientate his own actions and judgement autonomously without the influence of the worldly values of the palace. As Brombert explains, "La prison stendhalienne restaure l'individu privilégié à son propre moi; ou plutôt, elle lui permet de le découvrir ou meme de le créer. La geôle assume ainsi un role à la fois protecteur et dynamique: elle libère et elle fait connaître "(78; "The Stendhalian prison restores the chosen individual to his own self; or rather, it allows him to discover or even create his own self. The gaol thus assumes a protecting and at the same time dynamic role: it provides both freedom and knowledge" [my translation]). The main principle of the penitentiary is isolation—both from the external world and from fellow inmates. Nineteenth-century advocates of prison reforms extolled the beneficial effects of solitude not as a mere disciplinary measure, but as a positive instrument for the transformation of individuals. One of the authors of the civil code of 1804, Jean-Baptiste Treilhard, wrote: "The order that must reign in the *maison de force* may contribute powerfully to the regeneration of the convicts. The vices of upbringing, the contagion of bad example, idleness have given birth to crime. Well, let us try to close up all these sources of corruption, [so that] soon they will begin to know regret for the past, the first harbinger of a love of duty (qtd. in Foucault, *Discipline and Punish* 234). Julien has had experience of other institutions, such as his father's workshop, the seminary, and the palace de la Môle, that are founded on authoritarian principles of discipline. But, the cell, as it is imagined by Stendhal, has a precious quality that those other spaces do not possess: it underscores isolation. The cell shuts the prisoner in, but it shuts the world out as well. No longer constrained by the need to dissimulate his real feelings and by the fear of punishment he suffered in the panoptic surveillance system of the palace and the seminary, Julien is finally alone in the silence of his cell where he begins to question his conscience, to "regret the past," and finally discovers where his "duty" lies as Treilhard's model of the perfect prison.

But justice takes its course, and even if Julien has fulfilled his moral rehabilitation and his itinerary to recognition, the story offers him no real alternative to death. There is no place left open for him, and he has no desire to compromise his newly found freedom to fit again in the world down below. So, after pronouncing an inflammatory oration in the court, he walks gladly to the scaffold, on a sunny day of early spring. For his part, Pip is neither jailed nor sentenced to death, but he attends to Magwitch in a London gaol, and then lies for some months in his sick chamber, saved from death and from the debtors' prison by Joe's timely intervention. Besides, the jail (in all its possible forms) has been a constant in Pip's life represented by the hulks on the marshes, the indentures that have him "bound" to Joe's forge, Mr. Wopsle's recital of the *Tragedy of George Barnwell* to his visits to Newgate prison, and his connection to Jaggers and Wemmick.

From the moment when Magwitch appears, Pip's life is bound to his as if by leg irons and becomes one of reclusiveness and suspicion. On the night of his arrival, his first care is "to close the shutters...and then to close and make fast the doors" (Dickens 323), making sure that the returned transport is safe. The time spent in the secluded space of the cell, nursing Magwitch in the prison infirmary, offers Pip the opportunity to reconsider his opinion of the uninvited benefactor. His initial disgust for Magwitch changes into compassion and an almost filial devotion. Pip then begins to view things with more lucidity and pieces together the events that led to the creation of his great expectations. But as with Julien, Pip's recognition of his bond to Magwitch and the reconsideration of the value of Satis House are not enough to grant him a safe return to the home he is now longing.

Shortly before the tragic escape attempt on the Thames, Pip receives the ominous warning "Don't go home" (Dickens 366). It is only a precautionary note left by Wemmick, but it has a disturbing effect on Pip's visionary mind, as he explains: "It plaited itself into whatever I thought of, as a bodily pain would have done" (Dickens 367). From that moment on he acts like an automaton, in a hopeless and mechanical manner, carrying out the plan he conceived with Herbert without any real sense of purpose or direction. According to Frances Armstrong, with the note "Don't go home," "Dickens is emphasising Pip's earlier recognition that he has no real home, and that he is partly responsible for the destruction of other homes too" (138), such as the home he could have created with Biddy as his wife and Joe as his father.

Unsettled by Pip's refusal to conform to the prepared course of events, the situation at home nevertheless develops and finds a new balance with the marriage of Joe and Biddy. But this newly found harmony also means that the home is now closed to any further change. There is no place left open for Pip; so, when he eventually tries to "go back home," he finds that his allotted place beside Biddy has already been taken. Recognition does not imply the negation of what has happened in the middle phase of the story, in the confusion of the palace. In both novels, it is impossible for the hero to return smoothly to the initial stage since the home has changed during his absence and because the palace has influenced his character too deeply for him to fit again into the restricted space of the provincial town. After all, Pip's desire to become a gentleman has been fulfilled even if his expectations have lost their greatness, and, by the end of the novel, he is less common and has more experience of the wider world than before. In a sense, Pip's new social position is established, and there can be no return to a life with Joe and Biddy in the village.

In both *Le rouge et le noir* and in *Great Expectations*, the modern utopia of carceral reformation and the ancient memory of the hermit's den concur in the characterization of the cell as a haven for thought and a catalyst for recognition, which brings about a providential change of heart in the characters. In narrative terms, the cell resets the story to zero, through a contraction of the space that flattens the gain in elevation from the low provincial workshop to the heights of the metropolitan palace. From the cell, both heroes try to annul the narrative by returning full-circle to the beginning of their adventures, but their movements are blocked. One is condemned to immobility in death and the other is fated to carry on a life in which all energy has melted away, where only dissipated relics, a subdued Estella and an empty Satis House remain.

Conclusion

The same tripartite movement from home to palace and finally to the cell forms the structure of Stendhal's and Dickens's novels, and these three movements correspond to three stages in the hero's route towards recognition. At home, their mark of difference and their ambition push them away toward the palace, where the illusions of grandeur confuse their sight. Only when a sudden crisis precipitates them in the cell are they finally able to see clearly and complete the process of recognition.

In order to enact the simple pattern of the recognition story, the nineteenth-century novel develops a complex system of intersecting spaces that complicate the traditional trope of romance and myth. In *The Order of Things*, Foucault identifies the main characteristic of the modern *episteme* of the nineteenth century with the discovery of an "obscure verticality" (251) under the surface of things, an invisible substratum on which the visible rests, which contains the ultimate meaning and, so to speak, the kernel of reality. The idea of space that emerges from this new epistemological order is characterized by an increasing complexity and plurality of values: "A space without essential continuity. A space that is posited from the very outset in the form of fragmentation. A space crossed by lines which sometimes diverge and sometimes intersect" (Foucault, *Order of Things* 272).

The complex tapestry of the two novels evokes different, opposing worlds: the plot of Satis House and the plot of the marshes, Verrières and Paris, cold-blooded ambition and generous humanity. These spaces are linked by the movement of the hero across the border and finally made visible and recognized through the very experience of change. In this connection, we can reconsider Cave's definition of recognition as "a compulsive returning to the 'same' place...as if one were discovering it for the first time" (488): recognition can only take place in a space that allows mobility where people desire to rise and to change places, to be somewhere where they do not belong, and to become something that they cannot be.

The fact that Julien and Pip, like many other young protagonists of nineteenth-century novels, do not succeed in their transplantation probably tells us something about nineteenth-century society and the tensions that run through it. The revolutions have torn apart the orderly picture of the ancien régime, liberating the energies that were trapped by it. So, even after the Restoration imposes a return to order, the perception remains of a vertiginous depth below the ground on which Europe stands. It is an odd coincidence that Stendhal insisted on calling his novel "a chronicle of 1830," in spite of evident anachronisms in the story. In general, critics, such as Bradbury and Gilmour, agree on situating the beginning of Pip's story in the past with respect to the time of writing, approximately thirty years before 1860. The two novels thus reflect on the specific social context of Europe in the 1830s with Pip representing the Victorian middle class in its quest for redemption from menial work and social subordination. Julien, on the other hand, stands for the crushed hopes of many young Frenchmen in the post-Napoleonic era, when Stendhal sees the time of great ideals and social mobility come to an end and views France as dominated by conservatism and fear. Marshall Berman, in *All that is Solid Melts into Air*, describes the experience of modernity in post-revolutionary Europe as restlessly tending toward modernisation, opening up new perspectives and thus unleashing the ambition and energy of individuals. But, he observes, the possibility of expansion is not infinite and someone always has to be left out. What is more, the great changes in the social system brought not only enthusiasm but also fear, not only hope for a more just society, but also the looming threat of social chaos and anomie.

Ambiguity and contradiction are thus central to the experience of modernity. And they emerge also in the form of the novel in the nineteenth century, which continues to avail itself of the old machinery of the narrative tradition, but adapts it to a new conception of man and the world. In the nineteenth century, recognition has lost some of its power: it has become an instance of comprehension more than a force capable of reversing the direction of the events. The "mistakes of the middle" cannot be redeemed by the final recognition, characters and events can no longer simply pull back out of the muddle, and the initial truth and order cannot be completely recovered. Moreover, as Cave explains, modern anagnorisis is no longer total, but often partial and does not completely put at rest the desire for knowledge of both characters and readers. This is the case in *Le rouge et le noir*, *Great Expectations*, and in many nineteenth-century novels: "An ignorance which was never wholly innocent turns *for the moment* into an implausible and precarious knowledge; the apparent opposite poles of knowledge and ignorance meet in surreptitious complicity (complicity is, indeed, the prime index of Aristotle's 'complex' or 'twisted' plot)" (Cave 489, emphasis original). A complex and twisted plot is in fact what Stendhal and Dickens construct in their novels. And their recognition scenes are, accordingly, both complex, associated with a multiplicity of places and movements in space, and twisted since they do not assert equivalence, but a divergence and a lack of balance, between ideals and sordid compromises and between high hopes and a reality that proves to be less open and malleable than expected.

Works Cited

Aristotle. *Poetics*. Ed. Stephen Halliwell. Loeb Classical Library. Cambridge, MA: Harvard University Press, 2005. Print.

Armstrong, Frances. *Dickens and the Concept of Home*. Ann Arbor, MI: UMI Research Press, 1990. Print.

Berman, Marshall. *All that is Solid Melts into Air: The Experience of Modernity*. London: Verso, 1983. Print.

Bersani, Leo. *A Future for Astyanax: Character and Desire in Literature*. London: Marion Boyars, 1978. Print.

Bradbury, Nicola. *Charles Dickens' Great Expectations*. New York: St. Martin's Press, 1990. Print.

Brombert, Victor. *La prison romantique: essai sur l'imaginaire*. Paris: Corti, 1975. Print.

Brooks, Peter. *Reading for the Plot: Design and Intention in Narrative*. Cambridge, MA: Harvard University Press, 1992. Print.

Carey, John. *The Violent Effigy: A Study of Dickens's Imagination*. London: Faber and Faber, 1973. Print.

Cave, Terence. *Recognitions: A Study in Poetics*. Oxford: Clarendon Press, 1988. Print.

Collins, Philip Arthur William. *Dickens and Crime*. London: Macmillan, 1962. Print.

Dickens, Charles. *Great Expectations*. 1860–1861. Ed. Charlotte Mitchell. London: Penguin, 2003. Print.

Duncan, Ian. *Modern Romance and Transformations of the Novel: The Gothic, Scott, Dickens*. Cambridge: Cambridge University Press, 1992. Print.

Foucault, Michel. *Discipline and Punish: The Birth of the Prison*. 1975. London: Penguin, 1991. Print.

———. *The Order of Things: An Archaeology of the Human Sciences*. 1966. London: Tavistock, 1970. Print.

Gilmour, Robin. *The Idea of the Gentleman in the Victorian Novel*. London: Allen & Unwin, 1981. Print.

Hagan, John H. Jr. "The Poor Labyrinth: The Theme of Social Injustice in Dickens's *Great Expectations*." *Critical Essays on Charles Dickens's Great Expectations*. Ed. Michael Cotsell. Boston: G.K. Hall, 1990. 56–63. Print.

Lotman, Yuri M. *Universe of the Mind: A Semiotic Theory of Culture*. Trans. Ann Shukman. London: I.B. Tauris, 1990. Print.

Miller, D.A. *The Novel and the Police*. Berkeley: University of California Press, 1988. Print.

Stendhal [Marie-Henri Beyle], "Le rouge et le noir: Chronique de 1830." 1830. *Romans et Nouvelles*. Ed. Henri Martineau. Vol. 1. Paris: Gallimard, 1952. 193–730. Print.

———. *The Red and the Black*. 1830. Trans. Catherine Slater. New York: Oxford University Press, 1998. Print.

Wilson, Edmund. *The Wound and the Bow*. 1941. London: Methuen, 1961. Print.

11

RECOGNIZING OUR MISRECOGNITIONS
Plato and the Contemporary Politics of Recognition

CHRISTINA TARNOPOLSKY

The Contemporary Politics of Recognition

As this volume makes clear, recognition has been an important theme in religion, literature, and philosophy for centuries. However, renewed interest in this theme has arisen over the past two decades in the fields of social and political theory as a result of four intersecting developments, two occurring on the level of practices and two on the level of theory. On the level of practices, the widespread growth of social movements making demands for justice on the basis of ethnicity, race, language, culture, gender, and sexuality brought the theme of recognition to the fore in many countries (Markell 2; Gutmann 3; Habermas 581–83). Concomitantly, the fall of the Soviet Union in 1989 as well as the horrific genocides that took place in Bosnia, Somalia, and Rwanda all placed issues of ethnic conflict, immigration, citizenship, and nationalism at the centre of global politics (Markell 2; Taylor 25). All of these events in diverse ways and via very different means involved the demand for recognition of one's identity, both personal and collective, amongst one's neighbours, allies, and enemies.

During this period a number of political theorists began to approach these problems through the philosophies of Rousseau and Hegel. It was Hegel who first coined the term "the struggle for recognition" (*Kampf um Anerkennung*) and who provided the most influential philosophical treatment of this theme (Markell 2; Honneth, *Struggle* 5). While he argued that such struggles for recognition often involved "struggles unto death," he also provided a salutary model of mutual and reciprocal recognition: i.e., "to know what it means to be an 'I' and a 'me,' to know that I am an 'other' to you and that likewise, you are an 'I' to yourself but an 'other' to me" (Benhabib 340, 359; Cf. Honneth, *Struggle* 16). Many of these same scholars also began to talk about a shift away from a "politics of redistribution" towards a "politics of recognition." Where the "politics of redistribution" had focused on the injustice of material inequality and exploitation and advocated a redistribution of wealth, the "politics of recognition" now focused on the injustice of cultural domination and advocated an equal distribution of respect and esteem for society's diverse members (Fraser 68; Markell 2).

All of these themes came together in 1992 in two influential essays, one by the Canadian philosopher Charles Taylor, entitled "The Politics of Recognition," and the other by the critical theorist Axel Honneth, entitled "Integrity and Disrespect: Principles of a Conception of Morality Based on the Theory of Recognition." Taylor argued that "nonrecognition or misrecognition can inflict harm, can be a form of oppression, imprisoning someone in a false, distorted, and reduced mode of being....[Beyond simple lack of respect], it can inflict a grievous wound, saddling its victims with a crippling self-hatred. Due recognition is not just a courtesy we owe people. It is a vital human need" (25–26). Similarly, Honneth argued that "we owe our integrity...to the receipt of approval or recognition from other persons. [Negative concepts such as 'insult' or 'degradation'] are related to forms of disrespect, to the denial of recognition. [They] are used to characterize a form of behaviour that does not represent an injustice solely because it constrains the subjects in their freedom for action or does them harm. Rather, such behaviour is injurious because it impairs these persons in their positive understanding of self—an understanding acquired by intersubjective means" ("Integrity" 188–89). In his piece, Taylor established a norm of equality governing the distribution of recognition by looking to Rousseau's doctrine of the general will, which for Taylor did not eliminate the human need for esteem, but rather ensured its equal and uniform distribution (Taylor 49). Taylor argued that, for Hegel as well, the only satisfactory solution to the struggle for recognition is a regime of "reciprocal recognition among equals" (50). Modern polities, Taylor argued, must extend public recognition to all of their citizens, both as human beings worthy of respect and as unique individuals worthy of esteem (Taylor, 51–73; Cf. Markell, 3; Honneth, "Integrity" 189).

Taylor's and Honneth's accounts of the politics of recognition both identified instances of injustice or "misrecognition" as the failure arising either "out of malice or out of ignorance, to extend people the respect or esteem that is their due in virtue of who they are" (Markell 3). As Honneth puts it, "What the term 'disrespect' refers to is the specific vulnerability of humans resulting from the internal interdependence of individualization and recognition" (*Struggle* 131). They also identified the crucial element of recognition that underlies a notion of democracy as self-determination or self-rule: for a democratic regime to be a legitimate case of such self-rule all citizens must be able to understand the rules and decisions to which they are subject as in some sense expressions of their own will (Taylor 48–51; Markell 3). Polities that rely on persistent forms of identity-based inequality thus make it difficult for members of subordinated groups to understand themselves as part of the sovereign "people" and to understand political decisions as part of their own doing (Taylor 48; Markell 3). Even more problematically, this kind of disrespect or misrecognition can lead these subordinated groups towards violence (Gutmann 21).

Criticisms of the Politics of Recognition

Interestingly enough, in more recent years even this new politics of recognition has been criticized for performing its own kind of misrecognition of the very conditions of human social and political interaction. Patchen

Markell has questioned whether the transparent and mutual recognition valorized by Taylor and Honneth is either a possible or a desirable form of democratic intersubjectivity. As Markell argues, the pursuit of recognition involves a misrecognition that is much deeper than just the misrecognition of one's own or someone else's identity; it involves misrecognizing a fundamental aspect of our human finitude, understood not in terms of our mortality, but in terms of the openness and unpredictability of the future (10–11). Citing Hannah Arendt's work, *The Human Condition*, Markell claims that such a politics often involves misrecognizing the non-sovereign character of human action (5). For both Arendt and Markell, we are never fully in control of our identities, and the demand for a full recognition of who we are risks essentializing these very identities and binding us to them to our own detriment (Markell 14). Similarly, Anthony Appiah warns that, "Demanding respect for people as blacks and as gays requires that there are some scripts that go with being an African-American or having same-sex desires. There will be proper ways of being black or gay, there will be expectations to be met, demands will be made. It is at this point that someone who takes autonomy seriously will ask whether we have not replaced one kind of tyranny with another" (162–63). The desire for recognition also involves the desire for a kind of sovereign agency that may itself be at the root of a much deeper form of social and political injustice, such that successful exchanges of mutual recognition may in fact reinforce existing injustices or help to create new ones (Markell 5). Patchen Markell, Anthony Appiah, Michel Foucault, Wendy Brown, and Michael Warner have all argued that by always looking to the sovereign state or the law to fulfill their demands for recognition, certain groups end up increasing the power of these regulatory apparatuses at the cost of losing their own unique forms of existence and association (Markell 29; Appiah 163; Foucault 105–08; Brown 28; Warner, *Trouble* 192). Instead, such groups would do better to create and preserve their own "counterpublics" where they can embrace the notion of an identity that is fluid and unstable, risky and mysterious, and *for that very reason* supplies a rich and inexhaustible resource for political agency (Warner, *Publics* 122).

In contrast to a politics of recognition, Markell (32–38) calls for a politics of acknowledgement where democratic justice does not require that all people be known and respected as who they really are. (Such a thing is not even possible given the political ontology of thinkers like Markell, Appiah, Arendt, Foucault, Brown, and Warner.) Instead, it requires that no one be reduced to any characterization of his or her identity for the sake of someone else's achievement of a sense of sovereignty or invulnerability, regardless of whether that characterization is negative or positive, hateful or friendly (Markell 34–36; Cf. Warner, *Trouble* 218). Finally, it means "coming to terms with, rather than vainly attempting to overcome, the risk of conflict, hostility, misunderstanding, opacity, and alienation that characterizes life among others" (Markell 38). Similarly, Judith Butler argues that in the aftermath of events like 9/11, democratic theorists ought to begin to use this experience of loss, violence, dependency on anonymous others, disorientation, and recognition of our all-too-permeable boundaries to "think through this primary impressionability and vulnerability with a theory of power and recognition" (45).

Shame and Recognition

How then should we theorize intersubjective recognition within contemporary democratic polities in a way that can do justice to the respect, esteem, and dignity that Taylor and Honneth valorize, while also recognizing the fragile, conflictual, painful, mysterious, risky, and open character of these struggles for recognition valorized by Markell, Appiah, Foucault, Brown, Butler, and Warner? I believe that instead of turning to Hegel or Rousseau, we would do well to turn to Plato. Interestingly enough, many of these questions about the character of intersubjective recognition within democratic polities—its fragility and fluidity, painful and pleasant, conflictual and consensual character—were first addressed in Plato's dialogue entitled the *Gorgias*. In this dialogue, Plato turns his attention to the various ways in which the intersubjectivity characteristic of the emotion of shame can disrupt or enhance deliberations within a democratic polity.

Plato actually outlines three different models of a politics of shame in order to illustrate the various kinds of intersubjective recognition that can characterize democratic deliberations. These different models of a politics of shame come to light in the three-way "debate" between the rhetorician, Gorgias (and his followers, Polus and Callicles), the philosopher, Socrates, and the writer of the dialogue, Plato. I put "debate" in quotation marks because of the fact that Plato never speaks directly in his dialogues. The *Gorgias* itself contains a conversation between five interlocutors: (1) Socrates, (2) Gorgias, (3) Socrates's friend, Chaerephon, (4) Gorgias's student, Polus, and (5) the Athenian citizen and potential statesman, Callicles. One of the major themes of the dialogue is rhetoric, that is, how one ought to debate and comport oneself in the Athenian democratic assembly. However, I think that, especially in the middle and late dialogues, one cannot equate Plato's views with Socrates's. Instead, Plato's own views are articulated by the drama of the dialogue, by what is said and shown by all of the interlocutors in the dialogue. Accordingly, I actually derive three different models of a politics of shame from the dialogue, one of which is espoused by Polus and Callicles, one by Socrates, and one by Plato.[1] Before turning to an analysis of this dialogue, I need to first clarify the link between shame and intersubjective recognition.

Why was shame so central to intersubjective recognition for the Greeks and still, I would argue, for us today? Because shame is the emotion that is concerned fundamentally with sight and more specifically with being seen and recognized by an "other," both in a general and a concrete sense. In its most basic form it involves the "specific discomfort produced by the sense of being looked at" (Cavell 278). Here shame takes the form of a fear of censure produced by the gaze of a generalized other. However, as Bernard Williams reminds us, shame can involve the fear of censure from a much more specific and concrete other: i.e., we might not feel shame if people we do not admire and respect try to shame us (82). This is because shame depends in part on our thoughts about who is doing the shaming and what we are in fact supposed to be ashamed about. Shame thus is more than just blind feelings of unease. It has significant cognitive elements that involve both propositional truth claims—that such and such is the case in the world—and claims to normative rightness—that I ought to be ashamed of not keeping my promises or stealing from my best friend (Tarnopolsky, "Frank Speech" 51). Shame thus involves the cognitive-affective recognition of the gaze of an "other" that reveals a certain inadequacy in the self (Tarnopolsky, *Prudes* 18).[2] Shame is, in this sense, always social and relational because it involves the ways in which the self is seen or recognized by an other as inadequate.

It is also important to note that shame does not exclude respect, esteem, or dignity, but rather works against a background of these characteristic forms of recognition. It is precisely because one has a sense of dignity and respect for others and a sense of self-respect or self-esteem that one can then recognize in shame how one has (at least momentarily) lost this respect or dignity in the eyes of an other, or failed to live up to their own standards for granting such forms of recognition to an other (Nussbaum, "Shame" 404). Understanding shame requires understanding what we, individually and collectively, consider to be worthy or respectable aspects of human being. Finally, in shame there is always at least a momentary consensus between the self and the other: that is, that a certain ideal that has been transgressed. We might then disagree about whether one ought to be ashamed of falling below this standard, that is, whether the standard itself is false or unjust, but this disagreement goes on against the background of an initial consensus. In the latter part of this chapter, I will show how the kind of "respectful shame" that I derive from Plato incorporates these elements of consensus and disagreement, as well as shame's attunement to or desire for recognition from both general and concrete others, but first, it is important to confront head-on the suspicious character of shame.

Most definitions or understandings of shame (including my own) also point to the unease, discomfort, or painfulness of shame, and to the fact that there is an element of passivity, a loss of power, or a kind of coerciveness to shame. As Williams puts it, "the root of shame lies in exposure," not so much in the specific and paradigm instance of nakedness, but "in a more general sense of being at a disadvantage: in a loss of power" (220). These facts about shame are what have often marked it as an emotion to be *avoided* in any kind of democratic politics of recognition. Thus, in order to recoup shame as a positive emotion for the politics of recognition, it is necessary to address the concerns of those theorists who argue that the *avoidance* of pain, in both its physical and psychological forms, is what should be avoided when constructing models of democratic deliberation.

Plato's response to this kind of criticism of shame depends on his insight into the divergence of the pleasant and the good, the painful and the bad, in human life. This is one of the most important arguments of the *Gorgias*. Being shown in shame that you do not live up to certain ideals or exemplars of behaviour is psychologically painful because it sunders one's pleasant identification with the beloved object. Indeed, Socrates forcefully shatters the ideals and heroes of all of his interlocutors in the *Gorgias* by showing them that they do not live up to their beloved image of the tyrant. Yet this can be beneficial if, as the example of the tyrant illustrates, the object of one's longing is in fact fantastical or unethical (Tarnopolsky, *Prudes* 95–96). Plato shows us that *this* kind of psychological pain can be beneficial and is not equivalent to the kind of coerciveness that many democratic theorists of recognition are and ought to be worried about.

Moreover, Plato's dialogue, *Gorgias*, shows us that not all forms of shame are alike, and his distinctions between "flattering," Socratic "respectful," and Platonic "respectful" shame actually help us moderns to think about the different kinds of shame and shaming practices that can characterize human communicative interactions aimed at the always frail but salutary achievement of mutual and intersubjective recognition.

Plato's *Gorgias* and the Politics of Shame

The dialogue itself begins with a discussion between Socrates and Gorgias concerning the art of rhetoric. Here a certain kind of rhetoric is described as flattery because it aims solely at what is pleasant according to the existing prejudices of one's audience: it is analogous to a pastry chef who offers tasty treats to an audience of thoughtless children who think nothing of the potential dangers of consuming vast quantities of such treats (*Gorg.* 464c–465e).[3] In contrast, Socrates describes his own "political art" as being analogous to medicine because it knows the nature of the things that it administers and involves painful and bitter procedures that aim at the health of the patient (*Gorg.* 464c–464e, 465d).[4] Gorgias is then followed by his student, Polus, who explicitly espouses the life of tyranny and who argues that it is better to do injustice than to suffer it (*Gorg.* 470a–474b). Socrates, however, eventually shames him into agreeing that it is actually better to suffer injustice than to do it (*Gorg.* 474b–475e). Callicles, a promising Athenian citizen and potential statesman, then enters the discussion also espousing the life of tyranny. He argues that this life includes *pleonexia* (over-reaching/taking more than one's share) and indiscriminate hedonism (the pursuit of any and all pleasures), and Socrates is finally able to shame him into admitting instead that some pleasures are better than others and that some pleasures need to be restrained (*Gorg.* 490a–499b).

The first thing that the *Gorgias* teaches us about shame is that there are actually two moments to a shame situation: the moment of recognition and the moment of reaction (Tarnopolsky, *Prudes* 17–18, 57–58). Each of Socrates's encounters with his interlocutors in the *Gorgias* vividly illustrates these two moments. Under the critical gaze of Socrates, the interlocutor is eventually ashamed to realize that their specific definition of the best life is not consistent with other things that they also believe. They then react to this recognition either by squirming and trying to hide this discrepancy from themselves (e.g., Callicles) or, more positively, they try to transform themselves in accordance with the new insight that they achieve in and through the shame situation (e.g., Gorgias). In the dialogue itself, Gorgias illustrates the more positive reaction to shame by continually re-entering the discussion after he has been shamed by Socrates either to push the discussion forward and learn something new about rhetoric (*Gorg.* 506b1–3), or to contest the cowardly way in which Callicles is reacting to Socrates's shaming refutation (*Gorg.* 497b8–10).

Most contemporary theorists who speak about a "politics of shame" focus only on the reaction of hiding from or displacing the painful recognition involved in shame by displacing it onto others (Elster 153; Massaro 89; Warner, *Trouble* 3; Nussbaum, *Hiding* 183). The only people who ever feel shame in contemporary democracies, according to Warner and Nussbaum, are the misrecognized "perverts" and "weirdoes" who fall outside of and fail to assimilate to the norm of the "good" or "normal" citizen (Warner, *Trouble* 3; Nussbaum, *Hiding* 217–18). Indeed, like Taylor and Honneth, Nussbaum and Warner are right to worry that this kind of stigmatizing action is injurious to these citizens because it robs them of the respect and dignity owed to them as equal members of a democratic polity. However, Plato's *Gorgias* teaches us that this kind of reaction to shame (i.e., to hide from it or displace it onto others) is not the only possible one, nor is it the one that leads to salutary transformations within the public sphere. This kind of reaction depends on overemphasizing the *painfulness* of the experience and assuming that this painfulness is necessarily linked to its *perniciousness* for the person suffering shame (Tarnopolsky, *Prudes* 19, 106–07; "Frank Speech" 53–54).

Moreover, it can lead one to pursue the kind of flattering politics that is favoured by both Polus and Callicles in the *Gorgias*. When Polus and Callicles describe to Socrates how one should comport oneself in the Athenian Assembly, they tell him that one should gratify or flatter the audience and thus tailor their remarks to the audiences' existing prejudices such that this audience never has to hear anything unpleasant about themselves (*Gorg.* 462c–466a; 521b). The goal is the *avoidance* of the painful feelings of shame on the part of both the speaker and the audience. Flattery here aims at the pleasant without the best because it aims at the pleasures of mutual recognition as such, without regard to whether we ought to be so complacently pleased with this image of the "good" and "normal" citizen. As Socrates puts it, such orators are like pastry chefs who offer children the sweets they want without every considering whether these are beneficial and whether like doctors they might sometimes have to administer bitter and painful medicines to achieve the health of the patient (*Gorg.* 464d).[5] Much like Markell, Appiah, Foucault, Brown, and Butler, Plato felt that there can then be a problematic form of mutual recognition that occurs when citizens in a democratic polity are all oriented to maintaining a fantastical image of themselves as completely sovereign, omnipotent beings in complete control of their collective destiny.

In contrast to this, the model of politics that Socrates espouses involves a kind of shaming as an integral part of deliberation and debate. Here, it is important to note that in Attic Greek, the word *elenchus*, which is used to describe Socrates's incessant questioning of everyone he meets, means *both* a reproach, disgrace, or dishonour *and* a cross-examining or testing for purposes of disproof or refutation (Liddell and Scott 531). Socrates shames those he meets in an attempt to get them to think reflexively about themselves by recognizing the gap or distance between their self-images and their specific actions. His refutations are perplexing, discomforting, and painful because they always sunder the interlocutor's easy identification with his beloved ideals. It is simply a fact about human life that it is painful to have one's pretenses punctured and one's ideals shattered by another, but the positive outcome of such a painful experience is its ability to disrupt or unsettle one's blind or unthinking identification with such ideals. Shame involves the experience of having one's identification with such ideals disrupted and realizing that we are not who we thought we were. Producing perplexity in others was thus Socrates's way of prompting those around him to recognize their misrecognitions. This, however, can be a good thing if who we are cannot be fully captured by a unitary or fantastical standard. It is *this* potential in shame that underlies Socrates's elenchic or shaming encounters with his interlocutors in the *Gorgias* (Tarnopolsky, *Prudes* 95–96). Much like Markell's notion of acknowledgement (35), Socrates's "respectful" shaming is not as much about getting people to recognize and respect *other* people, as it is about getting them to understand and acknowledge something about *themselves*, which then underpins the way that they subsequently recognize others.

To repeat then, there are important differences between the "flattering" shame that Polus and Callicles preach (and that Taylor, Honneth, Warner, and Nussbaum criticize), and the "respectful" shame that Socrates practices and preaches. In the case of "flattering" shame, one fixates on the pain that is inherent to the recognition of losing one's ego-ideal under the disapproving gaze of the other, and it is this painful recognition that becomes the "shameful" situation that one tries to avoid in the future. But avoiding these painful recognitions might well amount to avoiding the recognition of our common human fragilities. The problem is that shame does involve a painful diminution of the self even when the other is pointing out our common vulnerabilities as human beings (Tarnopolsky, *Prudes* 157–58). It is painful to be shown that we are human and not omnipotent, sexless, bodiless gods. In other words, the false consensus or misrecognition that underlies this type of shame is the belief that we ought to be omnipotent, invulnerable beings, and the reaction then is always to conceal our vulnerabilities and to reestablish the mythic image of invulnerability. The speaker's sense of shame thus attunes him to the view of the other or audience, but in such a way that this other can never again reveal any inadequacies or criticisms of his self. Nor is he (the speaker) oriented to revealing any inadequacies in his audience. Instead, both parties to the debate are oriented to maintaining the mythic unity of an objectified public image of the "citizen." A false consensus and form of mutual recognition then occurs wherein "debate" becomes a kind of reciprocal exchange of pleasures or pleasantries, such that neither party ever has to endure the pain of having one's identity or ideals criticized by the other.

"Flattering" shame thus endangers democracy in at least two ways.[6] First, it aims at the pleasures of mutual recognition as such, thus foreclosing the possibility that the other we are addressing might actually show us something different and even unpleasant about ourselves. Second, it tries to move in a world of complete certainty, unity, and invulnerability, where there is one standard of the "normal citizen" that we all discern and follow. Those actions or aspects of the self that do not fit this mythic unity are then displaced onto other individuals or groups in the shaming practices of derision and stigmatization. The person whose sense of shame has fixated on the pleasures of mutual recognition, and who is oriented to restoring the lost unity that is always sundered by feelings of shame, will inevitably try to escape the "shame" of failing to live up to the norm by displacing it onto others. Here I think we can see why *this* kind of shame turns into a politics of humiliation or stigmatization of the other. If we are concerned with maintaining an inhuman or godlike invulnerability, then our very human weaknesses are displaced onto the marginalized other who becomes less than human if only because they always threaten to reveal our own humanness to us.

In contrast to this, Socrates's own sense of shame offers a model of respect that is grounded in preserving our very openness to judgement by the other that is present in the primary occurrence of shame. This kind of respectful shame is oriented to dissecting the mythical unity of these images of the "just citizen" in the ongoing project of mutual reflection. The morality grounded in this kind of "respectful" shame consists not in assimilating to a standard or norm, but rather in remaining open to the ongoing possibility that who you are cannot be captured by any particular norm or self-image you currently possess. It also requires understanding that the demands of morality might well run counter to the false moralism of the established norms of society and its conceptions of citizenship (Villa 3).

In this articulation, it might sound like we should simply replace a politics of feeling good with a politics of feeling bad, and then go around relentlessly shaming and perplexing everyone we meet. But I think that the *Gorgias* ultimately offers a third model of a politics of shame, which reflects Plato's own attempts to articulate a kind of respectful shame that goes beyond the limitations of the absolute negativity of the Socratic elenchus (Tarnopolsky, *Prudes* 167–71). Plato agrees with Socrates that shaming someone for their own benefit is necessary in light of the fact that the pleasant and the good are not identical in human life, and that a certain amount of pain is integral to the recognition of moral truths. However, his revision to this kind of Socratic shaming reflects two additional considerations. First, not all pleasures are bad, and, indeed, certain pleasures might well be beneficial as part of the more curative aspects of a noble rhetoric.[7] Second, although shame does involve the realization that we have fallen away from our ideals, it also involves an element of consensus between the self and the other. Socrates's absolute negativity overlooks the fact that certain experiences and standards are still shared between the self and the other even when this other is showing us that we have fallen below a specific standard.

Thus in the *Gorgias*, for the first time, Socrates does not just engage in a ruthless critique of every definition of a virtue and then throw up his hands and walk away. Instead, he shows his interlocutors that although or even because they fail to live by the standards of the tyrants they profess to admire, they do then agree with Socrates about certain ideals: e.g., suffering injustice is better than doing it and that restraining the desires is better than indiscriminately satisfying all of them. Also, as he reminds Callicles, these ideals are the same ones that are put forth by the Athenian demos (*Gorg.* 488e–489b). Thus, for Plato, the recognition of our misrecognition of ourselves as tyrants simultaneously involves the recognition of our own shared humanity and salutary *lack* of omnipotence and invulnerability.

Indeed, I believe that these criticisms and corrections depend upon Plato's own deepening understanding of the role of shame in communicative interactions. For Plato, Socrates's sense of shame was so attuned to the search for truth that it prevented him from *ever* uttering any pleasantries at all, or anything from within the viewpoint of his audience. In a certain sense Socrates's ironic comportment to others made him a radical other such that no real understanding could be achieved between him and Athens (Tarnopolsky, *Prudes* 168). But as Plato realized, shame quickly spirals into anger when the person who is ashamed does not fully accept or grasp the standards by which they are judged. Thus, for

Plato, "respectful" shame requires acknowledging the place or terrain of the audience in terms of both the experiences they have suffered and the standards they now use to interpret these experiences (Tarnopolsky, *Prudes* 139). Moving between different conceptual schemas requires a principle of charity, of acknowledging the shared standards upon which any meaningful disagreement or difference can even be perceived.

Plato and the Contemporary Debate
The Platonic model of respectful shame incorporates a number of the insights and criticisms of the politics of recognition outlined earlier. More specifically, it finds a salutary place for conflict, risk, and difference, even while retaining a place for reciprocity, respect, and consensus in a model of intersubjective recognition. First, then, Plato's model of respectful shame finds a place for the kinds of struggle and resistance that Markell argues is lacking in Taylor's view of transparent and mutual recognition (3). This is contained in the Socratic elements Plato retains in his own notion of respectful shame. Socrates's shaming refutations of his interlocutors are painful and discomforting because they are meant to show these people that they do not fully live up to their own conceptions of virtuous citizenship. Socrates comes across to most people, both then and now, as a rude and uncivil nuisance precisely because his elenchic activity is meant to disrupt the blind conformity to the norms of virtuous citizenship that he continually encounters in those he meets. Socrates's point is that being a rational citizen might actually involve *dissolving or contesting* rather than *affirming* our respective identities in a more agonistic politics of recognition (Tarnopolsky, *Prudes* 167).[8]

Secondly, Plato's own notion of respectful shame supplements this negative aspect of the Socratic elenchus with his own deepening reflections on the character of shame. As I mentioned earlier, these insights consist of the need to acknowledge the place of one's audience and the experiences and standards that are shared between the self and the other, even in moments of intense disagreement, struggle, and discomfort. In a certain sense, then, shame involves a negotiation between the self and a general *and* concrete other at the same time. This is because it involves the recognition of how one has fallen away from a certain ideal against the backdrop of a shared consensus. In the discussion with Callicles, Socrates shows him first that he does not live up to his specific image of the tyrant or the courageous leader understood as an indiscriminate hedonist (*Gorg.* 497e–499b). But in the very act of getting Callicles to recognize his difference from these concrete others, Socrates then gets him to see that he falls below these specific others only because like Socrates he *does* accept or lives by certain standards that tie him to the Athenian democracy and their ideals of debate (*Gorg.* 499b). This move is *not* equivalent to a blanket affirmation of Athenian democratic culture or tradition as the source of our moral values. Plato himself felt that Socrates's own brand of justice was superior to the Athenian one. Instead, it is an affirmation or acknowledgement of the ontological conditions upon which two non-sovereign agents can, through their very acts of intersubjective recognition, continually transform themselves.

Intersubjective recognition, for Plato, thus has both uplifting and unsettling qualities. Finding a salutary place for Platonic shame in a model of intersubjective recognition requires recognizing that without a certain amount of suffering, pain, and struggle there is no real possibility of transforming one's identity in and through the very process of engaging with others in the public sphere. Secondly, it requires acknowledging that consensus or agreement is instrumental to any kind of meaningful disagreement or struggle. Finally, it means that for Plato, to be truly radical, one cannot be simply a radical other.

Notes

1. For a full defence of the position see Tarnopolsky, *Prudes*, Chapter 1, 29–55.
2. I put "other" in quotes to connote the fact that this other can be individual or collective, and imaginary or actual. I omit the quotes in all subsequent references. For a discussion of the different forms that the other can take in a shame situation, see Tarnopolsky, *Prudes*, Chapter 2, 56–89.

3. All references to the Platonic text refer to the Stephanus pages. I have used the translation by Nichols (1998).
4. For the analogy to work it is important to note that Ancient Greek medicine involved painful procedures such as bleeding, cutting, and purging (and not, like many of our modern practices, simply dispensing painkillers).
5. One only has to think of the current economic crisis facing many contemporary polities to understand how much a flattering politics of pleasant and conspicuous consumption can ultimately endanger rather than foster the health of a polity.
6. For a fuller treatment of this theme and the five ways in which flattering shame threatens democracies, see Tarnopolsky, *Prudes*, 166.
7. In Tarnopolsky, *Prudes*, Chapter 4, 114–40, I show in detail how the myth at the end of the *Gorgias* combines the pleasures of sight and sound, so integral to Gorgias's epideictic rhetoric, with the more painful and negative aspects of the Socratic elenchus to elicit a more positive reaction to the experience of being ashamed. The myth incorporates the pleasures of going to see a spectacle (that is familiar to an Athenian audience) with the pain of the Socratic elenchus. The shaming mechanism of the Socratic elenchus is embodied in the familiar myths of the afterlife and the person, who withstands the painfulness of Socrates's just punishment, is released from the hideous tortures of Hades.
8. The notion of "agonistic" democracy comes from the Greek word, *agôn*, which means a struggle or contest (Liddell and Scott 18–19).

Works Cited

Appiah, K. Anthony. "Identity, Authenticity, Survival: Multicultural Societies and Social Reproduction." *Multiculturalism: Examining the Politics of Recognition*. Ed. Amy Gutmann. Princeton, NJ: Princeton University Press, 1994. 149–64. Print.

Benhabib, Seyla. Afterword. *The Communicative Ethics Controversy*. Ed. Seyla Benhabib and Fred Dallmayr. Cambridge, MA: MIT Press, 1990. 330–69. Print.

Brown, Wendy. *States of Injury: Power and Freedom in Late Modernity*. Princeton, NJ: Princeton University Press, 1995. Print.

Butler, Judith. *Precarious Life: The Powers of Mourning and Violence*. London: Verso, 2004. Print.

Cavell, Stanley. *Must We Mean What We Say?: A Book of Essays*. Cambridge: Cambridge University Press, 1969. Print.

Elster, Jon. *Alchemies of the Mind: Rationality and the Emotions*. Cambridge: Cambridge University Press, 1999. Print.

Foucault, Michel. "Two Lectures." *Power/Knowledge: Selected Interviews and Other Writings, 1972–1977*. Ed. Colin Gordon. New York: Pantheon, 1980. 78–108. Print.

Fraser, Nancy. "From Redistribution to Recognition: Dilemmas of Justice in a 'Post-Socialist Age.'" *New Left Review* 212 (Aug. 1995): 68–93. Print.

Gutmann, Amy. Introduction. *Multiculturalism and "The Politics of Recognition."* Princeton, NJ: Princeton University Press, 1992. Print.

Habermas, Jürgen. *The Theory of Communicative Action, Volume 2: Lifeworld and System: A Critique of Functionalist Reason*. Trans. Thomas McCarthy. Boston: Beacon Press, 1984. Print.

Honneth, Axel. "Integrity and Disrespect: Principles of a Conception of Morality Based on the Theory of Recognition." *Political Theory* 20.2 (May 1992): 187–201. Print.

———. *The Struggle for Recognition: The Moral Grammar of Social Conflicts*. Trans. Joel Anderson. Cambridge: Polity Press, 1995. Print.

Liddell, H.G.H., and R. Scott. *Greek-English Lexicon*. Oxford: Clarendon Press, 1996. Print.

Markell, Patchen. *Bound by Recognition*. Princeton, NJ: Princeton University Press, 2003. Print.

Massaro, Toni M. "Show (Some) Emotions." *The Passions of Law*. Ed. Susan A. Bandes. New York: New York University Press, 1999. 80–120. Print.

Nussbaum, Martha. *Hiding from Humanity: Disgust, Shame and the Law*. Princeton, NJ: Princeton University Press, 2004. Print.

———. "Shame, Separateness and Political Unity: Aristotle's Criticism of Plato." *Essays on Aristotle's Ethics*. Ed. Amélie Oksenberg Rorty. Berkeley: University of California Press. 1980. 395–435. Print.

Plato. *Plato: Gorgias*. Trans. James H. Nichols Jr. Ithaca, NY: Cornell University Press, 1998. Print.

Tarnopolsky, Christina. "Plato on Shame and Frank Speech in Democratic Athens." *Bringing the Passions Back In: The Emotions in Political Philosophy*. Eds. Rebecca Kingston and Leonard Ferry. Vancouver: University of British Columbia Press, 2008. 40–59. Print.

———. *Prudes, Perverts, and Tyrants: Plato's Gorgias and the Politics of Shame*. Princeton, NJ: Princeton University Press, 2010. Print.

Taylor, Charles. "The Politics of Recognition." *Multiculturalism and "The Politics of Recognition."* Ed. Amy Gutmann. Princeton, NJ: Princeton University Press, 1992. 25–74. Print.

Villa, Dana. *Socratic Citizenship*. Princeton, NJ: Princeton University Press, 2001. Print.

Warner, Michael. *Publics and Counterpublics*. Cambridge, MA: MIT Press, 2002. Print.

———. *The Trouble with Normal: Sex, Politics and the Ethics of Queer Life*. Cambridge, MA: Harvard University Press, 1999. Print.

Williams, Bernard. *Shame and Necessity*. Berkeley: University of California Press, 1993. Print.

CONTRIBUTORS

RACHEL ADELMAN completed her PHD in Hebrew literature at the Hebrew University of Jerusalem. She has taught Jewish studies at the University of Toronto, Miami University in Ohio, and Harvard University. Her first book, *Pirqe de-Rabbi Eliezer and the Psedepigrapha* (Leiden: Brill, 2009), is based on her doctoral dissertation. Rachel is currently working on a second book—*The Female Ruse: Women's Deception and Divine Sanction in the Hebrew Bible*—as a research associate in the Women's Studies in Religion Program at Harvard Divinity School. She is an assistant professor of Hebrew Bible at Hebrew College in Boston.

PIERO BOITANI is professor of comparative literature at the University of Rome "Sapienza." He is a fellow of the British Academy, the Medieval Academy of America, and the Accademia dei Lincei. He has received both the Feltrinelli Prize for Literary Criticism and the De Sanctis Prize. Among his most recent publications are *The Shadow of Ulysses: Figures of a Myth* (Oxford, 1994), *The Bible and its Rewritings* (Oxford, 1999), *Winged Words: Flight in Poetry and History* (Chicago, 2007), *Letteratura europea e Medioevo volgare* (Bologna, 2007), and *Il Vangelo secondo Shakespeare* (Bologna, 2009).

HARRY FOX (LEBEIT YOREH) teaches Judaism of late antiquity; Talmudic, rabbinic, and geonic literature; and modern Hebrew literature at the University of Toronto. He is the author, with Justin Lewis, of *Many Pious Women: A Yiddish Renaissance Defence of Women*, and the editor, with Tirzah Meacham, of *Introducing Tosefta: Textual, Intratextual and Intertextual Studies*.

RHIANNON GRAYBILL is assistant professor of Religious Studies at Rhodes College in Memphis, Tennessee. She received her PHD in Near Eastern studies with a designated emphasis in critical theory from UC Berkeley in 2012. She is currently writing her first book, a study of masculinity and embodiment in the Hebrew prophets.

ROLAND LE HUENEN is professor of French and comparative literature at the University of Toronto. Current concerns have led him to explore how the novel in nineteenth-century France creates its own tools to offer a critical representation of the social issues of the time. In 1973, he co-founded the Groupe International de Recherches Balzaciennes (GIRB), now located at the University of Paris 7. Other research interests have drawn on a number of issues found in travel narratives viewed from the perspective of an open genre.

ROSA MUCIGNAT is lecturer in comparative literature at King's College London. Her research interests include realism and the novel, literary geography and the idea of space in narrative, and Anglo-Italian cultural relations in the Romantic period. Her book *Realism and Space in the Novel, 1795–1869: Imaginary Geographies* is forthcoming with Ashgate in 2013.

JOSEPH RING is a lecturer in the English Department at the University of California, Berkeley. He is currently working on an article on second worlds in Shakespeare and a book-length manuscript titled *Wonderstruck: Early Modern Aesthetics of Astonishment in Spenserian and Shakespearean Romance*.

TERESA G. RUSSO has taught at The Catholic University of America and American University. She has written articles and papers on Dante, Boccaccio, Ficino, Antonello da Messina, and Matilda Serao, and her poetry has appeared in various journals, including *The Silenus* (Oxford, UK: Centre for Medieval and Renaissance Studies) and *Verbi Gratia* (Washington, DC). She is currently completing her dissertation on the art of memory in medieval literature, including Chaucer and Christine de Pizan, at the Centre for Comparative Literature at the University of Toronto.

JENNA SUNKENBERG received her doctorate in comparative literature from the University of Toronto's Centre for Comparative Literature in 2009. Her dissertation focused on a comparative study of medieval and contemporary hermeneutics. She currently teaches in the University of Toronto's Book and Media Studies Program in St. Michael's College and is working on a project that explores an ethics of social media through the cognitive function of the imagination.

CHRISTINA TARNOPOLSKY is associate professor of political science at McGill University. She is the author of *Prudes, Perverts, and Tyrants: Plato's Gorgias and the Politics of Shame*, published by Princeton University Press in 2010. Her research centres around three themes: Plato's relationship to democratic Athens; the role of emotions in democratic politics; and the aesthetic character of democratic politics. She is currently working on a book manuscript entitled, *The Rashomon Republic*, which reads Plato's *Republic* alternately through the lens of satyr-play, history, medicine, tragedy, epic, and comedy.

KEVIN FREDERICK VAUGHAN received his doctorate in theology from the University of St. Michael's College, Toronto, in 2009. His dissertation was a study of Thomas Aquinas's mystical interpretation of the Gospel of John, as found in his *Super Ioannem*. He is currently adjunct faculty at

St. Augustine's Seminary of Toronto and works in the area of Christian systematic theology, history, and spirituality.

JEFFREY NEIL WEINER is a doctoral candidate in comparative literature at the University of California, Berkeley. He is writing his dissertation on shock therapy, the experience of surprise as a rhetorical and spiritual attempt to resolve trauma in the romances of Cervantes and Shakespeare.

NAOMI A. WEISS is currently completing her PHD dissertation at the University of California, Berkeley, on the language and performance of music and dance in the tragedies of Euripides. Her other research interests include myth and ritual in archaic and classical Greece, ancient ethnography, and the use of literary theory in classics.

INDEX

Abraham, Joseph, 93n5
Abraham, story of
    Eco's village-fool agnition and, 14
    genealogies and, 51
    Mann's re-writing of, 18
    recognition of angels and God, 13–14
    See also Kierkegaard, Søren, *Fear and Trembling*
Adam and Eve, story of, 78–88
    Adam's first speech, 80–81
    bestiality, 83–84, 90–91
    "eureka" and breakthroughs (*yesh!*), 80–83
    Eve's creation, 81–83, 92n2
    gender hierarchy, 81, 83, 94n8, 95n16
    gendered terms and readings, 92nn2–4, 93n5
    heteronormative sexuality, 82–84, 88, 90–91
    heterosexuality, 81, 87, 90–91
    homosexuality, 84, 87
    incest prohibitions, 84
    Lilith and, 82–83, 95n19, 95n23
    miraculous elements, 84–85
    mutual recognition, 80–81, 85–88, 94n7, 94n13
    nakedness, 86, 87–88
    original sin, 96n26
    overview, xxii–xxiii
    Pandora myth, 86, 95n23
    Ricoeur on gifts, xxii–xxiii, 85–88, 95n22
    Ricoeur's stages of recognition, 78–80, 85–88, 94n7, 94n13
    self-recognition, 79, 81, 85
    shame, xxii–xxiii, 87–88, 91, 96n26

snake, 86–87, 96n26
Adelman, Rachel
   biographical notes, 261
   ethical epiphany in Judah and Tamar, xxii, 51–76
Aeschylus, 4, 6, 10, 33–34
Agamemnon, 108–09, 115
agnition
   double and single agnition, 6
   Eco's village-fool agnition, 6–7, 14, 20
   as term, 3, 30n2
   See also recognition
Albott, Robert, *Englands Parnassus*, 187, 191–92
Alter, Robert, 52, 68n4
anagnorisis, as term, 30n2, 53
   See also recognition
And Then the Tortoise Built Himself a Home (Katz), 81
Antony, St., and Augustine's conversion, 150–53
Appiah, Anthony, 244–45
Aquinas, St. Thomas
   divisions in works, 126
   on Job, 136
   original sin, 96n26
   on Paul's letters, 135–36
   quidditas-claritas in Joyce's *Portrait*, xvi–xvii
   recognition in *Summae*, xvii, 123, 125–26
Aquinas, St. Thomas, commentary on Mary Magdalene, 123–39

   charity, 136–37
   Commentary on the Gospel of St. John, 124–26
   gift of faith, 124, 129–32, 134–36
   Jesus's words to Mary, 127, 130–32, 135
   justification and recognition, 125, 132–37
   love, faith, grace, and recognition, xxiv, 124–27, 132–37
   Mary as model for all Christians, 124–25, 132, 137
   misrecognition of Jesus, xxiv, 20, 124
   mutual recognition, 135–37
   overview, xxiii–xxiv, 124–26
   recognition of God's gifts, 135–37
   seeing and believing, xxiv, 124–25, 127–30
   transformation of recognition, xxiv, 124, 127
   "turning" to Jesus, 127–30
   vision of Jesus, xxiv, 127–32
Archimedes' Bathtub (Perkins), 80
Arendt, Hannah, 244–45
Aristotle, *Poetics*, recognition
   anagnorisis, as term, 4, 30n2, 52–53, 77
   artistic perfection and nothingness, 12, 30n10
   catastrophe *(pathos)*, 4

comparison with Joyce's term, xviii
contrivance, not plot, 4, 6, 7
epic poetry, 4
error *(hamartia)*, 4
fear and pity *(phobos* and *eleos)*, 4–5, 169
French term, semantic range, 78
friendship *(philia)* and, 5
Hebrew term *(n.kh.r)*, semantic range, 77–78
hostility *(ekhthra)* and, 5
mechanisms, importance of, 4–6
memory *(mneme)*, 4–6, 9–10
mimesis, theory of, 4–5, 24, 142–43, 145
misrecognition, 53
on *Oedipus*, xiv, 4–6, 12, 16, 53
overview, xiv, 4–12
paralogism (false inference), 182, 212n5, 212n8
parody of, in *Faerie Queene*, 185–86
plot, 52–53, 59, 77, 155, 169, 239
reasoning *(syllogismos)* and, 4–6, 10–11, 30n10
return and rediscovery, 7–9, 53
reversal of events *(peripeteia)*, xiv, 4, 11–12, 52–53, 58–59, 169–70
Robortello's commentary on, 179–80

signs, xiv, 4, 9–10, 16, 53
surprise, 5, 11–12
theory of knowledge and, 5–6
tragedy, 4
wonder and awe, 4–5, 24, 169–70, 179–81
Aristotle, *Problems*
music and recognition, 19
Armstrong, Frances, 235–36
astonishment. *See* Spenser, Edmund, *The Faerie Queene*
Auerbach, Erich, 205
Augustine, St.
on allegory, 208
compelling of religious belief, 209–10
De Magistro, 152
faith and recognition, 21–22
memory and recognition, xxvii–xxviii
original sin, 96n26
Ricoeur on meditations, 153n2
shock doctrine, 209–10
Augustine, St., *Confessions*, and narrative identity, 141–54
Confessions, 146, 153
conversion processes, 150–53
distention of the mind *(distentio animi)*, 147–49, 151–52
memory, direct perception, and expectation, xxiv, 147–49
overview, xxiv, 141–42, 146, 153

paradox of human time, 142–43, 145–47
reader's dialogue with text, 149–53
reading Cicero's *Hortensius*, 149–50, 153
reading St. Antony's story, 150–53
time, narrative, and self-recognition, xxiv, 142–43, 145–53
awe. *See* wonder and awe

Babington, Gervase, 210
Barr, James, 93n5
Berman, Marshall, 238
Bersani, Leo, 225
Bible, Hebrew, and recognition
    genealogies and, 51–52
    Genesis, 12–16
    gluttonous cravings of Israelites (Num. 11), xxii–xxiii, 88–91
    God's struggle to be recognized, 12–13
    Hebrew terms (*n.kh.r; haker; jada'*), 13, 77–78
    Jephthah as tragic hero, 108–09
    story of Ruth, 66–67, 73n33
    See also Abraham, story of; Adam and Eve, story of; creation story; Job, story of; Joseph, story of; Judah and Tamar, story of; sexuality and biblical recognition
Bible, Christian, and recognition
    disciples as Eco's village fools, 20
    faith (*pistis*) and signs (*semeia*) as miracles, xxi, 13
    "fear and trembling," 119n4
    God's struggle to be recognized, 12–13
    Jesus's question, "Who do you think I am?," 19–20
    John's gospel, 12–13
    King Lear and I Cor. 3.18, 12
    Mary's recognition of Jesus at the tomb, 20–21
    misrecognition, 19–21
    Paul's letters, 135–36
    Peter's recognition as a "confession," 19–20
    sight and recognition, 21–22
    signs (*semeia*) as Jesus's miracles, 13
    Thomas's doubts and recognition, 20–21
    See also Aquinas, St. Thomas, commentary on Mary Magdalene
Bilson, Thomas, 196–200, 205, 209
Bird, Phyllis A., 93n5
Blackburn, Simon, xix
Blow, Douglas, *Orlando Furioso*, 194–95

Boileau, Nicolas, 180, 211n1
Boitani, Piero
　on Aristotle's anagnorisis, xv
　biographical notes, 261
　recognition and the divine, xxi, 1–32
Bowlby, John, attachment theory, 46n30, 47n36
Boyarin, Daniel, 93n5
Boyle, John F., 126
Boyle, Marjorie, 170
Boys, John, 194
Bradbury, Nicola, 238
Brombert, Victor, 225, 234
Brooks, Peter, 156, 226
Brown, Wendy, 244–45
Brownrig, Ralph, 209, 214n26
Buber, Martin, 113
The Bunyip of Berkeley's Creek, 80
Burke, Edmund, 181, 203, 211
Butler, Judith, 245

Carey, John, 230
Cave, Terence, xiv–xvi, 221, 237–39
cells and prisons. *See* Dickens, Charles, *Great Expectations*; Stendal [Marie-Henri Beyle], *Le rouge et le noir*
Centre for Comparative Literature, University of Toronto, conference (2008), xiii–xiv, xx–xxi

Cervantes Saavedra, Miguel de, *Don Quijote*, 155–77
　admiración and discovery of truth, xxiv, 168–75
　Aristotelian plot, 155, 169–70
　audience response, xxv, 156, 170–71
　Catholic ritual of purgation, 157, 173–75
　confession, xxv, 157, 171–75
　crying rituals, 174, 176n6
　destructive and restrained desire, 156–57
　Freud's repetition compulsion, 155–61, 165–69, 171, 174
　Freud's "uncanny," 157–59, 166, 172
　Frye's genres of comedy and romance, 155, 157, 162–63, 167–68, 171, 174–75
　Frye's hero and myth of Christianity, 167–68
　identity, 163–64
　Jesuit practice of sensual representations *(enargeia)*, 170
　marriage sacrament, 173–74
　marvellous *(maravilla)*, 156–57, 170–72
　overview, xxiv–xxv
　Pandafilando and sexual trauma, 164–66, 171
　paradox, 168–69
　parody, 162–64

plot and setting, 155, 157–58, 162, 170–71

repetition and doubling, 159–62, 165

repetitive trauma, xxiv–xxv, 171, 174

return and rediscovery, 174–75

signs, 163

space in narrative, 157, 161, 166–68, 175

storytelling as sacrament, 171, 175

time in narrative, xxiv, 157, 175

wonder and awe, 169–70, 172–73

Christianity

Eco's village-fool agnition and Last Supper, 20

faith and recognition, xxi, 13

Frye's hero and myth of Christianity in *Don Quijote*, 167–68

Jesus's astonishment in *Faerie Queene*, 196–200

Jesus's Transfiguration, 209–10, 214n26

resurrection of dead and *Winter's Tale*, 27–29

theory of faith and recognition, 21–22

See also Aquinas, St. Thomas, commentary on Mary Magdalene; Augustine, St.; Bible, Hebrew, and recognition; Bible, Christian, and recognition; confession; God

Chrysostom, John *(In Hebrew)*, 21

Cicero, *Hortensius*, 149–50, 153

citizenship

democracy, recognition, and self-rule, 243–44

identity and recognition, 241, 243

See also politics of recognition

Coleridge, Samuel, 27–28

Collins, John, 92n4

Collins, Philip, 232

confession

in *Don Quijote*, xxv, 157, 171–75

Jesuits and general confession, 172

in Judah and Tamar, xxv, 65, 72n29

Peter's recognition as a confession, 19–20

See also Augustine, St., *Confessions*; Christianity

Constable, Henry, 189

creation story

gendered terms and readings, 92nn2–4, 93n5

Ricoeur's recognition theory and, 78–80

See also Adam and Eve, story of

Crooke, Helkia, 213n21

culture, identity, and recognition. *See* politics of recognition

Dante Alighieri
   memory and recognition, xxvii–xxviii
   recognition as epiphany in *Purgatorio*, xvi, 20
   recognition in *Comedy*, xv
   rewriting of misrecognition of Jesus, 20
   signs in *Comedy*, 16, 22
Dawkins, Richard, 95n22
De Moor, Johannes C., 93n5
de Mornay, Philippe, 185, 188
democracy and recognition, 243–44, 257n6
   See also politics of recognition
Derrida, Jacques
   Gift of Death, xxiii, 95n22, 102, 107, 115
   on Job, 107
   on Kierkegaard, 102, 106–07
   paradox, absurdity, and suffering in ethical system, 102, 115–17
   on story of Abraham and Isaac, 113–14, 117–18
   suspension of the ethical, 113–18
Descartes, René, 10, 79, 211
Dickens, Charles, *Great Expectations*, 219–40
   Aristotle's recognition and, 221, 239
   cell's meaning in, xxvi–xxvii, 219–22, 231–33, 235–36
   home's meaning in, 219, 221–23, 225–27, 230, 235–36
   law and crime, 232–33
   overview, xxvi–xxvii
   palace's meaning in, 219, 221–22, 227–32
   plot and setting, 219–22, 225–27
   recognition as partial, 238–39
   recognition as reality check, 221, 231
   recognition stages, xxvi–xxvii, 237
   return and rediscovery, 221–22, 230, 236, 237–38, 239
   romance and, 221, 223, 237
   signs, 230–32
   social displacement and identity, 222–23, 225–29, 230
   social mobility, 237–38
Don Quijote. See Cervantes Saavedra, Miguel de
Donne, John, 204–05
Dostoevsky, Fyodor, 16, 22
Dumas, Alexandre, 6, 7, 9
Duncan, Ian, 220

Eco, Umberto
   types of recognition, 6–7
   village-fool agnition, 6–7, 14, 20
Electra, story of, 4, 6, 10–11, 33–34, 44n3

Eliot, T.S., 20, 71n24
epic poetry
    Aristotle's recognition and, 4–5
    sublime and, 205
    See also Spenser, Edmund, *The Faerie Queene*
epiphany
    Greek term *(epiphaneia)*, xvi
    literary epiphanies, xv–xviii
    See also recognition
ethnicity. See politics of recognition
Euripides
    Bacchae, 13, 30n11
    Electra, 10–11, 33, 44n3
    Helen, 1–4, 29, 34, 44n5
    Phaeton, 180–81
Euripides, *Ion*, 33–49
    fire and recognition scene, 45n6
    Freud's repetition compulsion, xxi–xxii, 34–35, 37–40
    identity of characters and audience's ancestry, xxi–xxii, 37–38, 41, 44n4
    memory and, xxi–xxii, 37–39
    misrecognition, 39, 42
    overview, xxi–xxii
    parody, 34, 44n3, 44n5
    plot, 35–36
    recognition scene of mother and son, 34
    repetitions and duplications, 36–42
    self-recognition, identity, and maturation, xxi–xxii, 34, 41–44, 45n15, 46n24, 46n30, 47n36

The Faerie Queene. See Spenser, Edmund, *The Faerie Queene*
faith
    Aquinas on gift of faith, 124, 129–32, 134–36
    Augustine's theory of faith and recognition, 28
    Bible and lack of proof of God, xxi, 12–13
    Christian theory of recognition and, 13, 21–22
    divine and recognition of loved ones, xxi, 3
    Donne on wonder and, 204
    recognition in Euripides's *Helen*, 2
    suspension of disbelief and, 27–28
    in *Winter's Tale*, 26
Fear and Trembling. See Kierkegaard, Søren, *Fear and Trembling*
Fisch, Harold, 73n33
Fletcher, Angus, 207–08, 212n8
Foucault, Michel, 232–33, 237, 244–45
Fox, Harry (leBeit Yoreh)

biblical recognition and
sexuality, xxii–xxiii, 77–100
biographical notes, 262
Freud, Sigmund
fire and recognition scene, 45n6
Mann and recognition theme, 18–19
pleasure principle, 35, 43, 46n18
repetition compulsion in *Don Quijote*, 155–61, 165–69, 174
repetition compulsion in *Ion*, xxi–xxii, 34–35, 37–40
"uncanny," 157–59, 166, 172
"From Ignorance to Knowledge: Recognition" (conference), xiii–xiv, xx–xxi
Frye, Northrop
comedy and romance in *Don Quijote*, 155, 157, 163, 167–68, 171, 174
heroic journey, 155, 167–68

gender
gender hierarchy in creation story, 81, 83, 94n8, 95n16
gendered terms in creation story, 92nn2–4, 93n5
See also Adam and Eve, story of; politics of recognition; sexuality
Genesis Rabbah. See *Midrash Genesis Rabbah*

genres
19th c. novel and Eco's agnition, 6–7
19th c. novel and romance and myth, 237
modern novel and recognition, 220, 238–39
See also epic poetry
Gilmour, Robin, 227, 238
Giono, Jean, 9
God
faith and recognition of, 13, 21–22
God's struggle to be recognized, 12–13
Job's recognition of, 13
recognition of God's gifts, 135–37
recognition of loved ones and, 3
recognition of Ultimate (*hodeh*), 65–66
religious epiphanies (*epiphaneia*), xvi
revelation-recognition process and, 16–17, 19–20
signs and, 15–16
theophany in story of Job, 102–03, 112–18
See also Bible, Hebrew, and recognition; Bible, Christian, and recognition
Goethe, Johann Wolfgang von, 11
Gordis, Robert, 112–13
Gorgias. See Plato, *Gorgias*

Index 273

Graybill, Rhiannon
   biographical notes, 262
   story of Job, xxiii, 101–21
Great Expectations. See Dickens, Charles
Green, William Scott, 95n22
Gregory the Great, 21, 28
Guenther, Genevieve, 212n8
Gwalther, Rudolph, 209–11

Haack, Susan, 93n5
Hagan, John, 230
Hale, J.R., 214
Harington, John, 187–88
Hart, Jonathan, xiv, xxi
Hegel, Georg
   influence on recognition theory, xix
   theory of recognition (*Anerkennung*), xviii–xix, xxii–xxiii, 78–79, 242–43
Helen and Menelaus, story of, 1–4, 34, 44n5
Hertz, Neil, 191, 206–09, 211, 214n24
Hesiod, 95n23
Hobbes, Thomas, 188, 194
home, meaning of. *See* Dickens, Charles, *Great Expectations*; Stendal [Marie-Henri Beyle], *Le rouge et le noir*
Homer, *Iliad* and *Odyssey*
   Aristotle's recognition and, 4–9
   heroic similes, 191
   memory in Joyce's *Ulysses*, 9–10
   misrecognition, 8
   return and rediscovery, 7–8, 79
   self-recognition, 79
Honneth, Axel, xviii, xix, 242–45
Hughes, John, 180–81

Ibn Ezra, Abraham, 82, 89
identity
   in classical recognition, xiv
   clothing and, 57–59
   in *Don Quijote*, 163–64
   as fluid and permeable, 244–45
   in *Great Expectations*, 222–23
   identity-based inequality, 242–43
   in *Ion*, xxi–xxii, 34, 41–43
   in *Le rouge et le noir*, 222–25
   and social displacement in *Great Expectations*, 225–28, 230
   See also Augustine, St., *Confessions*, and narrative identity; Euripides, *Ion*; politics of recognition; Ricoeur, Paul, narrative identity
Ignatius of Loyola, 170, 172–73
Iliad. See Homer
immigration, identity, and recognition, 241
   See also politics of recognition
injustice and recognition, 242–43

See also politics of recognition
Ion. *See* Euripides, *Ion*
Isaac and Abraham, story of. *See* Kierkegaard, Søren, *Fear and Trembling*

Jacob, Henry, *Treatise of the Sufferings*, 196–200
Jacob, story of
   recognition of angels, 77–78
   rewritings by Mann, 17–18
Jacobs, Mignon R., 93n5
Jegstrup, Elsebet, 103
Jephthah as tragic hero, 108–09
Jesuits
   general confession, 172
   practice of *enargeia*, 170
Jesus Christ. *See* Christianity
Job, story of, 101–21
   absurdity and, 102, 117–18
   alienation, 101–02, 117
   Aquinas on remission of sins, 136
   authorship, 118n1
   as classical tragic hero, 109–10, 113
   critique of normative theology, 110–11, 114–15, 118
   critique of universal ethicals, 101–02, 114
   Derrida on, 107
   failed speech, 101–02, 110–13, 116–18
   "fear and trembling," 106, 119n4
   Hebrew term "to know" *(jada)*, 13
   as Kierkegaardian hero of faith, 102–03, 107–08, 113, 117
   King Lear and, 12
   movement of repetition, 105
   mystery of undeserved suffering, 109
   overview, xxiii, 118n1
   paradox in, 117
   public struggle of faith, 105
   recognition of God, 13, 116–18
   teleological suspension of the ethical, xxiii, 111, 113–18
   theophany, 102–03, 112–18
   violence, 102, 111, 117
John, Gospel of
   Donne on wonder (John 5.28–29), 204–05
   See also Aquinas, St. Thomas, commentary on Mary Magdalene
Joseph, story of
   descent, 54–55
   Judah and Joseph, parallels, 52, 54, 65, 68n4
   Judah and Tamar's story and, 51, 57–60, 64
   misrecognition, 14–15, 58
   recognition act *(haker na)*, 68n6
   rewritings of, 17–19

signs, recognition, and
revelation, 15–17
Joyce, James
literary epiphanies, xv–xviii
memory and recognition in
Ulysses, 9–10
quidditas-claritas in *Portrait*,
xvi–xvii
Judah and Tamar, story of, 51–76
Aristotle's recognition, 52–53,
57
clothing, 57–59
confession, xxv, 65, 72n29
ethical recognition, xxii, 52,
53–54, 59–65
genealogy *(toledot)*, 51–52, 55,
65–66, 72n28, 72n31
God's intervention, 63–64, 67
identity, 57–59
incest and marriage laws, 56,
69nn13–15
as interruption in Joseph's
story, 51, 54
irony, 56–57, 59, 70nn16–17
Joseph and Judah, parallels, 52,
54, 65, 68n4
Joseph's story and, 51–52, 54,
57–60, 64
Judah's descent, 54–57
Judah's pledge to return with
Benjamin, 64
Levinas's ethical substitution,
52
misrecognition, 56–57

overview, xxii, 54–57
paradox of continuity/
discontinuity, 66–67
Perez and breach of ethical
norms, 65–66, 72n32
recognition act *(haker na)*, 13,
52, 54, 57, 59–64, 68n6
recognition of Ultimate
(hodeh), 63–64, 65–66,
72n29
reversal of events *(peripeteia)*,
xxii, 58–59
Ruth's story and, 66–67, 73n33
shame, 61, 70nn20–21,
71nn22–23
signs, xxv, 14, 16, 57–61, 65

Kahn, Victoria, 185
Kant, Immanuel, 203, 206
Katchadourian, Herant, 96n26
Katz, Avner, 81
Kawashima, Robert S., 93n5
Kierkegaard, Søren
authorship and authority,
103–04, 119n2
heroes of the faith, 102–03,
107–08, 113, 117
Repetition, 103–05
silences, 104–07
Kierkegaard, Søren, *Fear and
Trembling*, 101–18
Abraham as hero of the faith,
xxiii, 107–09, 111

Agamemnon and Jephthah as tragic heroes, 108–09
alienation, 101–02
authorship and authority, 103–04
faith, ethics, and religion, 108–09
"fear and trembling," 106, 119n4
Job as hero of the faith, 102–03, 107–08, 113, 117
Job's failed speech, 110
Levinas's critique of, 105
overview, xxiii, 101–02
paradox in, 102, 111, 115–16
parallels with Agamemnon and Jephthah, 108–09
role of language, 109–11
silences in his works, 102–07
silences of Abraham, 104, 109–11
suffering, 106
teleological suspension of the ethical, xxiii, 101–02, 108–09, 111, 113–15, 117–18
theophany, 112–16
title's significance, 106
violence, 102, 111
See also Derrida, Jacques
Kimchi, David, 84, 95n21, 96n24
King, Albion, 113
Klein, Melanie, 43
Klopstock, Friedrich, 22
Knapp, Steven, 203–04

Kugel, James, 60

Laban, 85
Lawee, Eric, 84
Lazarus, Richard, 42
Le Huenen, Roland
  biographical notes, 262
  on recognition, ix–x
Lemnius, Levinus, 213n12
Levenson, Jon, 68n4
Levinas, Emmanuel
  critique of Kierkegaard's *Fear and Trembling*, 105
  on epiphany, xvi
  ethical substitution, 52, 61–66
  recognition of Ultimate *(hodeh)*, 65–66
  story of concentration camp dog, 79
Lewis, C.S., 181–83, 187, 211, 212n4, 214n28
Licht, Jacob, 73n33
Lilith, 82–83, 95n19, 95n23
Lombard, Peter, 21
Longinus, *On the Sublime*, 179–81, 185, 191, 211n2, 212n3
Loyola. *See* Ignatius of Loyola
Lucretius, *De rerum natura*, 194–95

Macksey, Richard, 211n2
Magdalene. *See* Aquinas, St. Thomas, commentary on Mary Magdalene

Malory, Thomas, *Morte Darthur*, 187
Mann, Thomas, 17–19, 30n10
Markell, Patchen, 243–45, 251, 255
Mauss, Marcel, 95n22
Melville, Herman, "Bartleby the Scrivener," 106–07
memory
    Aristotle on *(mneme)*, 4–6, 9–10
    in *Don Quijote*, xxiv–xxv
    in *Faerie Queene*, xxvi, 208–09
    in *Gorgias*, 9
    in *Ion*, xxi–xxii, 37–39
    in Joyce's *Ulysses*, 9–10
    literary epiphanies and, xvii–xviii
    in *Odyssey*, 4, 9
    in Proust's *Recherche*, xvii, 9
    recognition and, xvii, xxvii–xxviii, 9–10
    Ricoeur on self-understanding and, 141–43
    in St. Augustine's *Confessions*, xxiv, 147–49
Menn, Esther Marie, 51, 68n7, 71n22
Midrash Genesis Rabbah
    Adam and Eve, 86, 88, 96
    Judah, 54, 63, 68n7, 69n14
Miller, D.A., 233
minority groups. *See* politics of recognition
Minsaas, Kirsti, 169–70
miracles and recognition
    creation story, 84–85
    in Euripides *(Helen)*, 3
    faith *(pistis)* and signs *(semeia)* as miracles, xxi, 13
    in Shakespeare's works, 22–23
misrecognition
    Aristotle's recognition and, 53
    clothing and, 57–60
    in *Ion*, 39, 42
    of Jesus, 20
    in *Odyssey*, 8
    in *Oedipus*, 53
    in *Othello*, 58
    politics of recognition, 242–45
    story of Joseph, 14–15, 58
    story of Judah and Tamar, 56–57
Monk, Samuel, 179, 206–07
Mucignat, Rosa
    biographical notes, 262
    on home, the palace, and the cell in *Le rouge and le noir* and *Great Expectations*, xxvi–xxvii, 219–40
music and recognition
    Aristotle's recognition of familiar music, 19
    in Shakespeare's comedies, 23, 26, 29
mutual recognition
    Aquinas on, 135–37
    Hegel's theory of, xxvii, 242–43
    Plato on, 251, 253

politics of recognition, xxvii,
  242–45
Ricoeur on, 80, 85–88, 94n7,
  94n13
in story of Adam and Eve,
  80–81, 85–88, 94n7, 94n13

Nachmanides, on Genesis, 84–85
Nagel, Thomas, 95n22
Nahmanides, 51
nationalism, identity, and
  recognition, 241
  See also politics of recognition
Nehorai, 90
Niskanen, Paul, 93n5
novels. *See* genres
Nussbaum, Martha, 250

Odyssey. *See* Homer
Oedipus, story of
  Aristotle's recognition and, xiv,
    4–6, 12, 16, 53
  comparison with *King Lear*, 12

Pandora myth, 86, 95n23
The Passion of Christ (medieval
  play), 30n11
Patrizi, Francesco, 179–80
Paul's Gospel
  Aquinas on letters, 135–36
  "fear and trembling," 119n4
Pedrick, Victoria, 45n6, 45n12,
  47n38
Peres, Shimon, on shame, xx

Perez, Judah's son, 65–66, 72n32
Perkins, David, 80
Phoenix myth, 96n24
Pirandello, Luigi, 9
Plato, *Gorgias*, politics of
  recognition, 245–56
  intersubjective recognition,
    xxvii, 245–46, 255–56
  knowledge as memory, 9
  misrecognition of self, 254
  moments of recognition and
    reaction, 249–50
  mutual recognition, 251, 253
  overview, xxvii, 246
  politics of humiliation of the
    other, 256n1
  questioning (*elenchus*), 251, 253,
    255, 257n7
  rhetoric, 246, 248–53
  shame, xxvii, 245–49, 255–56
  shame, respect, and self-
    recognition, 251–56
  shame and flattery, 246, 249–
    53, 256, 257n6
  shame as painful, 246–48, 250,
    252, 256
poetry, epic. *See* epic poetry
politics of recognition, 241–59
  critique of, 243–45
  due recognition as human
    need, 242
  gaze of the "other," 246–47,
    256n1

Index   279

Hegel's mutual recognition,
    xxvii, 242–43
identity as fluid and permeable,
    244–45
identity-based inequality,
    242–43
misrecognition, 243–45
overview, xix–xx, xxvii–xxviii,
    241–43
political harm and self-hatred,
    242–43
politics of acknowledgement,
    245
politics of redistribution *vs.*
    recognition, 242
Rousseau's doctrine of general
    will, 243
state powers, injustice, and
    mutual recognition, xxvii,
    244–45
See also Plato, *Gorgias*
prisons and cells. *See* Dickens,
    Charles, *Great Expectations*;
    Stendal [Marie-Henri
    Beyle], *Le rouge et le noir*
Proust, Marcel, *Recherche*, xvii, 9
Puttenham, George, 214n25

race, identity, and political
    recognition, 244
See also politics of recognition
Ramsey, George, 94n11
Rashbam, 84
Rashi, 83, 86, 89, 96n24

Recanati, 85
recognition
    agnition, as term, 3, 30n2
    anagnorisis, as term, 30n2, 53
    "by instinct," 5
    conference on (2008), xiii–xiv,
        xx–xxi
    "de facie," 4–5
    due recognition as human
        need, 242
    Eco's village-fool agnition, 6–7,
        14, 20
    epiphanies and, xv–xviii,
        xxvii–xxviii
    epiphany, Greek term
        (epiphaneia), xvi
    "eureka" and breakthrough
        (yesh!) moments, 80–83
    French term, semantic range,
        78
    gifts and, xxii–xxiii, 85–88,
        95n22
    Hebrew terms *(haker; n.kh.r)*,
        13, 77–78
    in Islamic literature, xv
    Mann's re-cognizing
        (wiedererkennen), 18–19
    narrative plots, setting and,
        220–22
    plot as loss and recovery of
        knowledge, xv
    return and rediscovery, 7–9, 53,
        79, 174, 221–22, 236–39

seeing *vs.* recognizing and
believing, 2–3
terminology, 30n2
See also Aristotle, *Poetics*;
Ricoeur, Paul
return and rediscovery
in Aristotle's *Poetics*, 7–9, 53
in *Don Quijote*, 174
in *Great Expectations*, 221–22,
236–39
in *Odyssey*, 7–9, 79
in *Return of Martin Guerre*, 8–9
in *Le rouge et le noir*, 221–22,
236–39
self-recognition and, xxvii–
xxviii, 79
Ricoeur, Paul
on Augustine's meditations,
152, 153n2
on gifts, xxii–xxiii, 85–88,
95n22
gratitude, 78, 85–86
Hegel's influence on, xix, 78–79
hermeneutics of the self, 143–
46
mutual recognition, 80, 85–88,
94n7, 94n13
natural recognition, 78
recognition stages, 78–80,
85–88
recognizing responsibility, 53
self-recognition, 79, 85
Ricoeur, Paul, narrative identity,
141–54

Aristotle's theory of mimesis,
142–43, 145
The Course of Recognition, xxiv,
141, 145–46, 148
hermeneutics of the self, 143–
46, 149
overview, xxiv, 141–42
reader's dialogue with text,
144–45, 149, 153n1
self-understanding and
memory, 141–43
time, narrative, and self-
recognition, xxiv, 141–46,
148–49
Time and Narrative, 141–43,
146, 153n2
Riley, E.C., 170
Ring, Joseph
biographical notes, 262
on Spenser's *Faerie Queene*,
xxv–xxvi, 179–218
Robortello, Francesco, 179–80
Le rouge et le noir. *See* Stendal
[Marie-Henri Beyle]
Rousseau, Jean-Jacques, 80,
242–43
Russo, Teresa G.
biographical notes, 263
introduction to recognition,
xiii–xxix
Ruth, story of, 66–67, 73n33
Rymer, Thomas, 184

Sarna, Nahum, 69n13

Scholem, Gershom, 95n19
self-recognition
   alienation and, 79
   in *Great Expectations*, 229
   in *Odyssey*, 79
   recognition as distinct from, 80
   in *Le rouge and le noir*, 229
   solipsism and, 80
   story of concentration camp dog, 79
   in tragedy, 46n24
   See also Euripides, *Ion*
Sewall, Richard, 109
sexuality
   identity and political recognition, 244
   Pandafilando and sexual trauma in *Don Quijote*, 164–66, 171
   sexual energy in *Faerie Queene*, 200–04
   See also gender
sexuality and biblical recognition, 77–100
   bestiality, xxiii, 83–84, 90–91
   Eve's creation, 81
   gender hierarchy, 81, 83, 94n8, 95n16
   gendered terms and readings, 92nn2–4, 93n5
   gluttonous cravings of Israelites (Num. 11), xxii–xxiii, 88–91
   Hebrew term *(n.kh.r)*, semantic range, 77–78
   heterosexuality, xxiii, 81–84, 87–88, 90
   homosexuality, 84, 87
   incest and marriage laws, 56, 69nn13–15, 84, 89–91
   Lilith, 82–83, 95n19, 95n23
   nakedness, 86, 87–88
   overview, xxii–xxiii
   Ricoeur on gifts, xxii–xxiii, 85–88, 95n22
   Ricoeur's recognition and, 78–80
   shame, 87–88, 91, 96n26
   story of Judah and Tamar, 56–57
   See also Adam and Eve, story of
Shakespeare, William
   comparison of *King Lear* and *Oedipus*, 12
   Cymbeline, 22–23, 31n16
   Hamlet, 11, 30n10
   King Lear, 12, 22
   miraculous events, 22–23
   music, 23
   Othello, 58
   Pericles, 22–23, 31n16
   recognition of old father and young daughter, 22–23
   rewriting of biblical recognition, 22–29
   The Tempest, 31n15

Shakespeare, William, *Winter's Tale*
  faith and recognition, 26–29
  indirect recognition, 23–24
  opposition of Nature and Art, 23–29
  suspension of disbelief and, 27–29
  wonder and awe, 24
shame
  genesis of, 96n26
  politics of recognition and, xx, xxvii, 245–48
  sexuality, shame, and biblical recognition, xxii–xxiii, 87–88, 91, 96n26
  story of Judah and Tamar, 61, 70nn20–21, 71nn22–23
  See also Plato, *Gorgias*
Sheba, Queen, 95n18
signs
  Aristotle on, xiv, 4, 16, 53
  in *Comedy*, 22
  in *Don Quijote*, 163
  in Electra story, 33–34, 44n3
  as essential to recognition, 15–16
  in *Great Expectations*, 230–32
  in *Odyssey*, 4
  parodies of, 33–34
  recognition and the divine/God, 15–17, 21–22
  in *Le rouge and le noir*, 231–32
  signs *(semeia)* as Jesus's miracles, 13
  in story of Joseph, 14–15
  in story of Judah and Tamar, 14, 16, 57–61, 65
social class mobility
  in *Great Expectations*, 219–23, 225–29, 230, 238
  in *Le rouge et le noir*, 219–25, 227–29, 238
Society of Jesus. *See* Jesuits
Socrates. *See* Plato, *Gorgias*
Sophocles
  Aristotle's recognition and *Oedipus*, xiv, 4–6, 12, 16, 53
  rewriting of Electra plays, 10–11
  See also Plato, *Gorgias*
Spence, Joseph, 214n28
Spenser, Edmund, *The Faerie Queene*, 179–218
  Arthur's shield and battle, 205–09
  astonishment and similes, 189–94
  astonishment as central to, 181–86, 198–200, 203–08
  audience, xxv–xxvi
  Blandamour and Paridell, 191–95
  Cambell and Trimond, 191
  Descensus Controversy and, 196–200

Index   283

epic and romance, distinctions, 186
epic combat, xxv–xxvi, 185–95, 203–04
epic similes, 183, 187–94, 199–204
guns and warfare, 194–95, 201–04, 214n22
Italian counterparts and, 182–84, 211, 212n4
Jesus's astonishment, 196–200, 213n19
letter to Raleigh, 190, 206, 210
marvellous in epic romance, 180–85, 187–88
memory, xxvi, 208–09
overview, xxv–xxvi
paradox, 200
parody of Aristotelian astonishment, 185–86
placement in structure of, 183, 200
Redcrosse and Orgoglio, 200–04
Redcrosse and Sansfoy, 185–91, 198–99
salvation paradigm, 203–04
sexual energy, 200–04
shock moments of knowing, xxv, 185–95, 204–05, 209–11
sublime and romance in, 179–85, 203, 211

sublime blockage, xxv, 183–84, 185–86, 206–07, 214n24
transformation, xxvi, 203–04
wonder and awe, xxv–xxvi, 182–83, 193, 195, 204–05, 211
Stendal [Marie-Henri Beyle], *Le rouge et le noir*, 219–40
Aristotle's recognition and, 221, 239
cave and self-reflection, 225, 233–34
cell's meaning in, xxvi–xxvii, 219–22, 231–36
home's meaning in, 219, 221–25, 227
identity problems and social displacement, 222–23, 227–29
overview, xxvi–xxvii
palace's meaning in, 219, 221, 227–32
plot and setting, 219
post-Napoleonic era, 238
recognition, plot, and setting, 220–22
recognition as partial, 238–39
recognition as reality check, 221, 231
return and rediscovery, 221–22, 236–39
romance, 221, 223, 237
signs, 231–32
stages in recognition, xxvi, 237
time and setting, 238

Sternberg, Meir, 55
Stock, Brian, 149–51, 153
Stordalen, T., 93n5
sublime
  epic poetry and, 205
  Kant's mathematical sublime, 206–07
  Longinus on, 179–81, 185, 191, 211n2, 212n3
  in Renaissance literary theory, 170, 179–81
  See also Spenser, Edmund, *The Faerie Queene*
Sue, Eugene (*Les mystères de Paris*), 6–7
Sunkenberg, Jenna
  biographical notes, 263
  on narrative identity, Augustine, and Ricoeur, xxiv, 141–54

Tagopoulos, Constance Vassiliou, xvii
Tamar. *See* Judah and Tamar, story of
Tarnopolsky, Christina
  on Adam and Eve's shame, 87–88
  biographical notes, 263
  on misrecognition, xxvii, 241–59
  on politics of recognition, xix–xx
Tasso, Torquato, 165–69, 205, 215

Taylor, Charles, xx, 242–45, 255
Testa, Italo, 78
Theweleit, Klaus, 201–02, 214n23
tokens. *See* signs
Tolstoy, Leo, *War and Peace*, 9
Torrell, Jean-Pierre, 138n5
tragedy
  and Aristotle's recognition, 4
  self-recognition and, 46n24
  tragic hero, 108–10, 113, 115
Traina, Cristina, 93n5
Treilhard, Jean-Baptiste, 234
Trible, Phyllis, 93n5

University of Toronto, Centre for Comparative Literature, conference (2008), xiii–xiv, xx–xxi

Vaughan, Kevin Frederick
  on Aquinas and Christian recognition, xxiii–xxiv, 123–39
  biographical notes, 263
Velleman, J. David, 96n26
village-fool agnition, 6–7, 14, 20

Wagner, Jenny, 94n13
Walzer, Michael, 94n8
Warner, Michael, 244–45, 250
Warton, Joseph, 181
Weiner, Jeffrey Neil
  biographical notes, 264

on traumatic doubling in *Don Quijote*, xxiv–xxv, 155–77
Weiss, Naomi A.
   biographical notes, 264
   on recognition and identity in Euripides's *Ion*, xxi–xxii, 33–49
Williams, Bernard, 246, 248
Wils, Jean-Pierre, 94n8
Wilson, Edmund, 232–33
Winter's Tale. *See* Shakespeare, William, *Winter's Tale*
Wolfers, David, 112–13
wonder and awe
   in Aristotelian theory, 4–5, 24, 169–70
   in *Don Quijote*, 169–70
   epic poetry and, 205
   in *The Faerie Queene*, xxv–xxvi
   John Donne on, 204–05
   in Renaissance literary theory, 179–81, 212n8
   in *Winter's Tale*, 24
   See also sublime

Zemon Davis, Natalie, *Return of Martin Guerre*, 8–9

OTHER TITLES FROM THE UNIVERSITY OF ALBERTA PRESS

Locating the Past/Discovering the Present
Perspectives on Religion, Culture, and Marginality
DAVID GAY & STEPHEN R. REIMER, *Editors*

224 pages | B&W photographs, bibliography, index
978-0-88864-499-2 | $39.95 (S) paper
Religious Studies/Cultural Studies

Response to Death
The Literary Work of Mourning
CHRISTIAN RIEGEL, *Editor*
JONATHAN HART, *Foreword*

304 pages | Notes, bibliography, index
Copublished with Canadian Review of Comparative
    Literature/Revue Canadienne de Littérature Comparée
978-0-88864-421-3 | $34.95 (S) paper
Literary Criticism

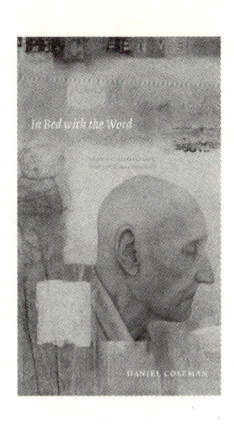

In Bed with the Word
Reading, Spirituality, and Cultural Politics
DANIEL COLEMAN

160 pages | Selected bibliography, index
978-0-88864-507-4 | $19.95 (T) paper
978-0-88864-647-7 | $15.99 (T) EPUB
978-0-88864-668-2 | $15.99 (T) Amazon Kindle
Literature/Criticism/Memoir